Childhood and
Art Therapy

Childhood and Art Therapy

Notes on Theory and Application

EDITH KRAMER

In collaboration with Laurie Wilson
Preface by Viola W. Bernard, M.D.

SCHOCKEN BOOKS • *NEW YORK*

First published by Schocken Books 1979
10 9 8 7 6 5 4 3 2 1   79 80 81 82

Copyright © 1979 by Schocken Books Inc.

Library of Congress Cataloging in Publication Data

Kramer, Edith.
    Childhood and art therapy.

    Bibliography: p.
    Includes index.
    1. Art therapy.   2. Child psychotherapy.
I. Title.
RJ505.A7K73   618.9′28′9165   79–14454

Manufactured in the United States of America

To My Mother

Contents

Illustrations

In each instance where a child gave a name to his work, it has been used in this list. To help the reader's memory, descriptive titles have been given to work that was left unnamed.

PLATES

Foreword

Art therapy, conceived and practiced for years in isolation, is rapidly becoming part of the academic scene. Colleges and universities are offering courses, and entire art therapy training programs are being developed in many parts of the country.

In my own work, training future art therapists has increasingly taken precedence over direct work with children. In the course of teaching and supervising, I have seen that it would be helpful to put into writing ideas that had been only lightly touched upon in my two earlier books as well as ideas I have developed since 1971 when my last book was published.

As I examine the theoretical framework upon which my understanding of art therapy rests, I find that although I have assimilated a great deal of new material, in essence my orientation has not changed. For psychological understanding I still rely mainly on Freudian psychoanalytic theory. The philosophical thinking of Susanne Langer continues to influence my general ideas about art. Langer conceives of the arts as highly disciplined modes of making available to contemplation experiences that cannot be encompassed by discursive thought. Thus the arts contribute substantially to our understanding of human existence. My understanding of child development in art and of methods of teaching art to children owes much to Viktor Lowenfeld, particularly to the ideas he formulated on the basis of his work with the blind.

In the realm of Freudian psychoanalytic thinking, recent developments in ego psychology have broadened our horizons. In particular, the work of Margaret Mahler and her collaborators has made us view the ego's integrative function in early infancy with greater respect. This in turn has brought into focus the importance of D. W. Winnicott's earlier investigations of the transitional object and of transitional phenomena. We have come to recognize as one of the roots of art the infant's earliest symbolic behavior as it emerges in the interchange between mother and child.

Reaching beyond human life into the natural history of behavior, the discoveries and theoretical formulations of ethologists, among whom Konrad Lorenz is the most articulate and well known, has also given much new food for thought. Ideas stimulated by their findings are incorporated in my discussion of art and play and on the source of pleasure in sublimation. Having burdened Part One of this book with a great deal of theory, I hope that the numerous illustrative examples that are interspersed will sustain the reader's attention.

Teaching and supervision have also convinced me that it is desirable to put into writing ideas on the practice of art therapy and on the art therapist's multiple functions. In Part Two I have devoted much space to the clarification of concepts such as transference and countertransference and of the therapeutic alliance as they pertain to art therapy. In this context the difference between art therapy and psychotherapy is discussed at great length. The art therapist's function as auxiliary ego and as facilitator of processes of neutralization and sublimation is described, and the role of various art materials in art therapy is also considered.

To illustrate my ideas, I have used case material both from my early experience as an art therapist and from my more recent work with disturbed children. The scope of this book has also been broadened by material contributed by students and colleagues. Case materials from work with the retarded and the physically ill and handicapped has been particularly valuable.

As they become acquainted with the many children whose work appears throughout this book, readers may feel frustrated by the incompleteness of the information about each of them. This is in part because extra care must be exercised to protect the children's anonymity when we present case material along with reproductions of artwork.

Like any writer who has dealt with the same subject for many years, I am faced with the problem that ideas presented in my later books are based on earlier formulations. To avoid encumbering the text with tired explanatory writing and boring readers already familiar with my work, I asked my friend and collaborator, Dr. Laurie Wilson, to contribute an introduction to my theoretical formulations. In it she has assembled and put into admirable order those already published ideas and formulations essential for understanding this book. Readers unfamiliar with my previous books will be saved from frustration and perplexity by reading this introductory chapter.

Although the experience of teaching future art therapists has been an important source of inspiration, this volume is intended to serve neither as a textbook nor a "how-to" book. I have made no attempt systematically to expound any methods or techniques of art therapy. Rather, I have presented ideas and illustrated them with case material— ideas which I hope will stimulate others to further thinking and to much-needed research. Above all, I hope to make all those who live and work with children aware of the many ways in which art and art therapy can foster growth and integrated functioning in childhood.

Acknowledgments

I welcome this occasion to thank a great many people for their help.

I am grateful to my collaborator, Laurie Wilson, for consistent support and constructive criticism, for advice on all matters pertaining to work with the retarded, and for contributing the Introduction to this book, the case study of Elena in Chapter IV, and the passage in Chapter VI on pre-art materials. I am deeply indebted to Erna Furman, child psychoanalyst, for exquisitely thorough criticism and clinical suggestions that have greatly enhanced the book's quality. My thanks to Rudolf Wittenberg for his advice and for expert criticism of my presentation of psychoanalytic theory, particularly of the concepts of transference and countertransference. For editing my writing with superb skill, I am profoundly grateful to Elinor Ulman, editor of the *American Journal of Art Therapy*. For contributing valuable case material and help in organizing it, I am indebted to Walter Carter, Betty Jo Clifford, Carol Smith-Daniels, Eva Jozan, Linda Eidelberg, Anne Hausman, Jill Schehr, and Elizabeth Stone.

My thanks go to the New Land Foundation for granting funds to the Department of Child Psychiatry of Albert Einstein Medical College, making possible the continuation of an art therapy program which has been the source of much valuable case material; to the nursing staff of Ward 9 West of Jacobi Hospital for actively supporting the art therapy program on the ward throughout many turbulent years; to the Wiltwyck School for Boys and to the Jewish Guild for the Blind for permission to use case material; to Eva Glaser, president of Schocken Books, for her confidence in my work; to Shirley Routten and Margo Colindreler for deciphering my handwriting and transforming it into typed copy. I am grateful to the students of the New York University graduate art therapy training program whose inquisitiveness and enthusiasm have been a continued source of inspiration; and to the faculty of the Department of Art and Art Education, of which the art therapy program is a part, and especially to its chairperson Angiola Churchill, for supporting the program and helping it grow.

Finally, I give thanks to the many children with whom I have worked, who have taught me how to practice art therapy and have given me joy in my profession.

Edith Kramer
January 1979

Preface

Viola W. Bernard, M.D.

Some twenty years ago I had the privilege of introducing Edith Kramer's first book: the exciting account of her ground-breaking development of an art therapy program at the Wiltwyck School for Boys, a residential treatment center for emotionally disturbed children.* Aged 8 to 13, most of them were black and from poor, disrupted ghetto homes in New York City. Now, two decades and two books later—years brimming with productivity during which Kramer successfully broadened and deepened her field—I find myself once again in the happy position of preparing an introduction to a book by Edith Kramer.

Reading this manuscript has been an intellectual, emotional, and literary delight. The author's theoretical ideas are presented with a degree of clarity that bespeaks their thorough assimilation. The relevance of her theoretical base to practice is vividly conveyed and brought to life by gripping case stories of art therapy sessions. The many illustrations, which show what the children actually produced, make the case histories all the more convincing and intelligible.

In reviewing Kramer's work over time, I am struck by how consistently she adheres to the basics of her approach,

---

Art Therapy in a Children's Community (Springfield, Ill.: Charles C. Thomas, 1958; New York: Schocken Books, 1977).

formulated early on, while she also continues to expand and enlarge her scope. The present book brings us the results of this expansion and enlargement. Laurie Wilson, Kramer's collaborator, prepares the reader to comprehend the new material with an excellent summary of the salient ideas from Kramer's two earlier books. In addition, Kramer herself tends to recapitulate early ideas as the foundation for the newer gestalts she presents, a stylistic device of explanatory value, in my opinion.

Kramer's widening and advancing of the art therapy field since that early Wiltwyck program has proceeded along several dimensions. Thus, she extended the application of this therapy to children who suffer from a much broader range of pathology. These include mentally retarded and blind children, youngsters with grave physical illness, and the severely disturbed inpatients and outpatients of the child psychiatric service of a municipal teaching hospital. This involved a greater variety of settings, with their differing patterns of therapeutic teamwork and conditions for conducting art therapy. By integrating what she has learned from these wider opportunities for observation and experience, Kramer has enhanced both her psychodynamic understanding and her therapeutic repertoire: treatment maneuvers appropriate for a more varied population of patients and settings have been invented or modified; new insights have been gained, and subtler differentiations made, within the theories by which she explains the intricate workings of art therapy.

Indeed, another major way in which Kramer's new book adds to and advances art therapy as a specialty is through the elaboration and further refining of theory. Her attention in this regard centers mainly on the process of sublimation with respect to artistic creativity. Building on the conceptual thinking she had already evolved, as expressed in earlier writings, she now has blended this thinking—and thereby enriched it—with findings from her own investigations and from the disparate literatures of ethology and early ego development. By infusing scholarship with creative imagination, she discovers and delineates how certain social behaviors of other species may foreshadow human sublimation. Through her educated powers of observation, she also identifies precursors of sublimation in the art of the very young and the retarded.

My reference above to art therapy as a specialty may be challenged by some and I, too, have had questions about designating it as such. The term is used all too loosely nowadays in the scramble for credentials with which to legitimize all sorts of activities, worthwhile or dubious. But, as Kramer reports in her Foreword, art therapy has now achieved a place on the academic scene. Largely due to her pioneering, it has become the teachable subject matter of courses in several universities. This has culminated in a graduate art therapy training program—Kramer was instrumental in establishing it—at New York University. As a further qualification for its status as a specialty, art therapy has gained, for its trained practitioners, employable membership in professional mental health teams, with distinctive roles and functions.

These developments are due, in the main, to the shift Kramer tells us she has made in the allocation of her time, from direct work with children to the training and supervision of future art therapists. I was concerned, originally, lest Kramer's remarkable therapeutic results depended so much on her idiosyncratic combination of talents and attributes that they could not be replicated. If so, the benefit from such treatment would be limited to the relatively few children she could work with herself. Clearly, in the light of events, my worries on that score were unfounded. On the contrary, she has multiplied her impact many times over by increasing the number of practitioners trained in her kind of art therapy. (In fact, some of these have contributed case material for this book.) To this end, she has constantly shared—through teaching and writing—her results, her treatment uses of art materials, and her understanding of what these occasion in the child, in the therapist, and between them.

I referred just now to Kramer's "kind of art therapy" because the concepts she has systematized as its rationale may not be completely shared by all workers in this field. I admire her scientific integrity in making her own theoretical position explicit and clear-cut, and also in accepting that others may differ. Thus, she writes, "Freudian psychoanalytic psychology...is the foundation of my work and thinking," but she also says, "We cannot categorically demand that art therapists adhere to one school of thought." She stresses, though, that since all art therapy deals mainly with visual rather than verbal expression, art therapists—whatever their psychological orientation—learn to see their patients' productions with a "third eye," much as psychotherapists, to use Reik's metaphor, need to listen with a third ear. It is evident that Edith Kramer has remarkable acuity of vision with her third eye.

Within the children we come to know in these pages, despair contends with latent hope; chaos, fear, and hate obstruct and obscure the innate push for healthy selfhood; and the urge to destroy threatens to stifle the potential for creative achievement and affectionate ties. Kramer's work, with its extraordinary blend of specialized understanding, patience, skills, and ingenuity, helps tip the scales of these bitter inner battles in favor of the child's imperiled thrust toward personality growth.

Intrinsic to this helping process, as poignantly evidenced throughout her book, is the immense value Kramer accords to each individual and the worth, to her, of even the slightest increment of progress toward maturation that a damaged child can make. Such a value system—over and beyond the specifics of this significant treatment modality for traumatized children—exemplifies at the societal level a crucial antidote to the dehumanization that abounds in our world, as inherent in mass starvation, mass persecution, mass violence, and irrational risking of mass annihilation.

From this perspective, I view Edith Kramer's practice and teaching of art therapy as *itself* a creative form of expertise in the service of humanization. Her focus is on understanding the detailed dynamics of personal growth, as well as the multiple uses of oneself as facilitator of growth through art. This demands of the therapists themselves a high degree of caring for others, ego strength, and effective sublimation—the same life-enhancing capacities of the human psyche which, to the extent possible for each, Kramer seeks to mobilize and strengthen in these afflicted children.

Thus, for me, this volume is not only highly informative and of absorbing professional interest, but it is also a profoundly civilized and civilizing statement.

VIOLA W. BERNARD, M.D.
Clinical Professor Emeritus of Psychiatry,
College of Physicians and Surgeons, and
Supervising Psychoanalyst Columbia University

Introduction:
Kramer's Theoretical
Formulations

By Laurie Wilson, Ph.D.

In two earlier books, published in 1958 and 1971,[1] Edith Kramer has presented her theoretical conceptions of art therapy and has discussed the functions of an art therapist working with disturbed children. In this Introduction I shall summarize both her basic theoretical position and her perception of the art therapist's functions, so that the reader may have some grasp of the fundamental ideas that have served as a foundation for Kramer's more recent thinking as it is presented in this volume.

In the Preface to *Art as Therapy with Children*, Kramer states her position as follows:

> My point of view is that of a practicing artist and educator who combines professional skills in the field of art with general knowledge of normality and pathology in childhood. The theoretical framework of my understanding of child psychology is based in the main on Freudian psychoanalytic thought. The emphasis, however, is on the idea of *art as therapy* rather than on psychotherapy which uses art as a tool. Thus, while the *therapeutic approach* is based on the awareness of psychic processes that include the unconscious, the *therapeutic maneuvers*...do not depend on the uncovering of unconscious material or interpretation of unconscious meaning. Instead art therapy is conceived of primarily as a means of supporting the ego, fostering the development of a sense of identity, and promoting maturation in general. Its main function is seen in the power of art to contribute to the development of psychic organization that is able to function under pressure without breakdown or the need to resort to stultifying defensive

1. *Art Therapy in a Children's Community* and *Art as Therapy with Children*.

measures. So conceived, art therapy becomes both an essential component of the therapeutic milieu and a form of therapy which complements or supports psychotherapy but does not replace it.[2]

In her first book, *Art Therapy in a Children's Community*, Kramer had defined art therapy as a means of making "available to disturbed persons the pleasures and satisfactions which creative work can give," and by means of insight and therapeutic skill, making such experiences meaningful and valuable to the total personality.

These two statements suggest that Kramer's idea of art and the creative process involves a complex comprehension both of the physical handling of art materials in order to form them so that they serve as symbolic equivalents for human experience and of the psychic processes that motivate creative work. Some understanding of these ideas about the nature of art is necessary in order to understand the function of *art as therapy*.

Kramer differentiates five ways in which art materials may be used. The first four do not qualify as art and are explained as either preliminary stages, symptoms of dysfunction which usually reflect psychological limitations, or limited communications. The first category consists of *precursory activities:* scribbling, smearing, exploration of physical properties of the material that does not lead to creation of symbolic configurations but is experienced as positive and ego-syntonic. The second Kramer describes as *chaotic discharge:* spilling, splashing, pounding—destructive behavior leading to loss of control. The third category, *stereotypes*, she named art in the service of defense. This may take the form of copying, tracing, or stereotypic repetition. Within this last area Kramer identifies three types: bland stereotypes that are dull and conventional, rigid or bizarre stereotypes that have personal meaning, and imagery displaying false sentiments, such as saccharine sweetness, hollow heroism, and false piety. The last and perhaps most controversial of this group is the *pictograph*

2. *Art as Therapy with Children*, p. xiii.

—a pictorial communication that replaces or supplements words. Kramer states that such communication occurs often in psychotherapy and art therapy or between people who know each other well and enjoy using a private code. They usually remain unintelligible to the outsider, and as a rule they are crudely executed, seldom attaining the integration and evocative power of art.

She calls the fifth category *formed expression,* and defines it as the production of symbolic configurations that successfully serve both self-expression and communication. For Kramer, only this way of using materials can be called art in the full sense because it derives from and evokes feeling and because it can serve as an analogue for a broad range of human experience.

The creation of an artificial world of symbols and conventions has the power to evoke genuine emotions. The experience can afford pleasure because the underlying content of unconscious feelings, conflicts, and fantasies is isolated from reality through these pictorial conventions and symbols so that these symbolic experiences do not normally stimulate any urge to act upon them in real life.

Kramer finds evidence of art as distinct from other types of pictorial expression in these general characteristics: economy of means, inner consistency, and evocative power.

The categories that Kramer has outlined are not rigidly separated. In the making of a single object different kinds of functioning may come into play: a child may progress from precursory playful experimentation to formed expression, may regress to chaotic discharge, retreat into compulsive defensive work, and move back again to formed, creative work. Although the art therapist's goal is helping people to produce work that is both expressive and formed, there are times when creative work is out of reach and situations when other modes of functioning are more helpful to the individual.[3]

3. *Art as Therapy with Children*, pp. 54–66.

Kramer's position on the dynamics of the creative process centers on her understanding of the psychoanalytic concept of sublimation. Both earlier books, as well as the present one, contain extensive discussions of this process. She has drawn on theoretical material from a number of sources and from it has synthesized formulations that constitute—especially in the area of artistic sublimation— an original contribution. Therefore, I shall quote at length from her earlier writings on this subject:

> To understand sublimation we must consider man's basic dilemma.[4]

Unlike the other species, whose behavior is regulated in the main by finely synchronized instinctive mechanisms, man can never unconditionally obey his instinctive drives or be guided by his primitive affects:

> Thus man's survival depends on the continuous appraisal of adjustment to reality. The drives, nevertheless, remain man's chief source of energy, and the gratification of instincts his basic source of pleasure. Yet, since they are no longer held in check by instinctive mechanisms which determine when they can be gratified and when they must be denied fulfillment, the drives are, in their primeval form, a source of mortal danger to man.
>
> The dilemma is inescapable. According to Freudian theory it has brought about a fundamental cleavage in man's psychic organization. It has become divided into the original primitive system, which Freud has named the id, and the more recently evolved ego. The latter is [conceived of as] an organizing force which develops anew in each individual and constitutes man's most indispensable organ of survival. To it are ascribed all the higher mental functions, such as the capacity to perceive and manipulate reality, to postpone gratification, and to maintain the inner unity of personality. Ultimately, the ego serves the drives, which through the ego's efforts, obtain the gratification they could never achieve through the impulsive discharge which is all the id remains capable of at this late stage of evolution.[5]

In the present book, Kramer takes up the difference between drives and instincts, but it is necessary here to

4. *Art as Therapy with Children*, p. 67.
5. *Art as Therapy with Children*, pp. 67–68.

provide the reader with a current statement about the drives: "A drive is a genetically determined psychic constituent. In present day psychoanalytic psychology, two drives are distinguished. The sexual or erotic (the energy of which is the libido) and the aggressive or destructive (the energy of which is the aggressive energy)."[6] Kramer states:

> As the individual matures, the superego develops, and social demands and inhibitions become internalized.... The ego could not fulfill its manifold and contradictory tasks of controlling impulses, avoiding dangers, warding off anxiety, and obtaining pleasure without the aid of simple repression as well as various more complex mechanisms. Among the latter, sublimation constitutes one of the most efficient means of dealing with dangers threatening from the drives and of making constructive use of their potentially destructive power.
>
> It is a process wherein drive energy is deflected from its original goal and displaced onto achievement, which is highly valued by the ego, and is, in most instances, socially productive. The obsessive single-minded quality that characterizes the drives in their original form is modified through sublimation, so that energies are freed for action beyond the narrow circle of infantile conflict and primitive needs. Because ego strength and autonomy increase in the process, we surmise that a shifting of energy from id to ego occurs and that aggressive and libidinal energy is neutralized. An essential feature of sublimation is the great amount of genuine pleasure the substitute activity affords.[7]

But Kramer reminds us that the pleasures of sublimation differ in kind from those of direct gratification, the latter being more intense but shorter lived. She also points out the difference between displacement and sublimation:

> In sublimation we expect a change of the *object* upon which the interest is centered, of the *goal*, and of the *kind of energy* through which this goal is achieved.[8]

In displacement only the object changes:

> Sublimation in art occurs when the artist replaces the impulse to act out his fantasies with the act of creating equivalents for his

6. Leland E. Hinsie and Robert Jean Campbell, *Psychiatric Dictionary* (New York: Oxford University Press, 1960), p. 235.

7. *Art as Therapy with Children*, pp. 68–69.

8. *Art as Therapy with Children*, pp. 70–71.

fantasies through visual images. Those creations become true
works of art only as the artist succeeds in making them meaningful
to others. The complete act of sublimation...consists in the
creation of visual images for the purpose of communicating to a
group very complex material which would not be available for
communication in any other form.[9]

Kramer identifies several sources of the need for this kind
of communication. Underlying all acts of sublimation is the
artist's "repressed material, which pushes to the surface and
demands fulfillment"[10] in the impetuous manner characteristic of primeval drives. At the core of every work of art are
internal conflicts which give it life and determine form and
content to a large degree. Thus conflict is formed and
contained, but only partly neutralized. In this way art
differs from most other products of sublimation which are
in themselves emotionally neutral. The artist's position
epitomizes the precarious human situation: while his craft
demands a strong ego capable of the greatest self-discipline
and perseverance, he must maintain access to the primitive
impulses and fantasies that constitute the raw material for
his creative work.[11]

The other reason that lies behind the artist's need to
make art is found in "man's great need to overcome the
isolation which is part of human life."[12] Thus through his
creation he can reveal and share his inner world with others
without losing his integrity as an individual or transgressing
the subtle boundaries that protect each person's inner life
from destructive intrusions.[13]

As Kramer sees it, the complex harmony of art mirrors
the precarious balance of inner forces that lies at the heart
of sublimation. The force that most frequently threatens
this balance both in art and in life is aggression, and in

9. *Art Therapy in a Children's Community*, p. 15.

10. *Art Therapy in a Children's Community*, p. 16.

11. *Art Therapy in a Children's Community*, pp. 15–18.

12. *Art Therapy in a Children's Community*, p. 16.

13. *Art Therapy in a Children's Community*, pp. 15–18.

Kramer's previous books she devotes considerable attention to this subject. For our present purposes, two paragraphs from *Art as Therapy with Children* suffice as a summary statement on aggression:

> Throughout our investigations we have encountered aggression in many guises: as disruptive violence that made work impossible; as threat that called forth defensive countermeasures; as destructive forces which, without disrupting the creative process altogether, interfered with the unity of a work of art; as emotional content that was expressed and contained. Finally, according to our theory of sublimation, we must assume that part of the constructive energy which goes into the making of art derives from neutralized aggression. Aggression seems to be both one of the most disruptive forces we have to contend with, and an indispensable source of energy for constructive work.
>
> Regarding the nature of aggression, both the psychoanalytic investigation of man and the study of the natural history of aggression as conducted by ethologists such as Lorenz and Tinbergen leave no doubt that it is a primary instinctive drive. Stresses such as frustration or danger call forth unusually intense aggressive behavior, but these stimuli must not be mistaken for causes. The drive is innate, not a mere response to external conditions.[14]

From Kramer's statements quoted at the beginning of this Introduction, as well as those that follow, we can see the relationship between her clinical aims of art therapy and her theoretical understanding of sublimation. To summarize: the art therapist "plans and provides the conditions under which the creative process can take place and be pleasurable, and substitutes his knowledge and deliberate acts in any area where the individual is unable to function fully,"[15] thus serving as a model of ego functioning and as an auxiliary ego. He modifies his working methods according to the patient's pathology and needs.

> The confrontation that creative work induces resembles the confrontation in psychoanalysis and psychoanalytically oriented

14. *Art as Therapy with Children*, p. 158.
15. *Art Therapy in a Children's Community*, p. 7.

psychotherapy in certain respects. The amorphous condition of the art material and the lack of specific directions for forming it are analogous to the blank quality of the therapeutic relationship. This freedom induces the child to form the art material or the relationship in his own image.... Each element in the child's work contains part of himself. The menace that confrontation with the self and its pathology constitutes is mitigated by [this] narcissistic gratification.[16]

The art therapist must recognize and respond to the hidden as well as the overt aspects of the child's production and will help the child produce artwork that contains and expresses emotionally loaded material. In addition,

he is trained to appraise the patient's behavior and production and to interpret his observations to the therapeutic team. He implements the team's therapeutic goals but does not ordinarily use his clinical insight for uncovering or interpreting to the patient deep unconscious material.[17]

Thus the primary function of the art therapist is to create and maintain a working atmosphere where the desire to make art prevails over all other concerns. With this general understanding of the process of sublimation and of the function of art in ego development, we can now turn to the specific issues that face the art therapist who works with children.

16. *Art as Therapy with Children*, p. 32.
17. *Art as Therapy with Children*, p. 25.

PART ONE

*Notes on the Theory of
Art as Therapy with
Children*

I

Art Therapy and Childhood

The child, considered in and for itself, with its equals, and in relations suited to its powers, seems so intelligent and rational, and at the same time so easy, cheerful, and clever, that one can hardly wish further cultivation. If children grew up according to early indications, we should have nothing but geniuses; but growth is not merely development; the various organic systems which constitute one man, spring one from another, follow each other, change into each other, supplant each other, and even consume each other; so that after a time scarcely a trace is to be found of many aptitudes and manifestations of ability. Even when the talents of the man have on the whole a decided direction, it will be hard for the greatest and most experienced connoisseur to declare them beforehand with confidence, although afterwards it is easy to remark what has pointed to a future.

—Goethe, *Truth and Poetry*

SOME ART THERAPISTS work equally well with children and adults and can enjoy the change of pace as they alternate between them. Differences, however, are so profound that the decision to specialize is entirely reasonable. Art therapists who work with children enjoy the vitality and energy that are at least potentially available for learning and growth, but they must contend with children's propensity to respond to any kind of stress with disruptive behavior, and the necessity unceasingly to control this is at times exhausting and monotonous. They will on the other hand

A condensed version of this chapter was published in the *American Journal of Art Therapy*, No. 2 (1975).

seldom need to wrestle with inertia, passive resistance, or distrust in the very idea of using art materials that we encounter so often in work with adults.

If we conjure up any session with almost any group of children two elements are immediately before us: discipline problems and the children's eagerness. Things happen at a higher key and at a faster rate, for children are possessed of enormous energies for development and change. We recall an all-prevailing urgency for us to function at once qua adult: upholder of justice, interpreter of reality, guardian of life and limb as a very special partner and helper in the children's creative ventures and as an admiring audience for their products. The most pervasive feeling is of pressure and of vitality.

We can never lose sight of two factors: the nature of childhood itself and the special relationship of childhood to the visual arts.

Because we work with children, our responsibility is absolute, residing in the adult status which makes us the guardian of any unprotected child who comes into our orbit. We note that this position differs fundamentally from the specific authority which is all an adult can attain over other adults or over adolescents. Among adults special qualifications such as specific knowledge, superior strength, or hierarchial position may confer authority while ignorance, illness, poverty, insanity, and other handicaps may diminish it. However, to disregard the *conditional, reversible* quality of one's authority, to *infantilize* them, constitutes the cardinal sin in any relationship with adults and adolescents. Conversely, it is unforgivable to *abdicate responsibility* toward children. This does not mean that we must attempt to maintain an unreal ideal of unassailable omniscience and omnipotence. Loss of control over unruly children and all sorts of mistakes and accidents are part of daily life with children and they are forever ready to forgive and forget occasional lapses. On the other hand the adult who sheds responsibility and virtually abandons the child creates panic and distrust. Such abandonment may take on many guises. The adult need not walk away—the one also abandons who truly (not playfully) becomes a child among children, who truly, not playfully or conditionally, treats the child as a fully responsible adult and partner, able to make final and fateful decisions, or reverses roles and burdens the child with responsibility for his, the adult's welfare.

It is noteworthy that the distribution of responsibilities is not essentially altered when children happen to possess specific knowledge and must inform their adult or even rescue him from certain situations. For instance, city children may sometimes know the dangers or the vocabulary of their own neighborhoods better than their group leader; country children may have essential information on territory, weather, animal and plant life, etc. If they trust him such children will be eager to share such knowledge with their adult in order to make him better able to fulfill his function, namely, to be responsible for them. It is endlessly fascinating to observe the ingenuity, sensitivity, and patience of children as they uphold and instruct their parents and guardians, adapt to their peculiarities and limitations, and yet continue to depend on them. Particularly, the profound dependence of school-age children on their parents which prevails in spite of the children's rapidly increasing range of autonomy must never be underestimated.

In this context it is interesting to note that a certain category of children's favorite books celebrates the relationship between the imperfect but nevertheless all-important adult protector and the competent but dependent child. These stories differ from the fairy tales rooted in the infant's fantasy of fusion with or power over the omnipotent parents such as those of Aladdin's command over the genie or Hansel and Gretel's usurpation of the witch's gingerbread house. They are distinct from tales that celebrate the adolescent hero's killing or superseding the evil parent–dragon, tyrant, giant, or devil. They also differ from those stories which celebrate childhood as a state of moratorium of sheltered innocence where conflicts and tragedies are scaled down to a child's capacities of comprehension and endurance such as *Winnie-the-Pooh* or *The Wind in the Willows*.[1]

I am speaking of stories which embody an attempt at coming to terms with childhood as a dependent and therefore precarious state. In these tales no dramatic change of roles is enacted. The child–protagonist is the companion, at times even the savior of the adult hero, for example, in *Treasure Island* and more recently in the *Saga of Batman and Robin*, but he never supersedes him. Wise and strong-minded children such as little Lord Fauntleroy and Heidi tame and reform their delinquent and intractable grandfather–fathers, and transform them into good parents —into adults who are ready and able to fulfill their parental function: to serve as protectors and providers, to help their children to grow up safely and prosperously.[2] These are consolatory tales. They reassure the child that it is possible to hold onto a good adult or to create oneself a good one by being virtuous, brave, patient, wise, resourceful (or mischievous and charming like Tom Sawyer). For no child can grow himself up unaided, and the great menace of childhood is failure to mature.

Any child who senses himself not growing up is virtually in a state of panic for his whole future is at stake. The same energies which normally push toward growth and change are then apt to be discharged chaotically, leading to destruction and self-destruction. This state of emergency does not necessarily make children more amenable to therapeutic or educative interventions. Indeed, it may

1. See Lilli Peller, "Daydreams and Children's Favorite Books," in *On Development and Education of Young Children*.
2. Anna Freud in *The Ego and the Mechanisms of Defense* has pointed out the element of reversal in these stories: "Not I, the adult is being tamed." These two aspects of meaning are not mutually exclusive, but complement each other.

constitute an additional obstacle to therapy. It does, however, make for a general readiness to hold onto any adult who the child feels may somehow be able to help him grow.

Naturally, adults also long for understanding, for trustworthy people. The hope of finding a good parent persists throughout life. But there is not the same urgency. The race against time is over, most of the damage done. Adults can hold themselves aloof without incurring fresh injury as empty days pass by. But there lives even in the most battered, disappointed, or cynical child some vestige of hope of finding a good adult. And so even while they rebel against our authority, distrust our good intentions, look through us, and ignore us, they continue to crave our company, particularly when we come bearing art materials. Indeed, the same children who would reduce the art room to a shambles and the art therapist to a nervous wreck will return again and again to the room where art materials and a person who knows how to use them are available, return in the dogged expectation that somehow something good will come of it. And following Freud's dictum "The patient is always right," more often than not good things do happen. Children's great affinity to art may be in part a manifestation of the general need for symbolic living which finds its immediate fulfillment in play. (We will investigate the relationship between art and play at greater length in Chapter III.) At this point let us just note that art has the power to mobilize considerable energies for constructive integrative functioning and that it seems to be compatible with a great deal of emotional disturbance and a wide array of social, intellectual, and physical handicaps.

While children's needs for good adults and their affinity for art facilitate our work, the effectiveness of all therapeutic labors is imperiled by their dependency on parents and environments that are frequently pathogenic. Even though children appear to be constantly in need of *more* good adults, all children, no matter how strongly they may invest the relationship to us or how wholeheartedly they seem given over to the immediate present, remain tied with bonds born of absolute necessity to their home and the adults to whom they belong. This bond, particularly the one to the mother or the mothering person or persons, cannot be broken without the gravest consequences. To survive as human beings children must manage to love those to whom they belong and feel themselves loved by them. The bond must survive the children's violent moods, death wishes, sexual fantasies, and dreams of acquiring different and better parents. It must also endure in the face of any inadequacies, character defects, or even vicious destructiveness on the part of the parents. It must survive any knowledge the child may have of the parents' faults or crimes. It must be preserved until adolescence, when the struggle toward full independence gradually alters the relationship.

So strongly is children's sense of identity linked to those who made them that even children who have been removed from home for their own protection seem to need to maintain some image of good parents, kept distinct from their avowed knowledge of ill-treatment and of their conscious anger and fear of them. Time and again childcare workers and teachers in children's shelters and foundling homes are puzzled by these children's unfathomable behavior concerning their families and the inextricable mixture of fantasy and fact which characterizes their ideas about them.

The absolute need for a parent's love leads to a double bind. Children's dependence makes them responsive to the parents' inner needs and their own immaturity makes them particularly receptive to the primitive components of the parents' personalities, their unconscious wishes and affects. Thus on a certain level children know their parents very well indeed, and the more difficult the parents the greater the necessity to know them well enough to be able to adjust to their needs, fulfill their expectations, and avoid head-on collisions. We know that such profound compliance can coexist with overt disobedience and rebelliousness. At the same time children must protect themselves against any awareness that would destroy their fundamental trust.

The more destructive the environment, the more difficult is the balancing of concomitant knowledge and oblivion. It is the lucky child whose parents are loving and sane enough so that he can afford to experience consciously a good portion (but never the whole) of the love and hate he feels toward them, and recognize some of the conflicting feelings they inevitably harbor toward him.

These fundamental conditions influence all our dealings with children. Not only psychotherapists but all those who aim to help a child must face the dilemma of how to induce children to relinquish immature or destructive ways of coping with conflict without endangering any adjustments and mechanisms that may be indispensable in the relationship between parent and child.

Next to laryngitis and chronic guilt feelings about not having done enough for them, the occupational hazard common to all those who work with disturbed children is the emotional strain of reconciling themselves to the children's environment. Some parents can be favorably influenced by counseling or family art therapy, but there are many others who cannot be reached by any therapeutic intervention. We all recall early mistakes and heartbreaks, incidents where the fine line between necessary support of the child and usurpation of the parental role was trespassed, bringing confusion and sorrow for all concerned, and we realize that we can never attain full immunity from committing new errors of this kind.

Luckily, even though we must not drive a wedge between children and their parents we may be and should be *different* from them. Children need many kinds of adults, just as they need playmates who are not their siblings and experiences which the family cannot offer. The quality that art brings to a child's life can be helpful even when the immediate family remains indifferent to art. Feelings can be expressed in art which could not and should not be put into words. Art therapy can inform a child even though certain conscious knowledge must be kept at bay.

Indeed, we find that children's ability to live in many different worlds, to adjust to different standards, to make do—as they must—with makeshift defenses contributes to the vitality and truth of children's art. Obviously, adults as well as children have phenomenal ability to live with contradictions. But from adolescence on the need for some consistency is felt and complex systems of defense are needed to sustain a semblance of unity. In this process, art may become subservient to the defenses and may be used mainly to lend conviction to conscious and unconscious deceptions. When the individual commands some skill and artistic sophistication his art may turn to saccharine sweetness, empty heroics, hypocrisy, and other forms of anti-art. Therefore, in order to produce valid art the adult's creative work must be beyond the reach of any defense mechanisms which would interfere with the perception of truth. This entails considerable moral courage, and because it constitutes a profound moral victory such art has the power to move us deeply. (Naturally, I do not mean to imply that the adult artist needs to be an honest person outside the realm of art, or conversely that very honest people's art cannot be exceedingly deceitful.)

Children can express the truth of the moment more readily not because they are morally superior, but because their statements need not add up to any consistent image of the world (artistically naive adults for whom art remains a playful activity beyond the pale of their defensive system enjoy a similar freedom). I also do not mean to imply that children's esthetic judgment is superior. On the contrary, they are undiscriminating and often their taste is atrocious. They are inclined to admire the slick or vulgar or the saccharine, but they cannot produce it on their own. This may be less because they lack skill than because they cannot muster sufficient energy in the service of a highly sophisticated kind of denial that is not age appropriate. Somehow, whenever images are made that require the use of imagination at all, the urge to gratify wishes and fantasies or to use the opportunity to master some aspect of reality seems to gain ascendance and enforce honesty. When children's art functions in the service of defense, work tends to be monotonous, obsessive, and as a rule impoverished. If defenses break down, work may become chaotic, or blatantly cruel or obscene. More often it disintegrates into playful or destructive behavior that leaves no product.[3]

Art therapists who work with children must clean up many messes, settle many fights, accept much repetitive, stereotyped work. Their duties seldom include accepting art that is elaborately and skillfully dishonest. As adults we can enjoy the refreshing sincerity and vigor of children's art as we take pleasure in their general eagerness for life, and we can learn from them. But we must guard against romanticizing. Those who extoll the virtues of childhood and deplore the tragic loss of spontaneity in adult life in the belief that it would be possible to maintain this pristine state inviolate fail to understand the fundamental difference between the adult and the child. Children's sheltered condition, their limited responsibility, their incompletely consolidated defense mechanisms, and their need to prepare for adult life through symbolic living in play and fantasy all facilitate artistic expression.

The adult state, on the other hand, precludes such easy freedom. Adult artists must struggle to develop the capacity to endure awareness of conflict and contradictions, at least within the context of their creative lives, and must battle to protect their creative efforts from the dominance of stifling mechanisms of defense. To maintain the candor of childhood as an adult artist while burdened with adult

3. For an extensive discussion, see Kramer, *Art as Therapy with Children*, Chapter VI.

responsibilities for the consequences of one's artistic statements becomes a difficult, at times a heroic task. To maintain responsible control over the conduct of life beyond the realms of art, even though denuded of the average adult's defenses that mask inner contradictions and establish unity at the price of diminished perceptions, presents additional difficulties. These may take on tragic dimensions.[4]

It is therefore not surprising that only a small percentage of the gifted children we encounter should choose to devote their adult life to art, and that among them only a tiny minority would be destined to attain excellence. The future of any artistic skills acquired in childhood, even under the most inspired guidance, remains unpredictable.

The profound reorganization of personality which extends in our culture from the onset of puberty to the beginning of adult life effects enormous changes both in attitude to art and in individual style. If art remains highly invested, the young adult must steer his way among conflicting styles and concepts. The outcome cannot be foreseen.

4. For a thorough investigation of these problems, see Kurt Eissler's *Leonardo da Vinci: Psychoanalytic Notes on the Enigma,* and *Goethe, A Psychoanalytic Study;* and Edith Kramer, "A Critique of Kurt Eissler's *Leonardo da Vinci.*"

II

Disturbed Children as Artists: Miracles

OUR INVESTIGATION of art therapy and childhood made us aware of the distinction between the art of children and of that of adults and of corresponding differences in the art therapist's tasks. We noted that the transition from the limited responsibilities of childhood to the full autonomy and accountability of the adult state entails fundamental changes in style, in the productive process, and in the function which the active pursuit of art assumes in people's lives. Our awareness of the discontinuity between the art of children and that of adolescents and adults must be tempered by the knowledge of the fundamental unity of art. Before we embark upon a more detailed investigation of troubled children's struggle for expression in art, I propose to contemplate work which, even though it was produced by troubled children, exemplifies this unity. We will investigate work that has evocative power and inner consistency and that has been made with economy and understanding of the medium, so that within the limitations of each child's age and talent it constitutes art in the full sense of the word.

Any work in which an individual attains the highest level of artistic eloquence of which he is capable has the quality of the miraculous. To function so fully is rare among children and adults, among the healthy and the disturbed. Much of the work produced in the name of art anywhere is trite—non-art, almost art, anti-art, once-alive art frozen into manner, secondhand imitation—or at best a commendable attempt. The examples I am presenting in this chapter were all collected in the practice of art therapy with disturbed children. Our search would not be essentially different if we were to look for similar material among healthier ones; miracles would probably be somewhat more numerous and the character of the work more varied, with a more even balance between victorious and joyful and aggressive and somber themes. We would, however, be looking for the same kind of phenomena and they would remain rare.

As art therapists we not only encounter the commonplace and the banal, we are also bombarded with manifestations of pathology, with fragmented, bizarre, chaotic, and abortive productions. We must learn to accept them and respond according to the child's needs rather than in terms of any extraneous standards of artistic excellence. However, the pressures of inner conflicts need not manifest themselves only disruptively. They can also become agents of extraordinary effort at integration culminating in unusually powerful artistic statements. To support such processes is the art therapist's most rewarding task. But the moment when the commonplace is transcended and something unexpected and evocative is born cannot be predicted or plotted. All we can do is to set the stage by providing art materials, time, and space; by being receptive to the unforeseen and respectful of the child's imagery and sense of form; by being understanding of the single-minded intensity, of the extravagance of creative fervor, and protective of the need for extra time and privacy during periods of heightened productivity, even if this interferes with the smooth functioning of scheduled activities.

I have come to designate work of this kind as *miracles* to myself and to my colleagues and students, both as a means of giving due recognition to their extraordinary quality and as a reminder of their rarity. This helps prevent our becoming impatient or feeling incompetent when we must work for long stretches of time without being so rewarded.

At this point it must be clearly understood that I am

speaking in this chapter of miracles of *artistic quality* rather than of miracles of *therapeutic success*. Evidently the most heterogeneous productions, including the chaotic, abortive, regressive, and even the trite can in the course of treatment herald unexpected, seemingly miraculous therapeutic gains. These issues will be discussed elsewhere. In the work presented in this chapter the relationship between artistic excellence and therapeutic gain varies.

Collecting miracles is not an easy task—it is most often the truly happy, victorious work that is carried home in triumph, or if the child lives away from home or cannot expect to find an appreciative audience in the family, such work frequently finds a place of honor in the office or home of some other beloved adult. Also, disturbed children's art tells more often than not of their troubles, and so in my own collection somber, tragic, and cruel themes far outnumber gay, tender, or triumphant ones. Yet—and herein lies the power of art—all the children took great pleasure in making their work, whether or not its content was painful.

The situations in which the miracles took shape differ in many ways, but they have some common features. Each of the works I am presenting was made by free choice. No subject matter was suggested. Each work was executed independently, or with only a minimum of technical help from me. All of them were produced in art therapy sessions held in informal groups. The situation was not conceived as group art therapy. The group merely provided an atmosphere of shared interest in art wherein each child was free to concentrate on individual work.

Remo: Even within my somber collection, eleven-year-old Remo's *Ghost House* (Pl. I) stands out as uncommonly perturbing. The imagery itself is commonplace, limited to well-known symbols of anxiety and suspiciousness: a house with heavily barred windows and a profusion of peering eyes. The handling of the paint and the superb placement of the images, however, sets it apart. When he painted it,

Remo had been a resident at the Wiltwyck School, a treatment home for emotionally disturbed boys, for more than a year. His symptons included truancy, stealing, and the compulsion to provoke flagrantly sadistic attacks, which made him a target of homosexual violence on the part of the older boys. Because his masochism made him court suffering and punishment, controlling his behavior and protecting him from abuse constituted an enormously difficult task for all staff members. In Remo's haunted existence the art room constituted something of a sanctuary. He was a frequent visitor but rarely able to concentrate on art, being too preoccupied with his fears and grievances.

Remo began his ghost house by covering a white eighteen- by twenty-four-inch sheet of paper with evenly applied black poster paint, establishing Egyptian darkness throughout. Using pure white upon the semi-dry black surface he unhesitatingly placed the ghost house in the upper right corner and painted the outlines of seven eyes and eyebrows floating in the dark. Next he painted yellow irises in all the eyes. Finally, instead of a black pupil, a black X shape was placed at each center so that the all-embracing darkness is aggressively repeated at each eye's focus. Since the background was not just a black sheet of paper but black paint, Remo's light brush lines have picked up some of this darkness so that background and super-imposed imagery intermingle.

The placing of white shapes on black ground sets the painting's mood. Such white configurations, no matter how clearly drawn, can never fully define a dark surface in the manner in which decisive dark lines easily give spatial organization to define and hold a light plane. Our dark background suggests undefinable spaces wherein neither house nor eyes can be unequivocally settled. The house, being tightly attached to the paper's upper and right borders, seems to be more securely held in place than the eyes, but even its heavily painted rectangular shapes might escape upward, for there is no roof, nor is there any baseline attaching the building securely to the ground.

Since the house is only outlined, the surrounding darkness appears to reign inside as well. No person is represented, but the size of the door and doorknob suggests small figures. The floating eyes, on the other hand, are lifesize. The onlooker is led either to feel himself a tiny figure scurrying for safety through uncharted darkness, beneath the gaze of seven giant eyes, or else he may conceive of himself as lifesize, confronting the eyes on equal terms. However, any attempt to focus on them must fail, for no pair can be constructed from the seven floating shapes. Each eye remains single and each can be interpreted as belonging to either the left or the right half of a face. This ambiguity corresponds to our own feeling of disorientation. To boot, Remo has told us that the eyes are dangerous, for he has attacked each iris and crossed it out.

The sense of danger, loneliness, and disorientation emanating from the painting is quite inescapable; we are moved, for we have experienced kindred states of mind. This power to touch us sets Remo's work apart from ordinary paranoid productions which may perturb us as evidence of pathology but leave us emotionally cold.

How has Remo achieved this? Was it because he was unusually gifted? Evidently, a child entirely devoid of talent could not have painted the picture, but at some felicitous moment even the moderately gifted may produce exceptional work. Remo was not an outstanding painter. Most of his production was empty, commonplace, or fragmented. By comparing *Ghost House* with another picture that is more typical of Remo's run-of-the-mill production we may learn something about what made it possible for the miracle to occur.

Remo painted *The Flag* (Fig. 1) in the mid-1950s before burning the flag had become a standard symbol of racial or political protest. At that time painting a flag had mainly a defensive function—to produce something that could not possibly convey personal meaning and yet must surely satisfy any teacher's demand for virtue.

In Figure 1 we note a progression from obsessive

FIGURE 1. *Remo:* Flag (18″ x 24″)

rigidity to angry gesture. Remo began with a green baseline; then he planted his flagpole into a meticulously painted brick base. Losing patience with the mathematical intricacies of the American flag, he contented himself with suggesting its main features. Around this meager factual statement, mood emerges—first in the three depressed dark-gray clouds and finally in an outburst of red flamelike brush strokes. The latter, however, respect all objects— even the flag does not catch fire.

The picture lacks integration. We note Remo's capacity for perceiving the logical intricacies of the brick base, his patience, and his manual dexterity. We note feelings of depression and anger, we see elements that could conceivably come together to convey a message, but as long as Remo hid behind the empty symbol of the American flag, he had no theme around which an evocative painting could crystalize.

This comes to pass when Remo was able in his *Ghost House* to give form to the anxieties and suspicions that pervaded his life without becoming helplessly enmeshed in them. His behavior testified to his state of autonomy. When he painted *Ghost House* he was neither compulsively bent on being a good boy nor was he subject to the frantic excitement that would usually build up after even a short period of controlled behavior. Instead he seemed at ease, absorbed in his work, fully in command of himself and of his art materials. The completed painting was greatly admired by his schoolmates. (This was in contrast to the violently hostile feelings which his person usually elicited.) He had done them a service, giving exquisite form to terrors common to them all. For the duration of this single session Remo seemed to have gained access to the most perturbed aspects of his emotional life in such a manner that his ego functions were not thereby disrupted or weakened. Instead he could create an image of his inner darkness. The painting seems to be born of a struggle against engulfment by persecutory ideation rather than being a symptom of any overt feelings of persecution.

The brief victory did not constitute a cure. Remo could not maintain the balance he had unexpectedly miraculously achieved. The episode may have given him a taste of what autonomous functioning can be like and this might conceivably help him mobilize energies for coming to terms with his troubles, but of this we have no knowledge. Meanwhile, his painting endures, to move and instruct us.

Harry: Twelve-year-old Harry also was a resident at the Wiltwyck School, but his behavior was less flagrantly pathological than was Remo's masochistic performance.[1] He had been raised by a paranoid schizophrenic mother and himself showed tendencies toward personality fragmentation. However, his controls were on the whole reliable and there was evidence of considerable ego

1. I have described Harry and his art more fully in two preceding books: *Art Therapy in a Children's Community* and *Art as Therapy with Children*.

strength. When Harry painted the group of pictures which he later arranged in a sort of triptych, he had been a resident for almost a year and had made a good adjustment.

The menacing ambiguity of Remo's *Ghost House* contrasts sharply with the sober cruelty of Harry's triptych of *Instruments of Execution* (Figs. 2, 3, and 4; Pl. II). Figure 3 (Pl. II), with its depiction of the guillotine's monumental structure, is the most impressive of the paintings, but the executioner's ax (Fig. 2) and the gallows silhouetted against a lonesome landscape (Fig. 4) contribute to the feeling of inexorable doom which emanates from the group as a whole. In each picture the execution is over. Two carefully outlined drops of blood tell of the head that only a short time ago filled the awful emptiness beneath the guillotine's bloodstained blade. The basket at the bottom is ready to receive the next head. The tick-tack-toe design surrounding the guillotine frame in rhythmic alternation of brown and black (maybe a count of heads?) emphasizes the empty space in the middle.

The droplets of blood on the executioner's ax dribbling onto the block, a single handcuff on the ground, and a bloodstained basket tell of a recent execution. The ax stuck into the block, its handle pointing diagonally to the left, seems ready for the next blow. A looped rope at the handle's end accentuates this feeling of poised immobility.

In the picture of the gallows the heavily braided rope and empty noose tell a similar story. The structure stands heavily planted against a faintly blue sky. We note a closed coffin beneath the rope.

We are in the presence of a logical, cruel, and cool mind. The killings have been legal. There is little gore, only just enough blood to tell the story. Each instrument of death is realistically and meticulously depicted. Unlike Remo's darkness which seems filled with mysterious life, Harry's *Instruments of Execution* convey a sense of finality. Even the dead have gone. In the absence of living beings, the instruments seem to have drawn all vitality onto themselves.

FIGURE 3.. *Harry:* Guillotine
(18″ x 24″)

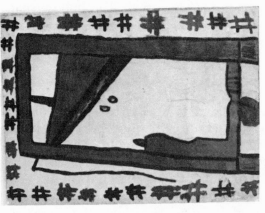

FIGURE 2. *Harry:* Ax
(18″ x 24″)

FIGURE 4. *Harry:* Gallows
(18″ x 24″)

Without their actual appearance having been changed in any way, they seem alive. Poised for action, they appear to be waiting for the next kill. Only the rope hanging importantly in each painting constitutes a link to the human agent who could set these engines in motion.

We cannot empathize with Harry as we could with Remo. The world he evokes is foreign and it chills us to the bone, but we must admire his superb sense of form, his moderation, and his artistic economy. The three paintings which form the triptych have unity. All objects—even drops of blood—are outlined in black. The same strong brown prevails in each painting. The hollow space in the guillotine's center carries over into the expanse behind ax and gallows on either side. The bold shapes are beautifully positioned so that each painting is distinct yet complements the others.

Unlike Remo, whose *Ghost House* was an unusual, unexpected event, Harry was an assiduous and successful painter. His cruel and precise imagery served him well as a container and defense against the floridly violent fantasies that forever threatened to invade his perception of reality. It seemed to fulfill the same function for the community of disturbed boys of which he was a member. Because Harry's overriding need for defense against the threat of personality fragmentation made it unwise to investigate the underlying fantasy at the time, I have no information about the criminals that presumably had been executed by ax, guillotine, and gallows, or about their crimes. The pictures inform us not of fantasy content but of a *state of mind*, which no narrative could have communicated as precisely.

Jesus: While our first two examples carried us into a world of fantasy, twelve-year-old Jesus's painting *Sunset over the Bronx* (Pl. III) tells of a specific environment. Anyone familiar with the tenements of the South Bronx must recognize the neighborhood.

Jesus had been admitted to a child psychiatric ward in a Bronx hospital because of uncontrollable aggressive outbursts culminating in threatening his mother with a lead pipe. He was mildly retarded, able to conduct himself well within established routines and limits, but he panicked easily under stress. In spite of his intellectual limitations he was eager to learn and to understand, and he responded well to instruction in the ward's special classroom. After several months of treatment he had attained the status of day patient, attending the hospital's school and afternoon activities and returning to his own home in the evening. His slow progress toward complete discharge was interrupted by the death of a brother which brought on a new crisis at home and threw Jesus into depression, and he was readmitted to the hospital. He painted his picture several months after his second admission, when he was again waiting for a partial discharge. The painting seems to be a composite of memories of his own street and the view from the ward's west window, where the rooftops and upper stories of dark brick tenement buildings were faintly visible beyond the hospital's immediate environment. The spectacle of a pollution-red sunset could be observed on any fair night.

A row of tenements stretches horizontally across the whole page, dividing the paper equally into buildings and sky. We seem to perceive the houses from an upper-story window, conceivably the ward's windows, for neither doors nor sidewalk are depicted. The houses' walls are painted black. Brown lines are superimposed vertically. The house at the right-hand end of the row appears to be smaller and set back a little; its windows and walls are painted in greater detail and it seems as if vertical rows of lighted windows are alternating with unlit ones. All windows in the picture seem to have been raised from the bottom up. The lower part appears open, while the upper half is divided into windowpanes by vertical or crossed lines. There are no curtains or other signs of habitation. Jesus has not painted the inside of the windows at all. The light-yellowish manila paper remains visible, brilliant against the surrounding darkness so that it looks as if the lights have been turned on at dusk. Two chimneys and several TV antennas are silhouetted on the rooftops, a whole group of them placed above the right-hand house singling it out from the rest. Against the regularity of the buildings the sky in blue, red, and orange appears wild and free. Jesus painted it just as the sun was setting, and went back and forth repeatedly between the art room and the west window in the hall to observe the colors and clouds.

Even though the buildings convey an impression of precision, Jesus evidently had no need to plan his painting in pencil or charcoal. There is no sign of any anxious attempt to stay within preconceived limits. Each line stands easily. He seems to have been in full command of his design, and indeed, even though the row of buildings conveys an impression of complexity, one single pattern prevails throughout. It is as if the inclination to perseverate, which is characteristic of the mildly retarded, had enabled Jesus to evoke the stark sameness of the South Bronx tenements to perfection.

But this sameness alone would not have made a painting. Its beauty depends on the juxtaposition of buildings and sky, order and freedom, drabness and glowing color. Jesus's personality also could not be characterized solely by his need for limits and for order. He was a boy of complex feelings, capable of love and hate, of despair, anger, and joy.

Inasmuch as we can conceive of a painting as a symbolic expression of personality, Jesus seems to have come to terms with life by separating the reality he must contend with from affect, confining the latter to the fleeting world of the sky. Yet Jesus has also given us an excellent image of the world he must live in, a barren slum where only the sky adds color and beauty. That he is able to perceive this beauty and make it part of his world constitutes a victory of the spirit, surviving in an arid and confining environment.

Dwayne: Twelve-year-old Dwayne's *Self-Portrait* (Figs. 5 and 6) is painted ceramic clay about twelve inches high.

FIGURE 5. *Dwayne:* Self-Portrait, front view (12″ high)

FIGURE 6. *Dwayne:* Self-Portrait, side view (12″ high)

Because it is meant to be perceived in the round, it is difficult to convey on the printed page the miraculous quality of any sculptural work. Therefore, I confine myself to a single example—Dwayne's three-quarters-lifesize *Self-Portrait*, which even survives being reduced to a photograph. It embodies a highly intelligent boy's search for an integrated self after experiencing a series of shattering traumatic events. To measure the distance Dwayne traveled within a period of less than three months, I present one of his numerous earlier attempts to create a sculptured face (Fig. 7). At this time Dwayne could do no more than assemble the various elements that make up the configuration *face* and connect them to a rudimentary slab of clay. He was himself distressed by the grotesque appearance and above all by the primitive sameness of these productions. Finally he made up his mind to get out of this impasse by devoting himself seriously to making a self-portrait in a more adult manner.

FIGURE 7. *Dwayne:* The Human Nose (7″ high)

He was taught how to build an armature of wood and plaster and how to apply the clay systematically around this solid core. Built in this manner, the finished sculpture could be cut into halves, detached from its armature, reassembled, fired in a kiln, and finally painted with poster paint. To look at himself, Dwayne used a reversible shaving mirror with both an enlarging and a reducing side. That by simply reversing the sides he could get very close to his face or move further away was endlessly fascinating to him. It seemed to help him to establish the right distance toward himself and to perceive himself as a whole. When the sculpture had been fired, Dwayne spent much time carefully mixing the colors for skin, hair, eyes, mouth, and sweatshirt to match his own.

The sculpture marked a turning point in both his self-perception and his perception of others. He blossomed into a sensitive portraitist able to produce excellent likenesses in charcoal, enthusiastically sketching friends and family and gaining recognition for his talent, and he produced a number of excellent self-portraits in charcoal.

Only a short time before, any complex procedure in making sculpture would have been beyond Dwayne's capacities: he could have used a shaving mirror only for endlessly repetitive play—casting light reflections on walls or making the world larger or smaller at will. It was essential that material, tools, and instruction in using them were available when Dwayne emerged from his withdrawn and fragmented state. At this juncture the workmanlike logic of building a substantial sculpture in clay paralleled and confirmed the psychic process of reintegration. Moving further away and closer could be practiced in order to study both detail and totality with the aim of achieving unity in his portrait. Thus the making of Dwayne's sculpture constitutes a perfect example of the unity of material process and product in art. Dwayne's success inspired a number of schoolmates to follow his example; thus his sculpture also helped him form relationships.

Formally, Dwayne's sculpture combines preadolescent and adolescent characteristics—the focus is still on the triangle formed by eyes, nose, and mouth, while the forehead is barely noticed. Yet the intense attempt to perceive his own particular features—the narrow, long-jawed facial structure, the strong nose, wide-open eyes, half-open lips—has resulted in successful capture of highly differentiated expression, bespeaking the adolescent need for full individuation.

This intrinsically new manner of conceiving of visual representation appears most vividly in Dwayne's treatment of lips and teeth. A child would either have kept the mouth closed or would have represented two rows of teeth bared aggressively or in a defensively aggressive smile. Dwayne, however, has left the schematic enumeration of features and the simplified expressive signaling of childhood behind. He arrives at a subtle expression of sensual longing in which the primitive aggressive element is transcended. This expression of intense search gives his sculpture its powerful emotional appeal. We are relieved at last to encounter among our miracles an image of a human.

Albert: I conclude my collection of miracles by presenting a sequence of four paintings which admirably exemplifies the precarious location of artistic creation—forever poised between the menaces of chaotic discharge and the menace of constricting defenses (Figs. 8, 9, and 10; Pl. IV).

Ten-year-old Albert[2] had been admitted to the Wiltwyck School because of persistent truancy, fire setting, and numerous reckless and at times self-destructive daredevil exploits. During his first few months at the school this behavior persisted. Although he set no more fires, he could rarely be contained in any classroom; he escaped into the woods, often spending nights outdoors. He remained nonchalant in the face of the many injuries he managed to incur as he scaled fire escapes, climbed trees, and provoked fights with boys much older and stronger than himself.

2. I have discussed Albert and his tree more briefly in *Art Therapy in a Children's Community*, pp. 149–51.

Figure 8. *Albert:* Man (18″ x 24″)

Even though he was constantly on the run, he often managed to pay a flying visit to the art room. He drew many quick sketches of trees from life, showing remarkable powers of observation but lacking the patience to pursue work beyond the swiftest of sketches. He also painted faces. Figure 8 is typical of his work of these early days. Albert had just discovered how to use a dry brush and was enjoying its possibilities. The method was greatly favored by the boys because it permitted them to cover large areas of paper quickly and freely without any danger of producing an unwanted mess.

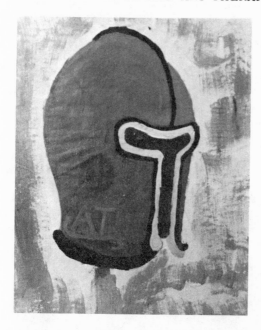

FIGURE 9. *Albert:*
Helmet (18″ x 24″)

FIGURE 10. *Albert:*
Autumn Tree,
sketch (18″ x 24″)

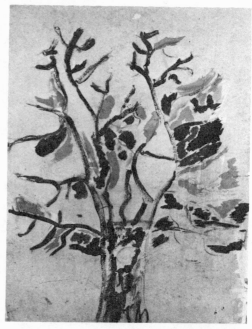

There is an intimation of talent in the rhythmic brush strokes that make up the strange apparition. The facial expression of pain and fear, which transcends any simplistic expressive schema, is particularly impressive, although the snowman-like body, rudimentary arms, and tiny legs seem incongruously immature. We note that this body, although lacking any well-defined boundaries, sports a row of solidly painted buttons down its front as if to affirm the possibility of buttoning up even in the face of rampant agitation.

Indeed, even during this period of driven restlessness Albert would function in a purposeful and controlled manner as long as he could choose his own tasks. I remember his arriving in the art room determined to help me clean it up and neither resting nor allowing me any respite until every scrap of paper was filed in the right child's portfolio and all materials and implements were restored to their proper places. When Albert had finished with the art room it radiated an unprecedented order and organization.

As time went on great efforts were made to induce Albert to settle down, stay in class, refrain from extravagant heroic exploits, and develop controls. During this time his art became exceedingly rigid and somewhat depressed.

He developed a great interest in medieval armor and drew many ironclad knights and shields; he particularly loved helmets. It was as if he were responding to his own lack of boundaries by growing a kind of protective lobster shell about himself, so that his individuality disappeared behind it.

Figure 9 was the acknowledged masterpiece of this period. The skillfully painted helmet is empty; Albert's person was reduced to a set of ornate initials on the helmet. Albert was inordinately proud of his achievement and insisted that the painting be given a place of honor in the rotating exhibition of the boys' pictures in the dining room. There the hollow symbol gave sinister testimony to the danger of establishing controls. But Albert was not to be depersonalized and confined for long.

In the last six months before his discharge from the Wiltwyck School he again began to sketch trees with much pleasure; his old impatience frequently overtook him, so most of them remained uncompleted. Figure 10 is a good example of these promising but quickly abandoned attempts. Naturally, I did all I could to encourage Albert in his new venture.

For a long time my efforts were in vain, but one day he entered the art room declaring that he needed to paint a beautiful picture to give to the head counselor. This was a stern but benign man, one of the school's pillars of peace and justice who had been instrumental in taming Albert's wild ways. The picture was to be a parting gift, for Albert knew that he would be discharged in the near future. He had spent several long weekends with his mother and a new stepfather who was showing much understanding of and interest in Albert, and the situation seemed reasonably promising.

I suggested that Albert paint a picture of the large maple tree he had previously sketched and that he try to complete it this time. It was a crisp, sunny October day and the tree was aflame with brilliant fall colors. Albert duly went outdoors to make the sketch which was to become *Autumn Tree* in charcoal. Returning with it to the art room, he seriously addressed himself to the problem of joining the well-observed branches to the tree's trunk. We note that his earlier sketch (Fig. 10) still consisted of a childishly conceived trunk complete with the obligatory squirrel hole and cut off at the height of the crown, from which more realistically conceived branches extend in many directions. The same was still evident in his new sketch.

As Albert had suddenly become aware of the intrinsic unity of trunk and branches, I suggested that he go outdoors once more to observe exactly how the trunk divided into several main branches. He was able to improve his drawing and on his return to the art room he painted trunk and branches a dark brown.

He then prepared a tray of yellow, orange, and red paint complete with an individual brush for each color and to my amazement began methodically to fill the spaces between the brown network of branches and twigs with irregularly spaced areas of pure yellow, orange, and red. These separate colors combined to create an astoundingly intense impression of the brilliance and variety of the maple's foliage (Pl. IV). Even though the manner in which he applied his colors was rhythmic and in no way compulsively precise, he was afraid he would not have the patience to complete his intricate painting. He managed it by working at it off and on throughout the day, with a little assistance on my part. Whenever I noticed his courage flagging I joined him briefly in painting in his colors, taking good care to leave all color choices and decisions about placement to him. The foliage completed, Albert bounded the tree's crown with a sky in intense variegated blues.

Finally Albert addressed himself to the grassy ground, and here he encountered difficulties. Albert had drawn his tree issuing from the bottom of his paper, so that the paper's edge constituted a primitive baseline. We are familiar with this spatial arrangement from the drawing of insecure or immature children. A linear strip of grassy ground below and a corresponding band of blue sky above would have been consistent with this developmental level, but Albert had outgrown these simplistic ideas. The placement of the tree trunk seemed a leftover from an earlier period. He helped himself by carrying the grassy ground upward and behind his tree, just as he had made the sky spread out behind as well as above his tree's crown. But the tree trunk constituted too heavy an obstruction and the grass appeared lifeless and dull. Albert tried to improve the area by scattering multicolored leaves on the ground, but the overall effect is not altogether satisfactory.

It is interesting that Albert reached an impasse in the pictorial area which tends to be expressive of the individual's footing in the real world (he was about to be discharged into a still-untried family constellation). In spite of this the painting constitutes an extraordinary achievement. It admirably conveys the spirit of the brilliant autumn day on which it was created. Its controlled vitality sets it apart both from Albert's earlier wispy and driven paintings and from the cold rigidity of the armor period that followed. We perceive the aggressive force that had driven Albert to fire setting and dangerous exploits neither extinguished nor imprisoned, but channeled into constructive expression, so we can, without hesitation, speak of sublimation.

The process whereby sublimation was attained does not essentially differ from that of the mature artist. The confluence of powerful impressions coming from the natural world and corresponding inner experiences leads to the creation of a painting which is at once an image of the artist's personality and an inspired interpretation of nature. A change of goal, of process, and of the kind of energy used had been achieved as Albert lovingly and patiently painted the woods which once had been his refuge from the demands of civilization. The woods are aflame with autumn colors but they are not consumed, for this is part of the natural cycle of growth and decay. Furthermore, Albert was laboring to make a present for the very person who had helped him establish controls.

The painting was duly hung in a place of honor in the head counselor's office, where it remained until Albert's discharge. Albert's gift differed from more emotionally neutral offerings such as a pair of bookends or any other useful object he might have made with his own hands. Such a present would undoubtedly also have been well received and would have served to cement and celebrate Albert's attachment to and identification with the controlling adult, but in giving his *Autumn Tree* Albert had made a present of himself. It was essentially a narcissistic gift, a means of symbolically remaining in the counselor's presence and of making his own person unforgettable to him. Inasmuch as Albert chose an object that was indeed interesting to the adult, who loved the woods dearly, Albert transcended infantile narcissism and fulfilled the artist's social function, to make the world more animated and meaningful to others through his art.

The ultimate destiny of Albert's tree also signifies something about the art therapist's position in the creative process. It is no accident that it was given to the admired counselor, the parental figure par excellence, not to me who had helped make it. As art therapists we are rarely the ones to be wooed or appeased with beautiful artwork. Rather, our position is that of a facilitator, an auxiliary ego, ready to serve the child, to supply some needed extra energy, patience, control, or skill when the child's own resources are wanting. Just because we are inextricably part of the creative process it rarely occurs to any child–artist to give us a picture as a present.

Albert's being able to make the tree gives no assurance that the kind of functioning he was capable of at that specific moment would be possible for him in daily life or even in his future artwork. Although the painting gives us ground for cautious hope, all we know for certain is that on one October day Albert, age eleven and a half, was able to attain an unusually felicitous balance between drive and control through the process of sublimation in art, that such functioning was therefore within his power, and that the experience is now part of his store of memories of joyfully constructive functioning. Even if the experience is forgotten, the memory of it for some reason repressed, it can never be entirely lost to him.

In more general terms, Albert's example demonstrates that temporary rigidity and loss of expressive powers need not inevitably be harmful. They can also be a necessary detour for the impulsive individual to attain the capacity for sustained and controlled expressive work.

We have devoted many pages to the description and analysis of exceptional work such as the practicing art therapist encounters only infrequently. What can we learn from these examples, particularly since we cannot claim that such miracles necessarily herald clinical improvement?

Each work we have contemplated has been unique in form, content, and mood; the common element is the intrinsic unity of process and product, of form and content, of overt and covert meaning in each of them. Each miracle constituted a model of integrated functioning whereby visual symbols came into existence that served as equivalents for exceedingly complex, multilayered experiences that touched upon the child–artist's innermost self.

The work had come into being without much outside influence. Each child had been motivated from within, and since their inner lives were burdened with and distorted by pathological processes, these elements helped determine the form and content of their work. Jesus and Albert transcend this self-absorption. Their paintings combine self-portrait and an inspired interpretation of the environment.

Even though the art therapist's special understanding contributed to the interpretation of the form and content of our examples, we have in this chapter on the whole learned more about art than about art therapy. We chose to open our discussion in this way because the vivid awareness of the integrative and expressive power of art is essential for the practice of art therapy; this vitally important principle can be most convincingly demonstrated by examples where emotional disturbance and heightened creative functioning coincide. Once we have become acquainted with them through unusually impressive instances we will be better able to recognize processes of artistic integration even when they appear in more fleeting and abortive ways.

Noteworthy in our examples has been unity between the child's handling of the materials and the resulting artwork. There was no evidence of the frequently evoked dichotomy between process and product. This raises the question of whether the commonly stated notion that art education is product oriented while art therapy is process oriented contributes to our understanding of art, art education, and art therapy. Perhaps such an oversimplification confuses more than it enlightens. Particularly when we speak of children, to whom the distinction between amateur and professional does not apply, these ideas seem misleading. Sometimes, of course, the creative process falters and therefore does not culminate in any product; nevertheless the artistic process, carried to its conclusion, does result in a product which in turn has a life of its own and may wield an important influence on both its maker and its audience.

Conversely, we cannot conceive of any genuine art product that is *not* the culmination of a creative process. Products that are manufactured by plotting and scheming to achieve preconceived results do not partake of art at all. They lack the dignity of even the most abortive artistic attempt and belong at best to the realm of commercially applied art. To designate art education as product oriented in the latter sense is demeaning to the profession.

The misunderstanding seems to have two separate sources. On the one hand there is the plight of the art educator who, faced with unreasonable demands from parents or administrations for easily demonstrable achievements, must sometimes compromise by diluting or perverting the creative process; he may become product oriented against his better judgment. On the other hand, it is true that art therapy is distinguished from art education by a much lower rate of finished work.

The art therapist who works with extremely handicapped children must vastly more often than the art teacher be contented with fostering processes that do not culminate in any lasting product. At times all thought of achieving finished paintings or sculptures may have to be abandoned while children endlessly experiment with art materials, vent their anger on them, or desert their work before it is finished.

Furthermore, disturbed children's preoccupations with their inner conflicts frequently make them inaccessible to conventional educative methods. Established ways of stimulating and focusing perception and of teaching techniques or of making children aware of the formal elements of art must be subordinated to therapeutic goals, must at times be modified or perhaps entirely set aside. In spite of everything, however, any discipline which partakes of art at all remains committed to processes that ideally culminate in art. To lose sight of this commitment is to deprive the disturbed child a priori of the possibility of experiencing the full creative process.

Naturally there are times when even the art therapist must connive in bypassing the process in order to manufacture imitations. It can be more important to help a child save face or fulfill some overriding need than to insist on any absolute standard, even the standard of honesty. For example, twelve-year-old Angel came to my studio clutching a snapshot of his forever elusive father who had left town that very morning without saying good-bye. Angel was determined to produce a handpainted oil painting of him from that very poor photograph. Angel was an excellent portraitist, advanced beyond his age. He could never have been satisfied with a schematic image such as a younger child might produce from memory. Only if his father had posed for a portrait could Angel's artistic and emotional needs have been properly fulfilled. Since this could not be, I did my best to help him concoct a likeness from the snapshot in order to satisfy his need to somehow restore his father. I even condoned his using oil paint on canvas board to lend the painting a spurious dignity, although I abhor such amateurish procedures on principle. I was not at this time working regularly with Angel and would have no opportunity to help him with his problem on a more profound level, either emotionally or technically. Therefore, I had perforce to remain product oriented, e.g., to help him produce an artistically worthless, emotionally shallow painting.

Returning to our miracles, beyond the quality of inner

consistency what other common characteristics can we find? We find in each instance familiar, well-worn, even trite formal components which, by some alchemy, acquire eloquence.

On the psychic level a similar transition from the well-worn to the extraordinary can be observed. Each child's pathology is of long standing, all-pervasive and repetitive. It appears that it is not essentially changed but rather *illuminated* by his miracle.

Remo's eyes and his house with barred windows are part of the commonplace vocabulary of the sinister. The arrangement of spaces in white on black makes the painting unique. The picture does not simply inform us of his paranoid tendencies, it conveys to us what it is like to feel observed, plunged into darkness, and to experience rapid changes of body size and position in space. Harry's *Instruments of Execution* are not in themselves remarkable; they acquire their peculiar life by exquisite spatial arrangement and great economy in the use of color. The triptych does more than document Harry's murderous and vengeful fantasies and feeling of depersonalization. It carries us into a world in which both aggressor and victim have vanished and only the inanimate instruments of death retain an eerie life. Jesus builds his cityscape out of simplistic, repetitive patterns; only their juxtaposition with a wild and glowing sky transforms the painting into an eloquent statement. Beyond informing us of the mildly retarded boy's tendency to perseverate and of his explosive emotionality, it conveys the sense of a life hemmed in by both intellectual and environmental limitations yet suffused with passion and longing.

Dwayne endlessly manufactured the single elements of the configuration face until he was ready to integrate them to form the individual countenance that speaks to us. His *Self-Portrait*, however, tells us nothing of his troubles, but only of his triumph. We are moved by its intense expression of search, but the preceding shattering of the self cannot be deduced from the sculpture. The same holds true for Albert's *Autumn Tree*. It mainly conveys exuberant vitality, giving only faint indications of his precarious position in the world and no sign at all of his previous destructive and self-destructive inclinations.

Can we fathom the intrapsychic processes that may have been active in the making of these works? Can we discern any specific elements that distinguish them from those that result in more ordinary productions?

Common to all our miracles is a transition from fantasy to imagination. These two words are often used interchangeably, but for our analysis we must make a clear distinction. When we speak of fantasy we have in mind a world that is fluid, protean, subservient to wish fulfillment, oblivious of contradictions and other stringencies of reality. Fantasy becomes imagination as the ego strives to impose some measure of stability and clarity upon these id-dominated productions. The ego in turn is enriched as the wealth of images and associations fantasy brings forth becomes available to the creative process.

Transforming fantasy into imagination is equally essential for the artist who strives to give form to the inner world and to the artist who depicts external reality. Even the fantastic attains its logic and visual organization through the ego's mediation. Conversely, the artist who is bent on realistic representation could not organize his perceptions and achieve the abstractions implied in creating visual images without resorting to preexisting inner representations of the outside world. These are of necessity not exact replicas of past perceptions but emotionally invested elaborations and condensations that partake of fantasy.

The outcome may be infinitely varied. Fantasy, bent on quick gratification, is apt to be oblivious of the contradictory complexities of psychic and outside reality and is ever ready to deny any unwelcome inner and outer truth. On the other hand, the ego's fear of instinctual forces is apt to impose radical repressions on fantasy. Depending on the distribution of forces, art is in danger of becoming either formless and flimsy or overly constricted and lifeless. In floridly psychotic art the ego's organizing propensities may be overwhelmed so that the work comes close to the fluidity of primary-process thinking. Or if reality is reinterpreted according to paranoid ideation the ego may be reduced to imposing rigid organization onto a world that nevertheless remains fragmented. If the proper balance is attained, art can become both expressive and highly organized.

Our examples are characterized by extraordinary integration and evocative power. It follows that psychic mechanisms that would have prevented such unity cannot have prevailed while they were being made. Instead, both denial and repression must have been to a large extent relinquished, without—and herein lies the miracle—causing either regression or anxiety. Far from being overwhelmed by intrusions from the id, the ego has been strengthened and its realm extended. The energy saved by the lowering of repressions and the abandonment of denials has become available to the ego for use in the productive process. In psychoanalytic terms, regression has served the ego and sublimation has been achieved.

The process informs and enriches the child not so much by uncovering the repressed as by illuminating what is familiar to him and in some instances restoring what has been lost. Remo's and Harry's paintings illuminate their state of mind. Dwayne's self-portrait helps to restore the unity of his personality that was temporarily lost.

The art therapist's experiences run parallel. Miracles seldom yield new facts. If we want to know about a child's family situation, about his body image or his areas of conflict, a simple house–tree–person or kinetic family drawing will tell us more than any evocative work of art. If, however, we desire to conceive of another human being, of those imponderables which transcend the circumstantial, the miracle informs us. To receive the message we need not resort to the specialist's skill at decoding visual productions. If we contemplate the work with an open mind we can partake of the child's inner world without violating his personal integrity by any intrusive act.

Are we justified in recognizing sublimation in all our miracles? We need not hesitate in the case of Jesus, Dwayne, and Albert. In each case, primitive acting-out, unproductive displacement, or paralyzing constrictions have been replaced by an act of integration and of communication. Libidinal and aggressive energies have been largely neutralized or tamed. Can we say the same of Remo's or Harry's work?

In Remo's case communication has replaced acting-out inasmuch as he was ordinarily inclined to provoke situations that would reduce him to the haunted, fearful state he evokes in his picture. He handles his art materials with the economy and serenity that speak of mastery and love, so we can speak of sublimation in the realm of execution. About the underlying fantasy we know very little, and it is entirely possible that it persists unredeemed. Indeed, the painting may well constitute a means of perpetuating the state it evokes and may even serve vengeful fantasies in which others are made to suffer as he himself is suffering.

The situation is similar in Harry's work. Sublimation is attained in the area of expressive communication, but the underlying fantasies persist unaltered as far as we know. Perhaps his pictures constitute even a kind of imaginary rehearsal of executions to be performed in real life. Nonetheless, Remo's and Harry's work permits each of them to contemplate his state of mind in serenity, a rare and precious opportunity in the impulse-ridden, chaotic life of a delinquent child. Art has fulfilled its function of transforming fantasy into imagination.

Our analysis leaves many questions unanswered. We have contemplated finished works, analyzed their content and formal quality, and from this evidence attempted to deduce the nature of the psychological processes that must have been active in their making. But we have learned very little about the inner reasons or the external circumstances that led to the making of each individual work.

Albert's story presents us with an example of the oscillation between fluidity and rigidity that occurs so frequently in art. It points to the necessity of finding a middle ground between these extremes. It also tells us of the importance of strong, positive relationships in mobilizing energies for sublimation. But even our information on Albert is scanty. Miracles are rare, and it is in their nature to be elusive. At this point our five examples can yield no further information.

We can learn more about the art therapist's work and more about the workings of sublimation by investigating instances where the creative process miscarries or remains incomplete, and we will encounter such work in subsequent chapters.

At present we will reverse our course and turn to the origins of image making—to work that is barely distinct from imaginative play—and observe the art therapist's role in facilitating the transition from play to art.

Art, Art Therapy, and Play

PLAY AND PLAYFULNESS

AS WE INTRODUCE children and adults to art, we find them coming to it from opposite positions. The child comes from a life still dominated by fantasy and play, the adult from the responsibilities of the real world. The adult must at once become more playful and more ready to expend serious effort in a pursuit that may at the onset seem mere child's play to him. The child, on the other hand, must transcend play and become more goal directed and workmanlike in his art. For both child and adult, art ultimately becomes an effortful seriously invested pursuit, which even as it touches upon the tragedies and griefs of life, as well as its joys, remains imbued by a playful spirit. Since playfulness is an essential quality of all the arts, as indeed of all cultural living, distinctions between art and play become easily blurred. Practicing art therapists who function beyond the pale of professionally established arts must forever navigate between these realms: encourage playfulness to stimulate imagination yet intercede when art threatens to dissipate into play; tolerate regression from art to play or assist in the transition from play to art, according to the exigencies of the various situations they encounter.

Our interest will focus on the kind of play where transition to art is fluid, such as playful experimentation

A condensed version of this chapter was published in the *American Journal of Art Therapy*, No. 1 (1977), under the title "Art Therapy and Play."

with art materials and imaginative play, while we need not consider games that are played according to rules. Also, we are not investigating the *emotional content* of play, the joys, anxieties, pains, and longings or the compensating fantasies which are its substance, or the gradual changes of content that can be observed in the course of maturation.[1] Rather, we hope to gain understanding of the inner laws which govern art and play, and of the different ego functions that are active in these related processes.

A lengthy study of the play of animals will be included since knowledge about the natural history of a function that has evolved before the advent of man can help us understand human behavior, providing that we avoid drawing any simplistic conclusions from the example of kindred phenomena among the lower species.

We will introduce this complex subject by describing an art therapy session in which play overshadowed art.

Sara: Ten-year-old Sara is seen in an evaluatory art therapy session at an outpatient clinic. She has been referred for disruptive behavior at school, truancy, and academic failure. The youngest of six siblings, she lives with her mother and five older brothers and sisters in an urban slum. The family is on welfare. Her mother has suffered repeated depressive episodes requiring hospitalization. She is anxious, ineffective, and overwhelmed by life. A visiting stepfather is in the picture and a new baby on the way. The family is close-knit. The children seem united in an effort to encourage and uphold their mother, for they dread her going to the hospital again.

Offered a choice of drawing materials, clay, and poster paint, Sara unhesitatingly chooses clay and sets out to prepare a Thanksgiving feast for herself and her family. Various lumps of clay are designated as representing the traditional foods. She pays little attention to giving them recognizable shapes. Next she fashions a set of identical

1. Lilli Peller, *On Development and Education of Young Children*, Section III; see also Susan Isaacs, *The Nursery Years,*

half-round shapes standing for the backs of chairs and attaches to each of them an identical round disc standing for the face of a family member. She carefully considers the seating arrangement: mother is placed in the center with the best-liked siblings close to her, grandmother sits at a distance, stepfather and stepbrother at a separate table. Sara has not represented her own person. When I ask, "But where are you?" she smiles disarmingly: "But I am *here*." However, she fashions a clay plate and serves herself first. Her mother is served next and then all family members are conscientiously supplied with food according to their tastes and appetites. When Sara has finished distributing the food, she goes through some playful eating motions. The session being over, she contentedly picks up the clay, rolls it into balls, and puts them back in the clay bucket. She smilingly declares that she expects the whole family to be together this coming Thanksgiving. Finally, she tells us that she and her siblings spent last Thanksgiving at a home (the children were placed in a shelter during their mother's hospitalization).

Sara's session had been a beneficial experience, but it was not an art session. Clay had been used as a toy, a vehicle for acting out Sara's wishes, not for symbolically representing them. The various pieces of clay acquired meaning by designation. It would have been impossible to guess from their shapes which of these lumps was turkey, corn fritters, or potatoes. Unless Sara informed us, we could never guess which of the moon-faces represented which person. Above all, Sara herself was not represented in clay. She was present in the flesh.

Energy had flowed into imagining the dramatic event. The clay vehicle had not become invested. Once Sara had finished playing, her play people and play food reverted to clay—emotionally neutral matter waiting to take on new meaning at another time.

Our playful Sara had used her opportunity well. Deprived and hungry, she had given herself a feast. Being the youngest, she had gratified her desire for ascendance and made her family obey her commands. Yet she had not regressed to irresponsible infancy but had maintained the attitude of a child in the latency period. Although she had usurped her mother's function, she had been tenderly protective of her; while bossing her siblings and other relatives, she had treated each one fairly and had provided them with sustenance.

Sara impressed us as a deprived but vigorous child engaged in a struggle, first to get enough for herself, next for her mother and family. At this point in her life she was still able to make up for missing gratifications via play and fantasy. However, her play was characteristic of a six- to eight-year-old child rather than a ten-year-old.

To play in the presence of a sympathetic and attentive adult had been helpful, but transition from play to art would probably be difficult for her. She seemed to be a pragmatic child, needing much real gratification, ready to state her needs playfully but unready for the more arduous task of image making.

Naturally I do not mean to imply that the difference between art and play hinges on skill in making recognizable objects. A three-year-old presents us with three shapeless lumps of clay, one of them bigger than the other two, and explains, "I made a cat and two kittens." A retarded blind boy digs a hole in a lump of clay and produces two flat pancake shapes to go with it and declares that he has made his mother's face (her mouth and cheeks). The enormous mental effort that went into singling out these specific shapes, connecting them to ideas, and establishing them as symbolic representations that can outlast the moment bestows on these creations the dignity of art at its most primitive level.

Sara, on the other hand, at the age of ten could very well have made recognizable objects, but she was not interested for she was only playing. Had she been offered a collection of lifelike toy people and toy foods, she probably would have been delighted. But such toys would have been a luxury rather than a necessity. Toys stimulate the imagination and help broaden the scope of play; to reign over a miniature world offers a delicious feeling of mastery while the very smallness of the toy objects gives assurance that all this occurs within playful sanctuary. But when play goes really well, children are incredibly self-sufficient. Sticks and stones, pots and pans, furniture—anything at all—take on life and meaning by a simple act of designation, and this is the *magic of play*. It is distinct from the *miracle of art*, which depends on the arduous creation of new objects whose sole function resides in their symbolic meaning. This transition from magic to miracle is the subject of our investigation.

Ten-year-old Sara's imaginative play is more complex by far than an infant's earliest playful activities; an even-wider gulf separates it from the play of wild or domestic animals. We nevertheless unhesitatingly use the word *play* for them all, for we sense their intrinsic community.

HUMAN AND ANIMAL PLAY

This realization is not new. As early as 1933 the psychologist F. J. J. Buytendjyk devoted an entire book to play in man and animal.[2] He exquisitely describes characteristics common to all play. Foremost he stresses the unending back-and-forth of play, the absence of any aim or goal. He notes that language precisely reflects this iridescent quality; e.g., we say the light plays upon the water, but we never say the rain plays against the windowpane. Second, he notes that play requires a plaything which embodies these iridescent qualities, either a living playmate or an inanimate thing or force that can be made to respond in a nonthreatening but also a not fully predictable manner. By virtue of being at once unpredictable and reliably in the

2. F. J. J. Buytendjyk, *Das Spiel von Mensch und Tier.*

player's control, the rubber ball constitutes the plaything par excellence. Finally, Buytendjyk notes that play needs the sanctuary of areas distinct from the larger environment, places where play can be enjoyed in safety. All this pertains to man and animal alike.

Historians as well as psychologists have noted that play antedates human culture and yet becomes an essential ingredient of it. The historian Johan Huizinga remarks:

> Animals play just like men. We have only to watch young dogs to see that all essentials of human play are present in their merry gambols. They invite one another to play by a certain ceremoniousness of attitudes and gesture. They keep to the rule that you shall not bite, or not bite hard your brother's ear. They pretend to get terribly angry. And—what is most important—in all these doings, they plainly experience tremendous fun and enjoyment. ...In play there is something *at play* which transcends the immediate needs of life and imparts meaning to action.[3]

Buytendjyk's and Huizinga's observations are confirmed and elucidated by the detailed study of animal play and its function in the evolution of mind conducted by ethologists such as Meyer-Holzapfel, Lorenz, Leyhausen, Tinbergen, and others. We find that animal play occurs only within a field of "relaxed tension."[4] The young play within the shelter of parental protection. Adults play when the environment is benign. Characteristically, animals at play spontaneously produce a broad range of behavior germane to their species—not just behavior belonging to the realm of hunting and food gathering, but, most important to our study, the whole repertoire of social signaling. These various sets of behavior occur out of context, seemingly at random, independent of the period of life in which they would be functional or the environmental or social stimuli that would elicit them in earnest. Indeed, situations that would generate any overriding impulses for specific social behavior—such as the urge to establish hierarchic suprem-

---

3. Johan Huizinga, *Homo Ludens*, p. 1.
4. G. Bally, *Von Ursprung und von den Grenzen der Freiheit.*

acy, to be submissive, to mate, to defend offspring—extinguish play, as does the pressure of hunger, rage, or fear. Conversely, only in play can movements belonging to entirely different realms of functioning follow each other swiftly. For instance, Konrad Lorenz notes tha a cat which arches its back because it has been seriously frightened needs many minutes to calm itself before it is at all ready to engage in any other activity.[5] At play the same arched back occurs at random, to be followed quickly by gestures belonging to entirely different situations. This is possible because the behavior is without consequences, not linked to any serious task. Herein lie both the opportunities and the limitations of play.

Paul Leyhausen points out that powerful "appetence toward the consummating act" can motivate an animal to put up with unpleasant experiences that are necessary for realizing its goal. For example, a lion might brave the hoofs of his wounded prey as he inflicts a final deadly bite, displaying all the while unmistakable signs of fear. He is nevertheless driven not only by actual hunger but by an instinctive need to complete the task. "In these facts lies the oldest and no doubt also the most important evolutionary root of all work and all effort undertaken voluntarily, in other words of 'duty.'"[6]

Play lacks this power. Not being goal oriented it can perpetuate itself almost indefinitely, but it has no energy available to push the organism beyond the threshold of unpleasure. The dichotomy of *play* and *necessity* thus seems firmly established before the advent of man.

The Functional Value of Play

The play of animals, then, seems to be nonutilitarian, energized by appetite for the behavior itself and independent of any immediate useful goal. Yet the vast energies

5. Konrad Lorenz, *Behind the Mirror.*
6. Konrad Lorenz and Paul Leyhausen, *Motivation of Human and Animal Behavior*, p. 235.

used in play compel us to conclude that play is somehow important to survival. The value of play becomes even more mystifying when we learn that perfecting coordination and strengthening the body through playful practice and exercise seem to be only a minor function of the play of animals. Experiments show that when animals are prevented from playing they nevertheless produce perfectly and on schedule the coordinated sets of movements they need. For example, jackdaws kept in cages beyond the period in which they would ordinarily make their first inept attempts at flight will fly expertly when released at the age in which flight normally reaches perfection.

It seems that the importance of play should be attributed more to the opportunity it affords the immature animal to become acquainted with its species' entire repertoire of behavior, including actions that would otherwise occur only under extreme stress. Behavior of attack and flight, of self-defense and defense of offspring, of giving warning and seeking cover are experimented with in safety and with pleasure. Social signaling can be rehearsed without serious consequence. For instance, a weak animal may make threatening gestures before its elders without being summarily punished for this impudence.

Another important value of play seems connected with its random quality. While necessity links stimulus–mood–response into rigidly programmed sequences for the animal, play induces experimentation with innumerable permutations. This makes play particularly valuable to those species which must adapt to changing environments, who are *opportunists* rather than *specialists* in the struggle for survival. Specialists are endowed with programmed behavior that is beautifully but narrowly adapted to specific environments and specific ways of life, with little leeway for change. Opportunists are able to accommodate to a great variety of environments and to draw sustenance from many sources. Their innate endowment is open-ended and must be synchronized with learned behavior to attain survival value. Information about the environment must be acquired by each individual. Animals of this kind tend to be both playful and curious. Evidently these qualities reach their highest development in man.

However, unlike play, curiosity is fraught with danger. (Curiosity, not play, killed the cat.) An unquenchable thirst for novelty will propel animals of the opportunistic species into situations where they experience fear and are poised for earnest flight. Lorenz describes this beautifully in the behavior of young ravens. These birds habitually approach each new object with extreme caution, attack it forcefully, and then retreat to a safe distance. Once the object has proved harmless, they experiment with it, vigorously applying their whole repertoire of hunting behavior. Once familiar with the object's properties, they have learned how to deal with it whenever they may encounter it again.[7]

We see that behavior motivated by curiosity is akin to play in being energized by an urge for pure experimentation rather than by any immediate physical need. It is, however, more stressful than play, for it has the power to propel the animal into dangerous situations. It seems that the distinction between the thirst for knowledge and the need to play is also established before the evolution of conceptual thought.

Those species which stay opportunists throughout life, such as felines, canines, or primates, must remain ready to perform an enormous variety of actions. The wish to carry them out must be programmed to exceed the demands that can be expected to be made on each kind of behavior in the course of any one individual's existence. Thus opportunists seem also to be driven to play by the pressure of appetite for actions that have not been sufficiently exercised in earnest pursuits, so that play seems to function as a safe way of maintaining inner equilibrium.[8] It is interesting to

---

7. Lorenz, *Behind the Mirror.*

8. Leyhausen describes this in great detail in the play of wild and domestic felines; Lorenz and Leyhausen, *Motivation of Human and Animal Behavior,* pp. 228-41.

consider that as the appetite for various kinds of behavior is gratified either in social play or in play with prey or toylike objects, the partner's or object's function continuously changes. Thus a playmate becomes the "one to be afraid of," the "one to be angry at," the "one to be chased," or the "one to be appeased." Prey used as plaything is treated in a similar manner.

Buytendjyk observes that wild animals as well as domestic ones are inclined to create toys for themselves.[9] It also seems that both wild and domestic animals respond vigorously to man-made objects that can gratify their varied playful needs more fully and reliably than either prey or accidentally found natural toys. Paul Leyhausen observed that his captive wild felines became readily attached to what the ethologists refer to as *supernormal objects*—for instance, rubber balls. Attachment increased with use. Such a ball would become "holed like a sieve," take on "an almost indescribable shape—become impossible to clean and quite irreplaceable." It was defended furiously and seemed to acquire territorial meaning.[10]

The phenomenon is strangely reminiscent of the human infant's long-lasting investment of what Winnicott termed *the transitional object*.[11] (Winnicott himself appears to have been aware of the similarity; he remarked in passing that "animals [too] have transitional objects."[12]) Thus we could venture to suggest that even art may have some roots in

9. Buytendjyk, *Das Spiel von Mensch und Tier.*

10. Lorenz and Leyhausen, *Motivation of Human and Animal Behavior*, p. 235.

11. D. W. Winnicott, "Transitional Objects and Transitional Phenomena," in *Through Paediatrics to Psycho-Analysis.* The transitional object is usually a blanket or a soft toy which the infant finds and over which "he assumes exclusive rights," developing a benign addiction to it. The object stands for the mother and holds a unique position between "the infant's psychic reality and the external world." It has for the infant a reality and life of its own, but it is not a hallucination. Rather, it constitutes the prototype of symbolic living, which later becomes a beneficial—even a necessary—area of illusion that can be shared with others.

12. D. W. Winnicott, *The Maturational Processes and the Facilitating Environment*, p. 110.

prehuman behavior. It seems that the human infant's propensity to endow certain inanimate objects with a wealth of emotional significance that endures over a considerable length of time stands in a precursory relationship to the capacity to create new objects that lastingly embody meaning to their creator and to his audience.

Application to the Play of Children

Can this analysis of animal behavior contribute to our understanding of the play of children? Even though the complexity of children's symbolic living in play is barely foreshadowed in the play of animals, nothing we have learned strikes us as alien. For instance, the basic rule that play for animals must be separate from life's necessity holds true also for man. The uneasiness we feel when the boundaries are blurred testifies to our intuitive knowledge of their importance. We worry when a child seems unable to relinquish play to attend to the serious business of life, or when a child imbues play with a sense of reality to the depletion of his relationships or experiences in the real world. We feel even more menaced and estranged when children seem unable to be satisfied by symbolic action and instead play in dead earnest—setting *real* fires; destroying *real* property; truly drowning, hanging, or maiming their playmates. The loss of the capacity to distinguish between the two realms of existence strikes us as profoundly ominous. We likewise feel more revolted when adults inflict serious injury playfully than when the same actions are carried out in earnest.

Finally, we are concerned when children are unable to play at all, when they retreat into inactive fantasy or when they seem like little old men and women focusing exclusively on learning or on practical achievement. However, we are not quite so seriously perturbed when preoccupation with some creative pursuit—drawing, sculpting, painting, play-acting, dance, music—or passionate interest in some branch of science supplants play at an unusually early age. We rightly feel that these pursuits include enough *playfulness* to safeguard the child's emotional balance.

While play that miscarries or lack of playfulness seem to signal danger, good play reassures us. Adults used to children sense the subtle difference between playful noise and serious commotion. They will be tolerant of the former no matter how wild it may seem and be wary about the indefinable change that indicates transition from play to earnest.

The danger is greater in man than it is in animals. While playful behavior can only on the rarest of occasions give an animal sufficient cause for earnest battle, children's play more easily crosses the threshold between make-believe and serious conflict. Yet insofar as it remains within its natural bounds, an intrinsic quality of irresponsible, luxurious pleasure characterizes play for us too.

The conditions under which play can occur thus seem to be similar for man and for animals. Fundamental differences become apparent when we compare the function of play in animal life and in man's psychic economy. Animal behavior is governed by a multitude of finely synchronized sets of instincts that have the power both to induce actions and to inhibit them. Man's behavior, on the other hand, is energized by global libidinally and aggressively charged drives that must be governed and tamed by the ego's mediation, and this implies the neutralization of great quantities of libidinal and aggressive energy. From early infancy onward the play of children contributes to this specifically human task.

According to Waelder, the playing child takes "a leave of absence both from reality and from the superego," finds sanctuary for enacting fantasies that cannot or must not be fulfilled in real life, masters overwhelming experiences through playful repetition, and comes to terms with the impact of passively endured frustration and pain by reenacting them actively.[13] This vacation nevertheless serves to strengthen the ego in its task of mediating between the inner forces of id and superego (or its precursor's) and the demands of the environment. The playing child practices ego functions within a sanctuary where conflicts are scaled down to the child's limited ego strength.

We perceive an analogous leave of absence from reality when playful animals enjoy the pleasures of the hunt even when there is no game. The child's vacation from the superego seems analogous to the animal's liberation from the stringencies of obligatory social behavior, e.g., animals can indulge in playful social signaling that has no serious consequences. The various functions which the animal's playmates and toys acquire as changing appetites are discharged in play seem to foreshadow the process whereby, to quote Waelder once more, the child's "play becomes fantasy woven around real objects."[14]

As we reach the realms of symbolic living and of fantasy the play of animals can no longer inform us. But we note that the rich symbolism of children's play makes it more prone to failure than is the play of animals. Even playfully enacted fantasies may become guilt-laden, and punitive elements may distort the pleasurable character of play. The attempt to master overwhelming experiences in play may fail and play may be disrupted by real anxiety, anger, or grief (an example will be presented on p. 61).

While practicing motor skills seems to constitute a relatively unimportant function in the play of animals, human play entails much practicing and learning. When children play, information is continuously absorbed and motor skills, social adaptation, and intellectual understanding are acquired. Yet any simplistic attempt to harness the vitality of play to disciplined, task-oriented learning is doomed to failure in man as in animals. For man and beast

13. Robert Waelder, "The Psychoanalytic Theory of Play."
14. Waelder, "The Psychoanalytic Theory of Play," p. 224.

the value of play hinges on pleasure and on freedom from necessity. As we have learned in the passage on behavior motivated by curiosity, to gain knowledge man and animal alike must endure frustration and risk danger. Even though children are on principle eager and ready to take these risks, adult attempts to insinuate earnest learning into play without warning are either ignored or experienced as deception. The adult has broken the rules, has high-handedly invaded the sanctuary of playful pleasure—an unforgivable sin.

At this juncture the distinction between playfulness and play becomes crucial. There are playful elements in learning and exquisite pleasures to be gained from the understanding of meaning and the mastery of skills. Common to the acquisition of knowledge and to play is an openness to the world, the inclination tentatively to apply a whole gamut of possible attitudes to the object or idea that is being investigated, and to perceive the object or idea in many different guises. However, this tentative back-and-forth which is the essence of play must ultimately give way to the systematic pursuit of possibilities that have been playfully discovered; this is not child's play. While the pleasures of play depend on sanctuary from the laws of necessity, the pleasure of acquiring knowledge implies acceptance of these laws. The pleasure of learning hinges on gaining the power to make reality more predictable or to bend its law to serve the individual's needs.

PLAYFULNESS AND ART

In contrast to learning, which is reality oriented, art resembles play inasmuch as it also enjoys sanctuary from the laws of time, place, and causality. Nevertheless, art is more stressful than play. Attempts to induce people to exert themselves in art by presenting it as a kind of play soon lead into dead ends; this is comparable to the fallacy of disguising learning as play. We will discuss this more fully later on, but first we will look at an example of an attempt at image making with clay and compare it to Sara's playful handling of the same material as I described it at the beginning of this chapter.

Matthew: Eleven-year-old Matthew was referred to the same outpatient clinic as Sara because of learning disability and aggressive behavior at home and at school. He too is seen in an evaluatory art therapy session. He enters the art room distrustfully, unwilling to commit himself in any way. After a while, he ventures to touch the clay and says he is glad there is plenty of it. I encourage him to gather several handfuls into a lump and to pat it into a solid ball with cupped hands. The ball suggests a head to Matthew, and he completes it by incising with a pencil a pair of eyes, a nose, and a mouth, and by adding a slab of clay for hair. He fashions a large, rather amorphous body complete with belly button, adds two arms and adorns them with muscle balls, but omits hands. Then he gives his man two rudimentary legs. He constructs three half-round clay loops and attaches one above the other in a ladderlike configuration. This airy structure stands almost as high as the whole figure. Matthew places it on the man's head. He explains, "It's a party hat." (See Pl. V.)

In front of his figure Matthew places a slab of clay upon which three phallic upright clay coils represent a fence. Finally he carefully paints his sculpture with poster paint. Head and features are colored realistically in brown and black; all of the body turns a solid red; hair and hat are fancifully colored in orange, red, green, and blue; the fenceposts are white, yellow, and orange.

Matthew works intensely throughout the session. He only needs to be encouraged to take enough clay and helped to keep his figure upright. He shows his work to his family and the staff members and returns periodically throughout the rest of the afternoon to visit with his statue.

Matthew has experienced an *art* session. It has been

good from his point of view, and it was highly instructive to us. The sculpture appears to be conceived at an eight-year-old level at best. Matthew's phallic strivings embodied in the pair of penis-shaped arms seem incongruous with the amorphous character of his figure. In addition, representing the nose by an indentation rather than by a protruding shape and including a belly button in a figure that is not represented as being nude signify immaturity. The unmodified phallic aspect of the figure's arms and of the three fenceposts indicates an ominously insufficient capacity for neutralizing his sexual preoccupations. The tall, airy structure crowning the head tells of an overactive, shifting, fantasy life. The fence informs us of an imperative need for protection. The sculpture's coloring reiterates Matthew's inner division: a rational head imposed directly without the intermediate structure of a neck on an affect-laden body, the whole topped by inflated, insubstantial fantasies.

However, Matthew's sculpture not only informs us of his pathology; it also testifies to his strength, his capacity to please himself through his creative work and to accept himself in it. We can reasonably expect that art therapy could be helpful to him.

If we compare Matthew to Sara, we see that Sara's session was entirely given over to wish fulfillment. Sara gave herself and her family a feast. She symbolically undid the deprivations they all had suffered, established a more advantageous position within the family structure for herself, and took on mothering functions. Beyond the value which these symbolic actions held for her there was no product.

Matthew, on the other hand, had produced a lasting image. His self-representation was motivated by his wishes —to make himself strong, to protect himself, to give himself leeway for fantasy. The idea of making a man was conceived in the course of playful manipulation of art material.

Both Sara's play and Matthew's art were motivated by

their neediness. Being bent on play, Sara required no prompting from me. Matthew, however, needed assistance at two junctures. First, I had to help him relinquish an unproductive, self-critical stance and approach the art material playfully. Later, when with a lump of clay held in his cupped hands he seemed poised between the desire to create and the fear of failure, I interceded. Drawing his attention to the way he had gathered the clay, I encouraged him to repeat this gesture more vigorously and purposefully. The resulting ball of clay suggested a head and this led to the decision to build a man.

In the pursuit of this goal Matthew had to take risks. He risked being confronted by the discrepancy between his concept and his skill. He also risked encountering the discrepancy between his ego ideal and his true feelings about himself. Indeed, this sculpture materialized as an uneasy compromise. It tells not only of Matthew's desires and aspirations but also of his unfulfilled needs, of his vulnerability, and the damage he has suffered.

Sara, since she was only playing, avoided such risks. Had she gone beyond play and attempted to sculpt herself and her family at Thanksgiving dinner, it would have been a very different matter. Her profound deprivation, her true position within the family, the unconscious conflict inherent in fantasies of usurping her mother's place would inevitably have influenced her art. The finished work would have expressed not simply her wishes but her relationship to these wishes.

Sara was in no way ready for such a complex undertaking. The need for immediate symbolic wish fulfillment dominated her actions. If Sara had continued to play in a therapeutic setting her inner conflicts would eventually have entered her play, but this would have been a slow process not inevitably inherent in the activity itself. Indeed, it would have required therapeutic intervention.

To return to Matthew, we find that he had good reason to feel that he had been successful. His confident belief that his statue deserved to be admired by his family and by the whole treatment center was justified. His sculpture had little esthetic value; he had not achieved the evocative power, inner consistency, and mastery of the medium that characterize art in the full sense. However, he had made the transition from play to image making. The iridescent back-and-forth of play had been stilled. Instead there was an object, rudimentary and primitive but embodying complex, many-faceted meaning far beyond anything Matthew could have deliberately planned. The finished image was inviolate—a thing to be cherished, an object in which new meaning could be *discovered*—not a toy to which meaning could be *ascribed* according to the owner's fluctuating needs and whims.

Matthew's ego strength was, however, limited. His capacity for expression in art could not sustain the pressure of adversity. In his twelfth year, Matthew was caught in a vicious circle. His mother was threatening to withdraw all love and interest, to send him away because of his troubles at school. This threat heightened his disturbed behavior in the classroom, and this in turn made his mother angrier.

He became unable to concentrate on art and retreated into repetitive play with toy cars and building blocks. He enacted endless chases between good guys and bad guys where roles changed erratically but no one could ever escape. He spent much time constructing tall buildings whose bases he gleefully knocked out, only to rebuild them again.

The play seemed to be at a four-year-old level at best. It was given over to enacting inescapable, continuous disaster, but it was the only thing that could hold his attention for any length of time, conceivably because it gave him the option of changing passive experience into active. Just as a nightmare fails to function as guardian of sleep under the onslaught of inner pressures, Matthew's play failed to provide sanctuary for wish fulfillment in the face of the dangers that threatened his very existence.

Under these conditions it seemed senseless to try to force Matthew to engage in art. He was allowed to play until the agency could intervene by engineering his admission to a class for learning-disabled children. When his situation improved he no longer needed to play obsessively.

The Distinguishing Characteristics of Art

Reviewing our investigation of the relationship between art, play, and the playful elements of art, we have found the fundamental laws governing play already established among the higher animals with even the toy in existence. We have also found that the motivations of play, work, and the acquisition of knowledge were distinct from each other before the advent of man and conceptual thinking. We have even found among animals precursors of the phenomenon of the transitional object.

The transition from play to art, however, seems to be exclusively human. It depends on the transition from *finding* a multipurpose plaything to *making* new configurations that permanently embody meaning, and this links it to work.

We recognize in the transitional object a forerunner of the work of art inasmuch as it has enduring symbolic meaning for the infant, but we see it as distinct because its meaning remains private. The transitional object is a found object. It acquires significance for the infant because something about it—its smell, its tactile quality, the sound it makes, or some other such property—links it to the gratification the infant has first experienced within the symbiotic unity with the mother. The infant makes no attempt to modify this object so that it will resemble the mother more or in some other way serve its purpose better, and the object's visual appearance is seldom important to the infant.

The serious quality of art seems to hinge on the

purposeful making of symbols. This holds true also of dance and music where no material objects are made. Play, like art, serves essential functions; we consider disturbances of the capacity to play as serious indications of pathology. If we speak of art as being more serious than play, we mean that art makes more stringent demands on the ego than does play and that art is more lasting than play. Since art is designed to be understood by others, it is more apt seriously to influence the conduct of life.

If we compare fantasy, play, and art in their relationship to life's exigencies, we find that fantasy affords gratification at the price of physical and emotional withdrawal. Play, on the other hand, implies vigorous action and thrives on contact with the world, but in this contact the world is reinterpreted to accommodate the child's needs and wishes. Within the real world certain spaces are designated as playspace. Miniature worlds are created with natural and man-made toys, and fictitious relationships are established with playmates. The reality principle is not entirely negated, for the unpredictable quality of real life is reflected in the shifting responses of the plaything or the playmates, to which the child must accommodate. Rather, reality is scaled down to manageable dimensions.

We find play admirably suited to maintaining equilibrium; it provides ongoing gratification of emotional and physical needs to counterbalance the frustrations imposed by nature and society. To a limited extent, elements of sublimation are present in play as well as in art. However, since play remains largely subservient to the pleasure principle, it cannot give a whole picture of the great contradictions of human existence. Although life's grief enters imaginative play, it is dealt with in a primitive manner, in many respects akin to the mechanisms of the dream. Like the dream, play utilizes displacement, isolation, projection, and denial. It has no means of representing the coexistence of conflicting forces but splits them into their antagonistic components. The profound ambivalence which characterizes all human relationship finds expression mainly in ceaseless vacillation, and this tends to prevent any full and painful awareness of internal tensions.

Both play and art afford reassurance by providing the opportunity to take the active role in reliving experience that actually had to be endured passively. But even at an early stage art is likely to encompass a broader truth. For example, after a painful medical examination a child will often *play the part* of the doctor. The child who *makes a picture* of himself in the doctor's hands usually shows himself as helpless before a terrifyingly powerful figure.[15]

Unlike play, art has the means to present truthful images of the conflicting realities of man's experience. At its highest level art establishes within the confines of its symbolic world states of harmony between antagonistic forces. This harmony is achieved without recourse to radically repressive measures that would obliterate the conflicting components.

To create such images it is necessary to face difficulties and dangers far beyond the enticing obstacles of play. The child–artist must face unwelcome truth, make far-reaching decisions, renounce easy gratifications. In psychoanalytic terminology he must become capable of extensive sublimations.

We see that inasmuch as it constitutes a truthful image of life, art is closer to reality than is play. However, art is a new creation, purely symbolic, clearly distinct from daily life, stable and predictable, exempt from the law of chance and accident. In this respect it is at a greater distance from reality than play, for in play chance constitutes an important element.

In considering play we must remember that even though it is largely devoted to wish fulfillment its pleasur-

15. For pertinent examples of the play and art of sick children, see Nancy Lewis, *My Roots Be Coming Back;* Emma Plank, "The Child Before the Operation," pp. 1–8; and W. H. Hitzing, and K. Kiepenheuer, "The Child and Death," pp. 1–10,

able quality is not (as we have remarked earlier) assured. The play of children who labor under severe pressures may turn joylessly compulsive, or, as in Matthew's case, catastrophic. However, painful and harrowing experiences need not inevitably induce regression from art to play. They can also furnish the impetus for exceptionally intense creative work.

The Transition from Play to Art

Eduardo: Eduardo was an educable retarded eight-year-old blind boy whose cancerous eyeballs had been surgically removed shortly after birth. He was much given to restless, playful exploration of the environment. He seemed driven by an urge to compensate for severe sensory deprivation suffered during the first four years of his life when, because his sinister eyeless appearance had frightened and depressed her, his mother had consistently isolated and immobilized him.

During art sessions Eduardo seldom went beyond assigning meaning to shapeless lumps of clay. For example, a number of clay lumps became his chickens which he fed little clay pellets, or similar lumps were used to represent cars and buses which he playfully pushed around.

When Eduardo's mother was hospitalized for gynecological surgery to prevent further pregnancies (Eduardo had six siblings), his longing for his mother and his concern for her mobilized him toward what was for him an extraordinary feat of image making. He laboriously formed all mama's most important parts. Her face included a large mouth, ears, nostrils, and two cheeks. (Congenitally and early blinded children's image of *face* is organized around the cavity of the mouth; soft, strokable cheeks frequently constitute another important facial attribute of a beloved person. The cavities of nostrils and ears are also of special interest. Eyes naturally could never serve as organizing factors for a blind child's concept of a face. They are frequently omitted, and when they are represented at all they are often a source of confusion and uneasy preoccupation.)

Eduardo also made his mother's long hair, her body, her arms and fingers, legs and toes. He worked hard at assembling all these parts into an integrated whole. Finally he placed two large clay bandages over mama's belly. He was immensely pleased and comforted by this creation, stroking it tenderly with an expression of wonder on his face.

Making the image seemed to have restored his inner representation of the absent mother, so that he no longer felt totally bereaved. When the figure had been fired in the school's kiln it became one of Eduardo's prized possessions. Having healed his mother (with the bandages) and restored his mother's image, Eduardo spent subsequent sessions sorting out his ideas about the purpose and consequences of her operation. Would mama return with another baby? Was there something bad inside her belly that had to be removed? Would there never be another baby? He made two more clay images: a fat mama and a skinny one. Making them seemed to help him bring into focus his confusion and anxiety about whether his mother was now pregnant or might never have another baby. Words were only of limited use to Eduardo, for his speech was mostly rambling and driven so that meaning was drowned out in endlessly repetitive meanderings. Thus Eduardo's clay figures alerted the school to his worries. Every effort was made to help him achieve understanding.

If we compare Eduardo's playful manipulation of clay with his goal-directed sculpturing, we note the concomitant transition from protean fantasy to imagination. Fancying himself the proud possessor of a flock of chickens—a fantasy that might at any moment give way to a different one—he was contented with the most rudimentary symbolic objects to help enact it. On the other hand, when in great longing and anxiety he tried to consolidate the fleeting memories of an absent mother into a substantial whole, fantasy was transformed into imagination. Shaping each remembered body part seemed visibly to enrich his inner life. It was as if the inner representation of his mother became more stable and integrated in direct response to the making of her person.

It is interesting that his ambivalence about childbearing and the unpredictable changes it brought about in his mother appeared only after he had made an unequivocally positive image of her and after he had symbolically contributed to her cure by placing the bandages on her belly. This latter action could conceivably have been acted out in play, but it attained more intense meaning because the bandages were applied not to a doll which fleetingly acquired the mother's role, but to the mother recreated and restored by Eduardo's sculptural effort.

We see in Eduardo's sculpture an unusually direct linkage between the work of art and the transitional object—a found object that stands for the mother's person, provides security in her absence, and also functions as a thing onto which conflicting feelings can safely be unloaded. Eduardo finds his mother as he creates his sculpture. At eight years of age it no longer suffices for him to adopt an object that can stand for her; he must make her image out of clay. Also, a single image can no longer serve multiple purposes. Eduardo had to make three sculptures to sort out his feelings, and he was destined to continue to create more images as life went on. This complex process gives his rudimentary productions the dignity of art.

Eduardo's primitive creation had meaning only to himself and to those who were with him while he made it. To the outsider it would be incomprehensible. Yet it was evident from Eduardo's behavior that he conceived of his work as something to be displayed proudly in the expectation that the whole world would understand its meaning and rejoice in the message. On principle his work constituted a gift to himself and to all of humankind, and in this sense it had the emotional significance of art. We might say that art in its full sense is reached when a work attains evocative power for the artist and for others, but it begins whenever a child or an adult manipulates art materials and thereby succeeds in evoking some experience for himself.

IMPLICATIONS FOR THE ART THERAPIST

We have come to understand a good deal about the origins of play and of the psychological processes which govern it. Comparing play with art, we have noted essential differences as well as overlapping areas. We have also considered the small child's transitional object and found it to hold an intermediary position between a toy and a work of art. How can these considerations help us in the practice of art therapy?

We can see that the transitional object, even though it may be the prototype of all works of art, cannot directly lead into their making. The object does not yet constitute a symbol for the mother; it has the quality of an illusion that stands for her in a more immediately physical way. The child's attachment is rigid (as rigid as his attachment to his mother herself). The greater freedom of symbolic play with toys must intervene to lead the child into the wider world where he can practice ascribing meaning to a variety of things. Once the capacity for symbolic investment develops (this coincides with the onset of the phallic phase), the child is ready to respond to the raw materials from which he will create a multitude of objects that will carry the permanent and intense significance initially confined to the transitional object.

As art therapists we value the playful attitude for its flexibility and openness to the world. We see that it can help prevent a premature narrowing of the range of ideas that can be expressed or of the materials that can be used in art, but we are also aware of its limitations. We will illustrate this with an example.

Michael: Michael, eight years old, whose seventeen-year-old half-sister has recently given birth to an out-of-wedlock baby girl, enters the art room with the professed intention of making a big clay elephant. He has previously been taught the technique of constructing large clay figures by giving them a core of crushed newspaper. Accordingly he produces a newspaper ball and wraps his clay around it. As he contemplates the resulting egg-shaped clay body, he decides that it suggests an Indian papoose in its carrier rather than an elephant. Delightedly he proceeds to define a baby's face at one end of the oval lump. Soon he becomes dissatisfied with the baby's bound and rudimentary appearance. He redefines the baby carrier as the baby's belly, squeezes out a neck to separate head and torso, adds arms and legs, and very seriously embarks on the difficult task of making a baby girl. To crown his effort he places a little clay doll in the baby's hands.

The completed sculpture (Figs. 11 and 12), eleven inches high, is a remarkable achievement for an eight-year-old. Michael named the sculpture *Josephine* after his recently born niece. Yet, strangely, the baby's posture and gesture (sitting up and holding a doll) seemed appropriate for an infant of at least twelve to eighteen months, older by far than the actual Josephine. Nevertheless, the sculpture was evidently based on close observation of real babies.

Further information about Michael's family helps to explain the mystery. Michael has a second half-sister, older than Josephine's mother, who gave birth two years before to Sophia. Sophia's birth had precipitated Michael's severe behavior problems. The sculpture then may have constituted an attempt to come to terms with the existence of both Josephine and Sophia.

Michael sculpted his *Josephine*'s baby belly and its herniated navel with loving realism. It seems very likely that at least one of the two baby girls in Michael's family

FIGURE 11. *Michael:* Josephine, front view (11″ high)

FIGURE 12. *Michael:*
Josephine, side view
(11″ high)

has such a navel, and at the same time Michael may have
taken special pains to make the protuberance substantial to
compensate for the absence of a penis. The baby's long
black hair, however, seems incongruously unrealistic, as if
the image of his two sisters had intruded upon Michael's
imagination. But then, to a little boy who had seen both his
sisters quickly turn into women bent on making babies, any
girl, even an infant, might have come to represent an
incipient woman and mother.

The making of *Josephine* was a stormy affair. Particularly as he struggled to make her legs, Michael was several
times on the verge of giving up. When the sculpture was
nearly finished the need to make air holes so that air could
escape from her paper-stuffed head and body in the course
of firing provided a rationalization for his viciously and
repeatedly stabbing the figure's head and belly.

The finished work still bears traces of Michael's ambivalence. While all that is massive and sculptural is endowed

with a feeling of solidity and warmth (this can be seen best in Fig. 12), the incisions defining eyelashes, mouth, fingers, and diaper are done in an impatient, aggressively slashing way.

Michael's attitude toward the completed work was a mixture of the artist's justified pride in achievement and a motherly tenderness for the clay baby. Aggression toward the sculpture seemed to be in abeyance. The work was taken home in triumph and was preserved as one of the family's proud possessions.

Michael's creation seemed to indicate that his jealousy at the birth of both babies had been twofold. He was jealous of the babies for getting the attention that had previously been lavished on him and he was jealous of his sisters' mysterious procreative powers. Even though ambivalence was not fully resolved, the making of *Josephine* constituted an important step in mastering conflict through sublimation.

We see that playfulness has been instrumental in leading Michael to a subject of intense personal concern. Playfulness has also helped him find the appropriate shape for it. Eventually, however, Michael had to complete his sculpture in all seriousness and struggle with the conceptual, technical, and emotional problems of his chosen task. Thus, even though we value playfulness as a means of gaining access to latent emotional material or of discovering new ways of expression, we must be careful to recognize the juncture where a playful attitude dilutes creative resolve.

In any expressive venture there comes the moment where each step is determined by the preceding one so that there is only one right way to continue, no longer a multitude of possibilities to choose from. Once Michael had hit upon his true subject matter, it would have been folly to try to persuade him to make the baby into a seal or some other legless creature to circumvent his difficulty in fashioning the baby's legs. Rather, I had to help him succeed in sculpting the legs and feet he had in mind.

Naturally, it is not always easy to determine exactly

when playfulness is helpful and when it becomes a distraction. Our best guides are the child's mood and our own esthetic sensibilities. Whenever we perceive a work attaining distinct character or when we perceive a child's mood becoming intense and profoundly serious, we will be inclined to support his efforts vigorously.

Beyond the usefulness of playful behavior for art, we also recognize the need for retreat into play under pressure. For example, children who feel threatened and exposed might use art materials at times simply to act out aggression and counterattack. The result may be no more than an incomprehensible tangle of lines, and yet they may have gained some measure of security from the experience. Matthew playfully enacted disasters when his life had become catastrophic. Sara's Thanksgiving dinner is a good example of a deprived child's imperative need to reassure herself by playing out a wish for nurturance.

While accepting such departures from art whenever they are necessary, we will be careful not to set up an environment which actively invites them, for playing is easier than creating. We will make every effort to keep both toys and materials that invite blatantly regressive pre-art activities out of sight of those children capable of the complexities of artwork. (Materials that cannot be given form, such as sand and water, are useful in play therapy but cannot be used to make artworks.)

However, our commitment to art must not blind us to the importance of social play in childhood. Even though art is more complex than play, it may be easier for a disturbed child to produce work that expresses profound conflicts than to tolerate the unpredictable exchanges of play with other children. For this reason, we sometimes welcome it when a child who has been exclusively given over to art turns to social play, even if this should mean a temporary loss of interest in art. An example follows.

Pierre: Pierre, a severely aggressive ten-year-old, was able to maintain himself without excessive outbursts in the art room. But he was entirely unable to accept the rules and regulations or the victories and defeats of competitive games. When, after one and a half years of almost exclusive immersion in the arts, Pierre joined the school's baseball team, everyone—including the art department—rejoiced. Even though it was unlikely that he would ever become an ardent sportsman, he would be better able to function in life and in art when he had become more tolerant of social give-and-take.

If we consider the difference between play and the playful element in art in more general terms, we see the value of playful experimentation as a preparation for art. Young children need to play with malleable and unstructured matter—with water, sand, mud, stones, finger paint, clay, and so on—before they are ready to use art materials symbolically.

When an individual's earliest sensual involvement with materials has been stifled or when adverse experiences have blocked access to playful sources of creative inspiration, it may be necessary to experience or reexperience the abandon of these earliest encounters, even as an adult. Playful activities that require only noncommittal rudimentary drawing, painting, or sculpting can be useful to break the ice for very shy or self-conscious individuals. Such activities can liberate them from narrowly conceived ideas of perfection and make them aware of the almost endless possibilities inherent in art materials and of the wealth of images and ideas within their own minds. Finger paint, for instance, can be used profitably with inhibited adults or with children who have been brought up with overstrict demands for cleanliness. The same material may have disastrous effects if it is offered to impulsive young delinquents.

But the shifting play with shape and meaning must eventually give way to the arduous task of giving definite form to matter. Therefore, whenever playfulness is encouraged, the art therapist must not fail to point out that there comes a moment when play ends and more serious exertion is required that may bring more lasting rewards but also entails taking greater risks. Otherwise the individual might feel that he has been tricked into encountering obstacles he had never intended to face. For example, we can induce a person to make a scribble on a piece of paper and confidently promise that it's easy and maybe even fun. We can suggest that he look for an image in his scribble and still treat the procedure as a game. But when we encourage developing the image into a picture we ask for exertion that requires moral courage, effort, and confronting manual and conceptual problems. We must acknowledge thàt this no longer is a game.

It is even more irresponsible to set up activities that instead of merely introducing people to the playful aspects of art rather limit art to play and nothing more. One such maneuver is to offer exclusively materials so impermanent and crude that they preclude the making of any work of lasting esthetic value—for example, finger paint, colored tinsel, play dough, and the like. By such unthinking tactics, the child is deprived of the opportunity to discover the exquisite pleasure which can be experienced only when the magic of play is relinquished so that the miracle of art can unfold.

IV

Notes on Sublimation

THE ETHOLOGY OF SOCIAL CONTROLS AND THE PROBLEM OF PLEASURE IN SUBLIMATION

IN THE PRECEDING chapter, we tried to broaden our understanding of the function of play and its relationship to art and art therapy by considering the play of animals. Can we find any other prehuman behavior that might foreshadow the intricate processes that combine in the making of works of art even though for art—unlike play—there is no precedent before the advent of man?

I suggest that some components of sublimation are foreshadowed in certain genetic modifications of behavior among those higher species that have evolved social organization. All of these changes occurred in the service of greater social cohesion within these species. Among these modifications are: the evolution of rituals whereby sets of behavior gradually lose their original function in favor of the new function of social signaling, displacement of aggressive behavior from the original object of hostility onto some substitute, and a reversal of meaning in which behavior that originally connoted antagonism serves instead to establish mutual bonds.

As we investigate analogies, we are aware of the fundamental difference between genetic changes that become hereditary and psychological changes that are achieved in the course of an individual's life.

To recapitulate ideas presented in the introductory

75

, according to Freudian psychoanalytic theory, we term *sublimation* to designate processes whereby primitive urges emanating from the id are transformed into complex acts that do not serve direct instinctual gratification and which are under the ego's control. Transformation occurs in such a manner that pleasure in performing these new actions replaces the gratifications that the fulfillment of the original urges would have afforded. In this process, drive energy becomes available to the ego.

Through sublimation, primitive behavior, necessarily asocial, gives way to activities that are ego-syntonic, and are also as a rule *socially productive* in the widest sense, although they may not always be *socially acceptable*. (We know of striking examples where heroic creative acts that undoubtedly came about through processes of sublimation were rejected by society.)

Sublimation is no simple mental act; it embraces a multitude of mechanisms, among them neutralization of drive energy, displacement, and identification. Always there is a threefold change: of the object upon which interest centers, of the desired goal, and of the kind of energy through which the new goal is attained. Sublimation invariably implies some element of renunciation. Yet sublimation somehow remains so linked to the urges that set the process in motion that the individual indeed attains through it at least partial gratification and partial relief from the pressure of libidinal and aggressive urges.[1]

The question arises: How can difficult, complex, demanding, often farfetched substitute activities afford pleasure that is at all comparable to the pleasure of immediate fulfillment of passionate physical and emotional urges?

We must state what we mean here by the word *pleasure*. It is a word frequently used indiscriminately to designate

---

1. For an extensive discussion of the concept of sublimation, see Heinz Hartmann, "Notes on the Theory of Sublimation," in Ruth S. Eissler et al., eds., *The Psychoanalytic Study of the Child*, Vol. 10 (1955).

both *joyful emotion* and simple *release* from the discomfort of instinctive pressures. For greater clarity I propose to reserve the term *pleasure* for subjective, emotional experiences perceived as such by the self and use the term *gratification* to mean relief from instinctive pressures. Naturally, these two positive experiences frequently take place together. Further, given the complexity of man's psychic organization, the same experience may also have different significance within various psychic realms. Instinctive gratification may be welcome to the id while terrifying to the ego. The aggressive superego may rejoice in the ego's painful humiliation—and so forth.

As art therapists working with individuals whose capacity for sublimation has often remained rudimentary or whose sublimations have broken down through the impact of illness, we can frequently observe sublimation at its very inception. We see individuals oscillate between sublimation and more primitve sexually and aggressively charged behavior, or sublimation may give way to painfully constricting defensive mechanisms under the impact of the frightening upsurge of primitive affects. We cannot doubt the interdependence among these different modes of functioning, or fail to notice that sublimation affords a very special kind of pleasure, distinct from simple instinctive gratification but somehow related to it. The intensity and power of the pleasure generated by sublimation remain nevertheless a cause of wonder.

Instinct and Drive

Implied in the concept of sublimation is the awareness that man's *instincts* are in a state of disarray—having lost their fine adjustment to reality, they can no longer be relied on to regulate behavior. We assume that this dissolution of a primitive yet exquisitely balanced structure has resulted in the accumulation of blind forces charged with undifferentiated libidinal and aggressive energy. These we call *drives*, and it is in their nature to push toward immediate discharge, oblivious of time, place, and circumstance, in nonrational actions that threaten to destroy the individual and his society.

We also assume that the gradual atrophy of the prehuman instinctive organization came about through the evolution of conceptual thinking. Since conceptual thought made human beings able to judge specific situations in a logical manner, it rendered obsolete the more global dos and don'ts of instinctive mechanisms. Man as a species could not have survived unless simultaneously with the faculty of conceptual thought new methods of controlling behavior in a more flexible, less mechanistic manner had not also evolved. It follows that a new psychic organization must have come into being, one capable of taming and binding the drive energies and channeling them into behavior that could assure survival. This organization capable of establishing order and structure—the ego—is man's most important means of survival. It is infinitely more flexible and resourceful than the ancient instinctive structures, but not as dependable.

Sublimation then serves a specifically human need to find ways of postponing instinctive gratification and channeling drive energy. Insofar as it fulfills these functions, we can subsume it under the broader concept of the mechanisms of defense. It is, however, distinguished from all other defense mechanisms by its unequaled economy. The amount of energy lost in unproductive maneuvers is exceptionally small and the pleasure generated in the new activity exceptionally great. Our investigation concerns the source of this pleasure.

Inasmuch as we are still inclined to describe unbridled, impulse-ridden behavior as animal-like, we adhere to obsolete, nineteenth-century notions about the nature of animals. The uninhibited human seeking immediate gratification regardless of every other consideration is actually further removed from our nonhuman ancestors than is civilized man. The healthy animal functioning in its natural habitat does not eat, mate, or fight incessantly and indiscriminately. Instead, behavior is very precisely regulated to assure that the right thing is likely to occur at the right time under the right circumstances with the right partner. Even though animal behavior must be aimed toward essential consummatory goals such as mating and ingesting food or protecting offspring, for the most part, it consists of a multitude of preparatory activities. Each of these must command energy commensurate with the work to be accomplished by it. Therefore there is no significant pressure for premature consummatory gratification.

For each species more energy must be expended in preparatory behavior than in consummatory acts, but the manner in which this occurs may vary greatly. For cattle, minute gratifications of hunger accompany endlessly laborious grazing, chewing, and rechewing as food is slowly ingested. At the opposite extreme, wolves gorge themselves and endure subsequent periods of hungry hunting in preparation for the next gratifying meal. A songbird like the cuckoo may be compelled to ward off competitors by almost incessantly signaling his presence, while a stag may establish hierarchical supremacy in a brief, dramatic showdown with his competitors. Both kinds of actions set the stage for mating.

Even though we find the magnitude of the energies available for the survival of the species awe-inspiring, we are impressed with the stringent rationing and programming that structures them into minutely synchronized and parsimoniously energized actions.

We see that as the ancient instinctive programming of behavior is replaced, more must be achieved than mere postponement of gratification. Man's newly evolved ego must effect a fundamental redistribution of drive energy such that this energy will not be dissipated in attempts at immediate gratification of libidinal and aggressive impulses. Instead, the better part of it must be neutralized and become available to the ego for the labors necessary for survival within the natural and social environment.

Even though we have gained some understanding of why mechanisms of defense evolved, we still remain puzzled by the way they work. How can defenses obtain the power to stem the tide of primeval impulses? How can pleasure be experienced in acts which depend on the inhibition of drive gratification, which indeed are instrumental in inhibiting it? Can we find analogous mechanisms among the lower species? Ethology teaches us that in the parliament of instincts that govern the life of animals, arbitrary—even nonsensical—kinds of behavior may attain key positions, endowed with absolute power over the release or inhibition of essential acts. This occurs particularly in relation to social behavior such as mating, rearing of young, and control of intraspecific aggression, where the species can evolve reliable signals for releasing or inhibiting behavior. For example, the male stickleback has evolved the faculty to make a red spot appear on his underside to signal mating intentions, while the female has evolved corresponding sexual responsiveness toward the red color.

Social Signaling and Subjective Experiences

Much social signaling appears to unroll automatically. However, it is in this area that we first encounter behavior that seems to be accompanied by subjective experiences that may be analogous to man's emotions of pleasure and grief. But are we justified in speaking of emotions in animals? To quote Konrad Lorenz:

> Similarities and analogies in the nervous processes of animals and men are sufficiently great to justify the conclusion that higher animals do indeed have subjective experiences which are qualitatively different from but in essence akin to our own....We are convinced that animals do have emotions, though we shall never be able to say exactly what these emotions are.[2]

2. Konrad Lorenz, *On Aggression*, p. 210.

Because we want to learn about the typical functioning of these proto-emotions, we will not turn to our closest relatives, the great apes, where it appears that instinctively regulated behavior is already in considerable disarray, but will confine ourselves to less intelligent species, such as the social birds, where instinct still rules supreme.

According to Lorenz, the capacity to experience subjective states of mind analogous to our own, in which attention is passionately directed toward a limited number of specific individuals, has evolved only among those species which in the course of evolution resolved the dilemma of how to form individual bonds among sexual mates and other conspecifics such as offspring, leaders, or particular companions in spite of a persisting inclination to act aggressively against all conspecifics. (This aggressive reaction corresponds to the ancient, instinctive heritage of these species, where equitable distribution of territory and mates was assured by mutual repulsion.) Furthermore, this peaceful cooperation must be established without effecting any general diminution of available aggression, for each individual must remain ready and eager vigorously to defend its companion against hostile conspecifics as well as against other intruders.

Lorenz describes the greeting ceremonial among friendly individuals of the Anatidae family (ducks, geese, and swans) as a classical example of the successful solution of this problem. The pattern consists of an initial threatening gesture performed by the stronger and more aggressive partner that corresponds to one which would initiate a serious battle. The gesture is, however, pointedly redirected past the partner and against a bystander—another bird, a person, or an inanimate object such as a twig—or even into empty space. After a real or fictitious victory, the bird turns to its partner, greeting it loudly and triumphantly, whereupon the partner joins in the celebration.

The greater the social cohesiveness of a particular species, the less the need for an actual enemy in order for the greeting ceremony to be successfully completed. In the more precariously socialized species, the male cannot perform the mating ritual in the absence of a competing male to serve as the object of his aggression. In the more fully socialized species, where the enemy may become entirely fictitious, the gestures of redirected attack are correspondingly more ceremonial—exaggerated, abbreviated, or both.

Lorenz writes:

> Among the highly socialized geese this triumph ceremonial constitutes the most important structural element of which the social life of geese is built...it is present in all their daily activities...on the reunion of partners that have been separated for an appreciable time...the full blown ceremony...is triumphantly performed...By the comparatively simple means of redirection and ritualization, a behavior pattern which not only in its prototype but even in its present form is partly motivated by aggression, has been transformed into a means of appeasement and further into a love ceremony which forms a strong tie between those that participate in it.... Like the performance of any other independent instinctive act, that of the ritual has become a need for the animal, in other words an end in itself. Unlike the autonomous instinct of aggression, out of which it arose, it cannot be indiscriminately discharged at any anonymous fellow member of the species, but demands for its object the personally known partner. Thus it forms a *bond* between individuals.[3]

The bond is charged with emotions analogous to the pleasures of friendship and of love and correspondingly the loss of the partner causes emotions analogous to grief.

Konrad Lorenz states:

> All the objectively observable characteristics of the goose's behavior on losing its mate are roughly identical with those accompanying human grief.... This applies particularly to the phenomena observable in the sympathetic nervous system.... John Bowlby, in his study of infant grief, has given an equally convincing and moving description of this primal grieving, and it is almost incredible how detailed are the analogies we find here in human beings and in birds....[4]

3. Lorenz, *On Aggression*, p. 173.
4. Lorenz, *On Aggression*, p. 209.

And so we find that ritualized behavior that has no immediate practical value can attain overwhelming importance and can become an end in itself, charged with pleasures that are independent of simple biological needs. Indeed it becomes apparent that these proto-emotions could never have evolved out of any primitive gratifications such as mating or victoriously attacking an enemy. Rather, they evolve as components of social controls which narrow the conditions under which gratification can occur but also make gratification safer and more permanently available.

Armed with highly pertinent information gleaned from an adjacent field, we return to our initial question: Can we find in prehuman life any behavior that can shed light on the riddle of sublimation?

To summarize: We found that the continuous pressure for gratification of drives is an exclusively human characteristic. Among animals, instinctive energy channeled into programmed preparatory activities normally exceeds the energy used for consummatory acts. Only man must strive to counteract a morbid inclination to rush continuously toward immediate gratification of drives. We recognize all mechanisms of defense, including the process of sublimation, as means of counteracting this self-destructive tendency.

We found that the faculty for subjective experiences analogous to human pleasure and grief did not evolve in conjunction with immediate gratification of basic urges. It came into existence in conjunction with actions that had the function of establishing cohesive social behavior *without loss of sexual and aggressive energy.* These actions entailed *a reversal of meaning,* so that an originally asocial aggressive act becomes a component part of an act of love and friendship. The change of meaning came about through the confluence of two contradictory instinctive tendencies: on the one hand, *mutual antagonism* between members of the same species in the service of equitable distribution over territory, and on the other, *mutual attraction* in the service of procreation. Behavior which originally led to direct action acquired new functions. This came about through ritualization, change of direction, and ceremonial abbreviations and exaggerations. The intensity and frequency with which such behavior occurs and the entirely new kind of rewards and punishment through subjective feelings of joy and grief it offers are a measure of the enormous amount of energy that is necessary to establish and maintain social cohesion.

We find that nothing we have described runs counter to the idea of sublimation. But naturally there are fundamental differences. First, animal behavior is genetically determined while sublimation is achieved by the individual. Second, sublimation entails partial renunciation of simple drive gratification. In nonhuman beings, which are not pressured by drives that demand immediate gratification, there exists neither the need for renunciation nor a psychic apparatus comparable to man's ego that could bring it about. Even though among animals one kind of behavior has replaced another, and even though behavior becomes more complex, the pathway is automatic and compulsory and the animal need not struggle to follow it in spite of an inclination to regress. Also, even though we find among animals behavior that has the power to influence the partner or the group, these actions do not carry symbolic meaning. Behavior never represents an idea such as "I am not your enemy, I am your friend, ready to defend you." Behavior and message are identical, response is automatic, and there is no leeway for individual inventions. Modifications of behavior occur only through the evolution of new species.

In contrast, sublimation requires that the individual establish a *symbolic linkage* between some primitive need and another more complex cluster of ideas and actions. This presupposes the capacity to evoke ideas and perceive analogies, a faculty involving both primary- and secondary-process thinking. The ability to perceive analogies belongs to primary-process thinking. As secondary-process thinking takes over, symbolic representations lose their protean, driven quality and become stable. We evidently cannot conceive of sublimation before the advent of conceptual thinking—a faculty that not only brought about the dissolution of instinctive programming but also made possible symbolization and the evolution of the ego.

For the advent of these interlocking characteristics which brought the radically new human species into being, Konrad Lorenz's word *fulguratio*[5] seems appropriate. The richness and variety of human cultural behavior cannot be foreseen from the behavioral models that are found among other species.

However, we can discern among other species certain phenomena sufficiently analogous to sublimation to assure us that the process as we conceive of it is not totally without precedent and does not constitute a biological impossibility. It seems reasonable to postulate: that man's subjective experiences can be linked to the physiological process of tension reduction, that actions which are linked only by a long chain of modifications to the gratification of basic urges can have the power to generate emotions and to reduce tension, and that man's heritage includes the faculty to channel considerable energies into such processes.[6]

Having initiated our investigations from the genetic point of view, we must next turn our attention to the earliest precursors of sublimation as seen in the art and behavior of

---

5. Konrad Lorenz, *Behind the Mirror.*

6. Because sublimation, which entails processes of transformation, was the subject of our investigation we have focused exclusively on animal behavior that serves social cohesion only after it has undergone a change of meaning. This does not mean that we underestimate the power of behavior which originally pertained only to the care of the young and serves social life when it is extended to embrace adult conspecifics. Analogous processes undoubtedly exist in human society and contribute greatly to peaceful social living. For an exposition of such phenomena, see Irenäus Eibl-Eibesfeldt, *Love and Hate.*

the very young, the retarded, and the emotionally disturbed.

PRECURSORS OF SUBLIMATION

Circles

Children learn to handle drawing materials before they are able to control paint or clay. We will therefore first investigate young children's drawing.

Children normally acquire a basic graphic vocabulary within the first four or five years of life. Transition from kinesthetically experienced formless scribble to the mastery of circular forms occurs with deceptive ease. Straight lines, zigzags, spirals, and the feat of changing directions at will are soon achieved. Meaning is ascribed to such production, only fleetingly at first. As the capacity to produce organized forms increases, meanings also acquire greater constancy. The entire development is easy for the normal child and ordinarily requires no educative measures beyond an opportunity to handle appropriate art material and benevolent adult interest in the productions. The significance of each separate step tends to elude us when we work with normally endowed children.

The circular shape borne of the rhythmically scribbled oval constitutes one of the infant's early victories of mind over matter. The hand allowed to move according to its own inclinations can do no more than meander over the drawing surface, moving somewhat more irregularly and intensely in early childhood when the experience is new and the hand unpracticed, and more softly and rhythmically in later life.

The primitive nature of scribbling and the regressive influence it exerts is well known to art therapists. It is often deliberately used in conjunction with projection to gain access to latent ideas not otherwise easily available for graphic elaboration.

Only when the mind directs the hand's movement can the line return to its origin as it travels around a dimly conceived center. Victorious young children often celebrate achievement by joyfully drawing multitudes of circles. From there it is a short step to making suns, faces, and complex radial designs. This progress might be slowed down or arrested because of intellectual retardation or emotional difficulties. Both kinds of impediments can teach us a great deal about the emotional and developmental significance of such circle drawings and of the configurations that evolve from them.

Arno: The story of Arno's temporary arrest at the scribbling stage and the manner in which he got beyond it[7] affords a glimpse at the possible emotional significance of the circular configuration.

Arno was a normally endowed little boy born out of wedlock to a teenage girl. He had known little stability in his brief life; his mother had frequently abandoned him to the care of a variety of relations and friends, many of whom were entirely unsuitable guardians for an infant. At age three years and five months he was placed in a foster home with a young, childless couple who later adopted him. At this time he explained to his new foster parents that he had lived in "too many houses" and that some of them had been "very bad houses."

The foster father, himself an artist, observed Arno's handling of art materials with much understanding. His production at that age was limited to scribbling. The vigor and variety of his lines and the manner in which he used the whole drawing surface testified to his vitality and kinesthetic enjoyment. However, in most instances, a brief period of free-moving scribbling soon came to a halt as Arno seemed to be stuck at some particular area of the paper. As he scribbled again and again over this narrow

7. The material for this passage was supplied by Walter Carter, artist, art educator, and student at the Master of Arts program in art therapy at George Washington University, Washington, D.C., 1975.

space, an ominous dark knot appeared (Fig. 13). Often he ended up by rubbing a hole in the paper. If a new sheet was offered, he could again scribble with abandon until his movements once more became frantically confined to a narrow space and another dark knot came into being.

At a time when his drawing seemed thus at a developmental deadlock, Arno confided to his foster father that he sometimes dreamt of "circle houses" and that these were good dreams. When the father asked him if he could draw such a house, Arno produced a pattern reminiscent of a sun, placing a number of tiny dots inside the circle (Fig. 14). This unprecedented feat proved that Arno was developmentally capable of more than scribbling, that he was ready to move on to controlled configurations. In order to make this step, however, it had been necessary for him to evoke the image of a "good house." This dream house presented itself to Arno as a circular form, accentuated by short radial lines that seem to penetrate toward the center as well as to extend outward.

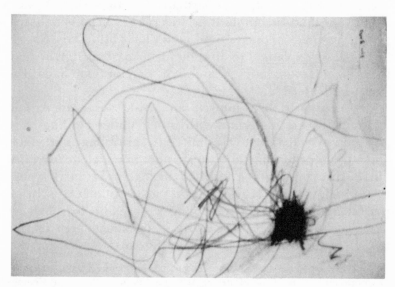

FIGURE 13. *Arno:* Scribble (18″ x 24″)

Could the large, dark, circular knots that literally paralyzed all further actions in his scribbles have signified the bad houses in his life? This must remain conjecture, for Arno ventured no information about them.

Developmentally, Arno's *Circle House* belongs to a group of related configurations based on a circular shape observed in detail by Rhoda Kellogg.[8] She groups them into "mandalas" with radial shapes inscribed within the circle and "suns" with lines issuing from the circle's boundaries. Arno's *Circle House* seems to be a hybrid, more sun than mandala. Kellogg perceives both kinds of configurations as a combination of the earlier achieved gestalts of crosses and circles, and observes that they immediately precede the drawing of the human figure. She observes their first appearance within the second half of the third and first half of the fourth year of life. She avoids all psychological interpretation of these configurations and also points out the absence of any statistical study confirming the sequential development she postulates.

Our single example does not permit us to draw any general conclusions about the emotional significance of circular or sunlike shapes. We can only be certain that for three-and-a-half-year-old Arno, the circle house he drew meant something good, that he became able to dream of good things and to evoke goodness in a drawing at a time when his life had taken a good turn, that when he had drawn *Circle House* he was not overtaken by any compulsion to produce a dark spot on the paper.

Even though Kellogg is not ready to ascribe emotional significance to the circular shapes produced by young children, psychologists who apply projective drawing tests agree on their significance for school-age children and from there on into adulthood. In such tests the preponderance of circular and of softly rounded shapes and a scarcity or absence of decisive straight lines and of angles is considered characteristic of the dependent personality seeking

8. Rhoda Kellogg, *Analyzing Children's Art.*

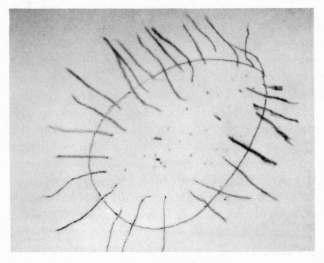

FIGURE 14. *Arno:* Circle House (18″ x 24″)

oral gratification. Such a frame of mind would of course be entirely appropriate for a three- to four-year-old child whose dawning strivings for individuation and independence need to be anchored in a securely gratifying environment. Although some elements contributing to the oral significance of round shapes may elude us, we can safely assume that the round and soft quality of the first gratifying agents in the infant's life importantly contribute to it. Breasts and the mother's face are rounded and the baby's oral cavity is a round, hollow shape.

According to René Spitz, "The first percept to be crystallized out of the shifting nebular masses in the world of the baby is the human face...the nursing baby stares unwaveringly from beginning of the feeding to the end of it at the mother's face."[9]

We also know from his study of "the smiling response"[10] that the three-and-a-half-month-old baby reacts with the

9. R. A. Spitz, "The Primal Cavity," p. 218.
10. R. A. Spitz (with the assistance of K. M. Wolff), "The Smiling Response."

so-called social smile not only to the human face but even more vividly to any dummy consisting of a large oval shape adorned with two eye-like dots.[11]

The baby then seems to be endowed with an innate appetite for perceiving and responding to large round shapes accentuated by smaller, inscribed configurations. This innate reaction mechanism, parsimoniously programmed to respond to a limited set of gestalten, is soon superseded as the infant memorizes his mother's individual features; he now reacts with distress to the simple schema which he so recently greeted with a smile.

Thus it seems reasonable to postulate that an enduring linkage between round shapes and oral gratification is established in the first months of life even before the capacity to recognize individual faces becomes significant. From this moment onward, we see the infant already tending toward two opposing modes of perception: on the one hand, the inclination to perceive and respond to simple and regular gestalten and to single out and automatically correct the irregularities of imperfectly formed natural objects so that they are perceived as more regular than they really are; on the other hand, the capacity to note and remember very precisely the individual features of the environment in all their idiosyncratic irregularity. These opposing ways of perceiving will intertwine and contribute to his understanding of the world and to the organization and style of his art.

When the ability to produce circular shapes matures in the third or fourth year, we can well imagine that this should be an intensely gratifying achievement. We can also imagine that the child would be inclined to relate all other graphic configurations he is capable of, such as the straight

11. According to Paul Leyhausen (Lorenz and Leyhausen, *Motivation of Human and Animal Behavior*, Chapter 11), there exists a period in the baby's development when a dummy with four or six eyes elicits the classical "supernormal response," as demonstrated by R. Ahrens's 1953 experiments: "Beitrag zur Entwicklung der Physignomie- und Mimikerkennens."

line, loop, and the cross, to this supremely satisfying shape. But while we can easily imagine that the child will soon be moved to create the all-important human face from the circle, we have no equally convincing explanation for children's inclination to produce radial patterns and sun shapes. Yet they prevail both as simple designs and in the guise of the obligatory sun in the art of children well into the eighth or ninth year.

Circles and the Art of the Retarded

> The innocent Stevie, seated very good and quiet at a deal table, drawing circles, circles, circles; innumerable circles, concentric, eccentric; a coruscating whirl of circles that by their tangled multitude of repeated curves, uniformity of form and confusion of intersecting lines suggested a rendering of cosmic chaos, the symbolism of a mad art attempting the inconceivable.
>
> —Joseph Conrad, *The Secret Agent*

Many retardates endlessly repeat simple circles unadorned by any additional configurations. We also find that those retardates who have achieved the simple circle are as a rule somewhat more mature in other areas of life than those whose graphic repertoire is limited to repeated hooklike scribbles or only to controlled up-and-down motions. It can be easily observed that pleasure is generated by repeating any of these configurations, but the nonverbal retardate cannot tell us whether any idea is evoked as they are produced.

Even though some forms of retardation are accompanied by emotional blunting, a great many educable retarded individuals and even a considerable number of trainable ones are capable of intense feelings. They suffer greatly from the discrepancy between their capacity for differentiated emotional experiences and a correspondingly subtle perception of the moods and feelings of others and their inability to comprehend the ways of the world or to make the world understand them. For them a passion to repeat certain simple configurations over and over again may be partly motivated by the desire to satisfy an undifferentiated need for action in a manner which is certain to keep them out of trouble. Having learned that the inscrutable powers in charge of their lives approve of drawing, these retardates eagerly pour their energies into the activity for the pleasure of feeling safe and liked while doing something. Yet their behavior strongly suggests that such endlessly repeated forms may also have emotional significance. Laurie Wilson's article "Theory and Practice of Art Therapy with the Mentally Retarded" suggests that meaning may be linked to such graphic productions.[12]

Elena: Elena had been institutionalized by her parents at age four. At this time the clinical record reported an IQ of 15. She suffered from hydrocephalus and epileptic seizures. The hydrocephalus was arrested but seizures continued up to the time of her treatment by art therapy. Institutional records indicated prolonged fixation on the oral phase. She could not be weaned from the bottle until age five, and collected and swallowed bits of string and buttons until the onset of adolescence, when she abandoned this habit and instead developed a fixation on a ball-like clump of metal jingle bells which she wove together with wire and carried around her neck. Separation from this precious possession, which bore all the characteristics of a transitional object, caused extreme anger and distress. At age twenty-two, when first seen in art therapy, Elena had achieved the mental age of three to six and an IQ of 20. Her vocabulary, however, was considerably below this age level, consisting of very few almost unintelligible words. She had, however, a repertoire of facial expressions that could denote pleasure

12. Laurie Wilson, "Theory and Practice of Art Therapy with the Mentally Retarded." The following condensed version of that article has been prepared with Dr. Wilson's cooperation.

and grief and a number of expressive gestures that included stroking her cheeks, mouth, and nose, or holding and rubbing her breasts. These soothing gestures seemed to be attempts at comforting herself with caresses that had in her past experiences been given her by others. Her art production was, at this time, entirely limited to a radial pattern superimposed on a circle and usually drawn in red, repeated over and over again in various sizes (Fig. 15). The pattern seemed complex and specific beyond the shapes usually produced by similarly retarded people. It seemed to afford more than pleasurable release of tension, indeed to embody some particular meaning to Elena.

Elena's attachment to her clump of bells was another unusual characteristic in one so profoundly retarded. It seemed as if Elena's potential developmental level might somewhat exceed her actual performance and that psychosexual fixations might be impeding intellectual growth.

Wilson conjectured that Elena might be arrested at the period of life when transitional objects make their first appearance: at the developmental stage preceding the moment when the infant begins to perceive the mother as a separate person and concomitantly begins to establish his own body image. She decided to direct concerted efforts toward developing Elena's body image through art therapy.

In the course of two years of skillful and patient work Wilson and her collaborators succeeded in bringing about considerable changes. Elena developed a second graphic pattern consisting of concentric circles. While radial and concentric patterns were at first used interchangeably, the circles were gradually used more consistently to denote the various parts· of body and face, while the radial pattern became located more often in the region of the breasts (Fig. 16). Later on when Elena had achieved a relatively rich combination of circles, triangles, and squares, radials were also used to denote eyes (Fig. 17). Radial patterns also appeared as separate groups drawn next to circle images

FIGURE 15. *Elena:* Radial Pattern (18" x 24")

FIGURE 16. *Elena:* Circular Head and Radial Breasts (18" x 24")

FIGURE 17. *Elena:* Head (18" x 24")

FIGURE 18. *Elena:* Circular Self-Portrait with Bells (18" x 24")

representing Elena's person (Fig. 18). On these occasions, she made it understood that the radial patterns represented her cluster of bells. Throughout her treatment, communication remained for the most part limited to gestures; e.g., Elena would point alternately to her own body and to various configurations on her pictures.

In one crucial session the connection between Elena's drawing and the idea of her mother and of her mother's breasts was unequivocally established. Elena had begun the session by drawing a fairly well-organized arrangement of circles denoting a person, but was overtaken by an overflow of circles which covered the whole paper. She identified these circles as breasts and later named the whole drawing a "mommy." When the therapist suggested that she draw a house where such a mommy would like to live, Elena enthusiastically set out to draw a configuration of squares. When asked who else would live in the house, she said the word "me," and later said, "baby." She ended the session by drawing a radial configuration enclosed in a square. Following this session her imagery became much richer and more flexible.

Eventually Elena was able to relinquish her fixation on the clump of bells. She learned to string beads and to make simple jewelry. She transferred her interest to the bracelets and necklaces she made for herself as well as to a pocketbook which she carried with her at all times. These precious possessions were more socially acceptable than the bells. In general she became more independent and more able to care for herself within the shelter of the institution.

The crucial session in which Elena finally named three of her drawings mommy, house, and baby gives us the clue to the success of art therapy. The art therapist's patient and enlightened work with Elena had made it possible for her to reestablish connection with early experiences of being mothered that must have occurred before she was institutionalized at age three. It is unlikely that art therapy could have been as successful as it indeed was without a foundation of early libidinal satisfaction.

We do not know whether her mother ever encouraged three-year-old Elena's scribbling, or even whether Elena was able to scribble at this age. But we can assume from the evidence of Elena's transitional object that while still in her mother's care she had made some steps in the direction of individuation and symbolic behavior.

Work with Elena could take up where her mother had left off. As the art therapists shared Elena's pleasure in her rudimentary art activities, symbolic behavior was once more invested with libido. Elena would therefore respond to the therapist's encouragement toward change and growth.

Art and the Transitional Object

Elena's uneven development affords unusual insight into the connection between the phenomenon of the transitional object and art. At the time when babies normally develop their first attachment to a transitional object they obviously can neither tell us about it nor draw any image that they may conceivably connect with their experience of it. At the period when the capacity to draw any controlled configurations usually evolves, the transitional object has either passed into limbo or undergone extensive modifications of meaning and often of appearance. Children are by this time at the onset of the phallic phase and the linkage between their drawing and their early attachment to a transitional object is overshadowed by their immediate concerns. Elena's emotionality, on the other hand, remained arrested at the level of a preverbal infant still dependent on oral gratifications, while her capacity to draw controlled configurations had reached the level of a four- to five-year-old and her manual dexterity was at an even higher developmental stage. (For example,

Elena was able to thread her jingle bells on wire unassisted.) We can, therefore, directly observe the equating of her mother's breasts, her own breasts, her jingle bells, and her radial and concentric shapes. We also see the transitional object losing importance as Elena reaches a level of individuation where she can restore the lost object by evoking her own image and the mother's image in art, both of them complete, with the all-important breasts now perceived as an integral part of the whole body.

Even though we cannot prove the general validity of the symbolic meaning of the young child's radial configuration solely on the evidence of Elena's story, Wilson's suggestions are highly persuasive. Since the symbol is universal, i.e., it appears in children's art worldwide, further study correlating psychosexual development, ego development, and graphic configurations would be extremely interesting. Also worth further study is Wilson's suggestion that a lag of approximately two years may regularly separate the time when a developmental landmark is reached in children's psychic development and when it becomes manifest in their art. In support of this conjecture, Wilson mentions that according to Mahler and her collaborators, children normally achieve an inner sense of body image at age three and that most children can draw a human figure, including head, trunk, and limbs, at age five.[13] We can add that children become aware of sexual differences between age two and three, but that the three-year-old's first rudimentary representations of people as a rule lack gender differentiation, which is usually added in the fifth or sixth year.

Whatever the relationship between specific graphic configurations and transitional objects may be, what is important for our investigation is mainly the linkage between the transitional phenomenon and the phenomenon of art per se.

13. Margaret Mahler, Fred Pine, and Anni Bergman, *The Psychological Birth of the Human Infant.*

Winnicott has introduced the terms *transitional object* and *transitional phenomenon* to designate "the intermediate area of experience, between the thumb and the teddy bear, between the oral eroticism and the object relationship...." He summarizes the special qualities of the relationship as follows:

1. The infant assumes rights over the object, and we agree to this assumption. Nevertheless some abrogation of omnipotence is a feature from the start.
2. The object is affectionately cuddled as well as excitedly loved and mutilated.
3. It must never change, unless changed by the infant.
4. It must survive instinctual loving, and also hating, and, if it be a feature, pure aggression.
5. Yet it must seem to the infant to give warmth, or to move, or to have texture, or to do something that seems to show it has vitality or reality of its own.
6. It comes from without from our point of view, but not so from the point of view of the baby. Neither does it come from within; it is not an hallucination.
7. Its fate is to be gradually allowed to be decathected, so that in the course of years it becomes not so much forgotten as relegated to limbo. By this I mean that in health the transitional object does not "go inside" nor does the feeling about it necessarily undergo repression. It is not forgotten and it is not mourned. It loses meaning, and this is because the transitional phenomena have become diffused, have become spread out over the whole intermediate territory between "inner psychic reality" and "the external world as perceived by two persons in common," that is to say, over the whole cultural field.[14]

Winnicott sees the necessity of paying attention to a specific area of functioning that lies between the individual's inner reality and his interpersonal relationships. "A third part of human life we cannot ignore, an intermediate area of experiencing to which inner reality and external life both contribute. It is an area which is not challenged because no claim is made on its behalf except that it shall exist as a resting place for the individual engaged in the perpetual

14. D. W. Winnicott, *Through Paediatrics to Psycho-Analysis*, p. 233.

human task of keeping inner and outer reality separate yet interrelated." He suggests that there is a need to study "the substance of illusion, that which is allowed to the infant and which in adult life is inherent in art and religion."[15] This evidently is the realm in which the art therapist encounters the client, patient, or student. Perceived so broadly we can consider even the repetitive scribblings or circles of the profoundly retarded as belonging to the realm of art at its very inception.

Can we speak of *sublimation* as we contemplate Arno's scribbles and his *Circle House,* or Elena's chaotic attempts at constructing the image of a woman from her limited repertoire of circles and radial shapes?

Both Arno and Elena take pleasure in an effortful activity through which they evoke experience. No practical gain is attached to these activities. Instead, effort is rewarded by illusions becoming available at will and conceivably taking on reality in a very special way. Even though the periodic absence of some gratifying agent such as the mother's breasts or her person may initially constitute an incentive for seeking such alternate pleasures, once the capacity for evoking illusions is established, it is not experienced as second best, a substitute to be abandoned when the real thing becomes available. It is cherished as an independent source of pleasure, for which the individual develops an appetite.

It is interesting that even though our artists of the circles may need no help in drawing their images, the presence of some nurturing person remains essential. Arno makes his *Circle House* for his new foster father. Elena needs enormous amounts of attention to be able to draw at all. However, in the shelter of these benign presences our immature artists are engaged in a pursuit that will give them some measure of emotional autonomy so that each of them is less dependent on gratifications provided by the nurturing adult whose presence is still needed.

15. Winnicott, *Through Paediatrics to Psycho-Analysis,* p. 230.

We are reminded of Winnicott's suggestion that the adult's capacity to be alone, to concentrate on a task, to be benignly isolated without being *insulated*, has its origin in the infant's experience of "being alone...in the presence of mother."[16] According to him the capacity for concentration in the older child or in the adult signifies that object relationships have been so well internalized that contact with the world can be maintained even in solitude. He envisions the situation from which this capacity is born as one in which the child is in contact with a mother who is benignly available but not at all intrusive. Because he needs neither to stimulate his mother's attention nor to defend himself against unwanted interference but can be calmly certain of her continued availability, the infant reaches a state of relaxed tension. In this state impulses and sensations can emerge without causing any disruption of the relationship to the mother. Experiences belonging to the realm of impulsive, instinctual living, or, to use Winnicott's terminology, id experiences, can occur within the framework of a relationship anchored in the ego, rather than arising from the id, serene rather than passionate. Instead of being overwhelmed, the ego is strengthened by the experience.[17]

The process Winnicott describes constitutes the prototype of more complex ones that are essential for all successful creative efforts. Such processes are characterized by a benign contact with the primitive mind that enriches and energizes the ego. Repressions are lifted and older modes of functioning activated. Ideas and memories belonging to the ego's realm are briefly subjected to the mechanisms of primary-process thinking.

To be beneficial rather than destructive this dipping

16. D. W. Winnicott, *Maturational Processes and the Facilitating Environment*, p. 30.

17. Winnicott has coined the term *ego relatedness* to denote these kinds of relationships. To explain their meaning he compares "liking" to "loving." He considers the former ego related while the latter "is more a matter of id-relationships either crude or in sublimated form" (from "The Capacity to be Alone," in *Maturational Processes and the Facilitating Environment*).

into the domain of the id must occur when the individual is able to resist the pull toward permanent regression. Psychoanalysis has adopted Ernst Kris's concept of *regression in the service of the ego* to describe these benign creative processes.[18]

The term can cause confusion, for it denotes a complex and contradictory state. Even though prelogical primary-process thinking prevails and ancient libidinal and aggressive strivings which have been superseded in the course of maturation are reactivated, the ego continues to function on a mature level. Indeed, if all goes well regression in the service of the ego brings about new maturational spurts. However, if the ego should be unable to withstand the pressures arising from the id, there may be regression in the pathological sense. Long before it was described in psychoanalytic terms, it has been known that creative work entails this risk.[19]

Undoubtedly the companionable solitude which Winnicott describes for us in terms of psychoanalytic understanding constitutes the ideal situation for producing art or for vicariously experiencing it. As practicing artists we recognize it as infinitely precious. As art therapists we strive to establish this atmosphere as we conduct sessions. We must frequently be much more active than the mother Winnicott envisions. Often our work begins at a more primitive level. We must directly participate in the child's efforts and thereby libidinize the creative process. We must, nevertheless, constantly strive to maintain a balance between ego support and respect for the child's need for unmolested introspection. We must forever remember that only what emerges within an ambience of supportive but nonintrusive contact can feel real to the person who brings it forth, for he

18. Ernst Kris, *Psychoanalytic Explorations in Art.*

19. Silvano Arieti suggests the term *tertiary process* for the creative synthesis that occurs when benign contact with primary-process thinking lends vitality to secondary-process mental functioning. For an extensive discussion of these questions, see Arieti, *Creativity: The Magic Synthesis.*

has achieved it himself. Enforced productions or information obtained through coercion can rarely be fully assimilated and can therefore have no lasting effect on the individual's life.

To summarize our findings: We see direct, instinctive gratifications receding in importance as more complex, effortful, symbolic actions gain ascendance, provide pleasure, and contribute to ego development. Can we detect any renunciation of instinctual gratification or any resolution of conflict enacted in the kind of art we have described in our examples? Can we expect anything of this nature to occur in the art of anyone functioning on the developmental level of an Elena or an Arno?

On the whole we see more repetition than change. Elena relinquishes a fixation on a cluster of identical jingle bells for the making of endless arrays of similar bracelets and necklaces. She changes from drawing stereotyped radial shapes to a more variegated repertoire of simple configurations but continues to repeat them untiringly.

The story of Arno's productions comes closer to sublimation as we know it. His initial scribblings seem to express emotional distress. The *Circle House* appears to be a victory over the stranglehold of compulsive repetition. We can envisage a subsequent blossoming of art that will have all the hallmarks of sublimation. His subsequent history confirms our expectation. At age seven Arno is still greatly concerned with houses, their stability, and all the good, nurturing things that happen at home. An elaborate drawing shows an X-ray image of a brick house, its bricks carefully drawn, with kitchen stove and refrigerator, and a meal being cooked, and himself smiling broadly among these reassuring objects.

In the art of children who have reached the representational stage we are inclined to associate sublimation with variety and change and to see repetition as a symptom of conflict at a deadlock. The very young and the retarded, however, are inclined to practice any achievement endlessly and joyfully. Their graphic repetitions need not signify constricting mechanisms of defense or deadlocked conflicting emotions. Rather, pleasure may be reigning supreme, unimpaired by any intrapsychic conflict. But because we perceive no inner struggle we hesitate to designate such benign repetitive productions as sublimations.

For our present discussion it would seem to me profitable to designate the very earliest ego-building art activities that are pleasurably repetitive as *precursors of sublimation* and to reserve the term *sublimation* for those instances where we can perceive a struggle between ego and id from which the ego emerges victorious, having effected some fundamental changes in the balance of inner forces.

If we adhere to this distinction we can say that the young child discovers the pleasures of the evocative power of art and its capacity to create illusions before he is ready to use this faculty in the service of sublimation. To arrive at this level he must learn to take pleasure in evoking not only what is desirable; he must also be ready to contemplate what is painful and conflicted and to take pleasure in finding a way of mastering such feelings through his art.

THE BOUNDARIES OF SUBLIMATION

Good and Evil

As the child's capacity to sort out opposites develops, simple repetition loses attraction. The need for clear-cut distinctions motivates mastering many different configurations in art.

Anton: Anton's paintings of *Heaven* (Fig. 19) and *Hell* (Fig. 20)[20] are good examples of the successful expression

20. Case material and pictures for this passage were supplied by Eva Jozan, teacher of special education.

of opposing ideas on the part of an intellectually handicapped individual as he uses his limited mental capacities to the hilt.

When the teacher of a class for educable retarded young adults suggested that they paint pictures representing the things they liked best and those they feared most, Anton complied enthusiastically, quite in contrast to the majority of his classmates, who were ready to depict good things but inclined to deny the very existence of any fears and dislikes. This is not unusual among the moderately retarded who have learned the advantage of presenting a compliant and cheerful front to the world and are fearful of risking the displeasure of the authorities by showing any sign of discontent or rebellion.

The two tempera paintings on twelve- by eighteen-inch white paper complement one another. Equally impressive are the clarity of Anton's message and the simplicity of his pictorial vocabulary. Triangles dominate both paintings, but the neatly drawn church doors and windows demonstrate that he has also mastered rectangular shapes. We see that he can draw crosses and semicircles as well. His figures are limited to simplistic stick men, their top-heavy circle-heads perched on frail, linear bodies. For his heavenly church, Anton has used his paper vertically, filling the whole space with a compact triangular structure composed of four separate triangular shapes, each outlined in blue and filled in with a light bluish-green. The inside areas of doors, windows, and bell chambers are left white. The whole structure is planted on a green baseline. Each of the three upward-pointing triangles constitutes an individual church complete with bell tower and cross, while the central inverted triangle unifies these structures into one hierarchical whole. The severity of the triangular composition is relieved by three black crosses, the top one crowning the structure's apex, the other two ingeniously displaced sideways to serve both as the crowning glory of the two

FIGURE 19. *Anton:*
Heaven (12″ x 18″)

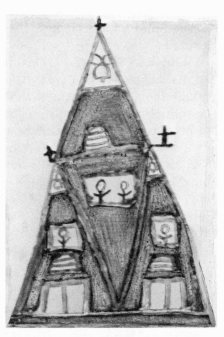

FIGURE 20. *Anton:* Hell (12″ x 18″)

lower churches and as ornamentation for the total structure. On the inside the blue outlines of bells, windows, doors, and four stick people extending their arms in greeting add a touch of gaiety.

Anton uses triangular shapes also for depicting hell. While the church painting's verticality expresses a feeling of upward striving, horizontal organization establishes the downward pull of hell. The hellish stronghold is symbolized by a group of three brown triangles resting on a brown baseline. The central one dominates the two smaller ones at the sides. Poised precariously between the apex of each of the two smaller triangles and the large one's flanks are two black, bridge-like perches straddled by two grim-faced devilish stick figures. One of them sports horns and claws and both are armed with pitchforks.

Simply by a different arrangement of three triangles and different color choices, Anton creates diametrically opposite impressions—in his church solidity, cohesion, and upward striving relieved by moderate gaiety, the whole conceived in the blue color of heaven and of control and supported by a hopeful green. In hell, we discern earthiness, brown anality, and a feeling of precariousness and danger. While the central inverted triangle of the church painting unites the three separate churches, two inverted triangles of negative space separate the three hellish mountains. The people inhabiting the church seem both protected and confined. They could almost be taken for flowers growing in pots at the windowsills. In contrast, the devils appear to be endangered but to have the power to move, as they tower above hell's stronghold.

We can assume that Anton had become familiar with the triangle in the course of his classroom experiences, since the use of form boards and stencils of the basic geometric shapes is standard in teaching the retarded. This skill gave him the freedom to express potentially disruptive feelings of aggression and anxiety within the protective structure of strictly organized configurations. We see a mind able to establish for himself a world that he could handle both conceptually and emotionally. It is a world that allows for complexity and conflict; for even though Anton clearly separates good from evil, he also shows their complementary relationship. Even though we cannot ascribe any abstract understanding of moral dilemma to his limited mentality, his painting expresses his intuitive awareness that safety and goodness are attained at the sacrifice of aggressive freedom—conceivably of manhood. Considering the retardate's dependence on clear-cut rules and regulations, we must conclude that Anton's somewhat rigid image of the world is consonant with his needs.

In this connection it is interesting to contemplate the different mental functioning implied in making various geometrical shapes. The circle requires no abrupt change of direction; movement is soft and potentially endless. To draw triangles it is necessary to change directions, take aim, make decisions three times. To undergo such exertions four times in order to draw a rectangle demands yet greater effort. We often find that young children who have in principle mastered the rectangle are nevertheless inclined to produce a rounded loop in lieu of the last corner of their houses, windows, or doors, as if they lacked the energy to take yet a fourth direction. More energetic children, on the other hand, often practice the newly achieved square as victoriously and joyfully as younger ones repeat the newly mastered circle.

Can we conceive of processes of sublimation being active in the making of Anton's pictures? The struggle between contending inner forces is solved by establishing separate areas for each, but neither is denied expression. Unity of form and content, of conscious and unconscious meaning, has been achieved. At their own childlike level the two paintings attain moderate esthetic dignity. Thus we can safely assume that Anton did experience sublimation.

The Realm of Illusion

Eduardo: If we look back on the examples of children's art presented in the previous chapters, blind Eduardo's clay image of his hospitalized mother provides us with the most rudimentary production that can be unequivocally ascribed to sublimation. His anger at her desertion, his confused and sadistic fantasies about the nature of her illness and of the operation to be performed on her body, his longing and grief all energized the act of making her image and of symbolically healing her wound. This helped him endure the separation, to keep in touch with her and to keep her image whole rather than splitting her into a good and a bad mother. We see Eduardo able to endure ambivalent feelings. We observe insatiable infantile demands transformed into protective tenderness. It also seems likely that single-minded sexual curiosity is being transformed into a more mature attempt to understand his mother's previous pregnancies and the nature of her operation.

If we had asked Eduardo whether the mama he had made was *real* or "only" a statue, the question would have been destructively disenchanting. He evidently knew that mama was not in the room, but somewhere at a place called a hospital; the feeling of her actual presence had not intruded into his perception of the real world. He willingly left her image in our care to be fired in the school's kiln. Rather than cast doubt on the benign magic we had witnessed, we could rejoice with him for having brought it about.

Eduardo's creative experience occurred in the realm of *illusion* as described by Winnicott: "an intermediate area ...to which inner reality and external life both contribute ...a resting place for the individual engaged in the perpetual human task of keeping inner and outer reality separate yet interrelated."[21] Can we speak of sublimation

21. Winnicott, *Through Paediatrics to Psycho-Analysis*, p. 230.

when the subtle borderline between illusion and reality, or the one between illusion and delusion, is transgressed or becomes blurred?

Certain distinctions are easily made. Attempts at gratifying unregenerated sexual or aggressive impulses through image making are usually crude and rudimentary. They are undertaken as second best to doing the real thing in the real world, preferred only because they are safer.

Destruction in Effigy

Margaret: When Margaret was absent from her art therapy group the remaining children, who disliked her, guickly drew a crude image of her and proceeded to attack it gleefully with paint. They acted much like a mob burning a hated and feared public person in effigy. The incident unrolled so rapidly and forcefully that I could not intercede in time. Only when sufficient rage had been siphoned off could order be restored and the besmeared image relegated to the wastebasket where it belonged.

Aggression had been displaced and discharged without causing bodily harm, but this positive achievement was offset by the children's excessive sadistic gratification. The session had been a therapeutic failure and most certainly it had been devoid of sublimation. Deplorable though the incident was, it was well within the common range of group behavior.

The Image as a Substitute

Morris: Image making as a shortcut to sexual and aggressive gratification can take on an ominous character among severely disturbed children. For some of them art may indeed become a means of practicing seriously destructive and perverted deeds with every intention of performing them in dead earnest should the occasion present itself.

Morris had lost the remnants of his defective eyesight in

the first years of his life. He had been abandoned shortly after birth and had been raised in institutions. At age ten his behavior had become unmanageably psychopathic.

During several art therapy sessions in a day school, Morris made innumerable rudimentary clay figures and gleefully beheaded them. He also constructed crude trees and cut them into small pieces while he enacted the sounds and motions of a chain saw. Occasionally he could be induced to leave the last person or tree he made during a session intact, but these were inevitably killed off at the beginning of the following one. It seemed that he spared them mainly for the pleasure of looking forward to their impending doom.

Later on Morris also constructed realistic lifesize penises and buttocks. These he allowed to be fired in the school's kiln so that they could serve as props for enacting sodomy. In this play the big penis became personified as "Jumping Penis," able to move about on his own. The buttocks remained stationary and never acquired a name.

We can understand Morris's act as a desperate attempt at turning passive experience into active, the cruelty of his fantasies corresponding to his desperate, utterly destructive life experiences. His sculptures of sexual organs can be understood as expressing his fragmented body image as well as the sexual excitement that possessed him. Yet we would be in error imagining that acting out his murderous and perverse ideas in art could serve as a safety valve that would diminish his need for direct action.

On the contrary, Morris perceived the art room as an arena where he could safely practice what he intended to do to the best of his ability in real life. Morris had become truly dangerous to children weaker than himself, and he roamed the dormitories at night offering his body to the older boys. Only his blindness made it possible to control him at all.

Sublimation evidently played no part in Morris's art and would remain out of reach in the foreseeable future.

Image and Idol

Samantha: Morris never invested his clay images very highly. He produced them rapidly, characterizing them just enough to be able to enact and reenact his fantasies on them. Samantha's images were made with loving care and considerable skill, but she too used her products as a means of giving substance to very explicit sexual strivings.

Samantha was admitted to the child psychiatric ward at age nine. A scrawny, undersized little girl, she appeared indefinably strange. The fifth child in her family, Samantha had been deprived of mothering at the age of fifteen months when her mother gave birth to a profoundly retarded baby girl whose care absorbed all her time and energy. Samantha's psychological tests revealed mild retardation (IQ 73) and brain damage. She was diagnosed as suffering from childhood schizophrenia.

Samantha was habitually truant from school. She frequently ran away from home and she believed herself to be a dog. She walked on all fours and barked, bit, licked, and sniffed at people, and insisted that her meals be served on the floor. The police often found her sleeping among stray dogs.

On the ward Samantha gradually relinquished her impersonations of dogs, reverting to them only at times of stress. She enjoyed art and showed skill and imagination far superior to her academic performance.

Memorable above all was a group of two clay images each standing approximately four inches high. These represented her psychotherapist, Dr. M, and herself (Figs. 21 and 22). These two personifications of sexual organs, shaped with tender care and painted carefully in bright colors, exude an indefinable archaic power, so that we could easily imagine them to have belonged among the ritual objects of some very ancient culture.

Dr. M's combination penis–body is painted brown. Arms have not been sculpted but are painted on the body

FIGURE 21. *Samantha:* Samantha and Dr. M, front view (4″ high)

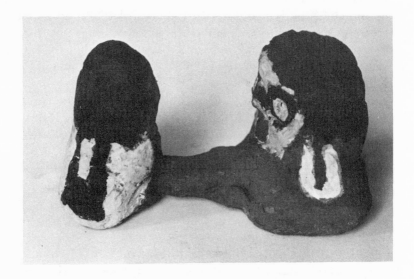

FIGURE 22. *Samantha:* Samantha and Dr. M, side view (4″ high)

with white lines. Dr. M's face is painted a pink skin color. He is adorned with eyeglasses that are incised into the clay and then painted over in black. His eyes are incised and painted white to stare straight at Samantha. His mouth is red and smiling, his hair black. In spite of sculpture's primitive quality, Samantha somehow succeeded in producing a definite likeness of her doctor.

Samantha presents herself as no more than an upright, somewhat cone-shaped lump onto which features have been incised. Close to the bottom of this lump a hole has been provided that perfectly fits the male's penis. The little figure is neatly painted. The face and front of the body are painted a brown skin color. The mouth is red and the vagina bright yellow. The hair is black. The white dress covers only the back and sides of the figure, leaving the front exposed. Arms and hands are indicated by black outlines.

Samantha kept her two idols permanently hidden on a shelf in the art room closet. At the beginning of each art session she ritually visited with them to play at intercourse between them. She performed the act solemnly, not in an obscene or flippant manner, and I never saw her masturbate while she was engaged in making her figures join in the sexual act.

After this ritual Samantha could return her figures to their shelf and turn to more conventional artwork. Mainly, she painted and sculpted little girls and horses. She never represented any dogs at this time. It seemed as if the symbolically enacted sexual closeness to her therapist gave her the strength to behave in a more controlled and conventional manner during the rest of the session. Dr. M had evidently come to be an important and stable person in Samantha's world.

Later on Samantha made another group of clay images that served as a means of keeping in touch with other beloved persons who, like the doctor, were conceived of as sexually active. These represented her siblings, each consisting of a clay disc that supported a prone, gingerbread-

FIGURE 23. *Samantha:* Family (approx. 8" in diameter)

like figure with a smiling face (Fig. 23). The clothes of each little person were arranged so that the genital area was exposed. Samantha attached a kind of handle to each work in order to be able to carry her family around with her. Unfortunately, I do not know exactly which of the four siblings each of the three figures represented. What is interesting for us above all is that although they were represented as stripped for action, they were never used in any overt sexual play. Rather, Samantha treated them as proud possessions, conceivably as her own children. Carrying two heavy clay discs by their handles in her right hand and the third one in her left, she looked much like a little girl busily imitating mommy by carrying several of her pocketbooks.

Can we imagine that sublimation played any role in the making of Samantha's sculptures or in the part these objects played in her life? Compared to Morris's jumping penis and disconnected buttocks, Samantha's images were conceived on a much higher level. While Morris's sculptures embodied his pathology unredeemed, Samantha's productions did not express her most severe symptoms. At her most bizarre she removed herself entirely from humankind, assumed the guise of a being that has license to indulge in primitive oral pleasures—to lick, bite, sniff, and bark without restraint (her impersonations rarely stressed a dog's more appealing aspects). Returning to humankind, she fashioned her own breed of people. Although their bodies were strangely condensed and sexualized, their faces belonged to real persons—her doctor and herself, and later on her siblings. The sexual play enacted with these images seems tender rather than aggressive, serene rather than climactic. This seems to indicate that the experiences which found expression in Samantha's sculptures had actually been tender rather than crudely sexual ones. It seems unlikely that she had been sexually abused. When children who have been so treated communicate these experiences in their art the work is rarely well organized; chaotic and fragmented work prevails. Samantha's work is bizarre but well integrated. We can rather assume that Samantha's primitive mentality made her perceive any positive relationship in sexual terms. She evidently conceived of her relationship to Dr. M as a kind of intercourse.

Can we liken Samantha's archaic sexual idols to the vast domain of serious erotic art, a realm of imagery which is distinct from pornography which facilitates masturbatory short-circuiting of the sexual act, imagery which in a great many cultures contributes to the process of integration and sublimation which must be reached if genital love is to be fully gratifying?

Evidently she achieves full perception of neither her own body nor of that of her lover and partner. Her idol's bound and confined appearance precludes the idea of any tender contact beyond simple sexual union. The situation Samantha created suggests fellatio. But we find that she has made an effort to sort out the functions of various body openings. She did indeed provide the female with a separate opening below the mouth to accommodate the penis (a second mouth, so to speak).

The yellow color of the opening, suggestive of urine, seems consonant with a sexually undeveloped girl-child's range of physical experiences. Displacement of sexual material onto more neutral subject matter that would be characteristic of a normal latency-age child has not occurred. Nevertheless, we cannot entirely exclude the idea that Samantha has used her artistic talent in the service of taming and civilizing her sexuality, that the pleasure she derived from making her idols and from playing with them belonged more to the ego than to the id, that some archaic process of sublimation or what we might at least call proto-sublimation may have been at work.

Since these idols are not ritual objects firmly anchored in the Weltanschauung of some ancient culture but the private invention of a child of the twentieth century, it is hard to fathom their exact position in Samantha's perception of the world. Do they belong to the realm of illusion that normally mediates between the individual's inner perceptions and his perception of the environment? Do they belong to a magical world that serves to exclude the environment or to reinterpret it according to her private needs?

We can answer the question only in an impressionistic manner. Many children who live in private worlds do not invest their art at all; it remains meager, perfunctory, lacking integration and energy. Others are inclined to use their art to express and uphold ideas that contradict the evidence of their senses. In the latter cases I have observed a tendency to produce redundantly repetitive work. It differs in a subtle manner from the compulsive repetitions of neurotic children whose art serves as a defense against unacceptable impulses. Although less elaborate than the well-known productions of adult schizophrenics, these works seem to serve the dual purpose described by Kris: to impose a private kind of organization upon a chaotic inner world buffeted by archaic libidinal and aggressive strivings and to protect these private structures against the influx of perceptions that might cast doubt on their reality.[22] Children's drawings produced to serve such need tend to

22. Kris, *Psychoanalytic Explanations of Art.*

be massively overcrowded, leaving no breathing space—no opening, so to speak, for intrusion of any extraneous material. The need to fill the world to overflowing with their private images keeps some of these children busy manufacturing innumerable similar clay objects. Figure 24, for example, is a collection of anal people mass-produced by ten-year-old Gregory, a boy whose universe at the time was confined to personages inhabiting the toilet bowl and sewer system. Had Samantha proceeded to create a population of similar penis and vagina idols I would consider her productions as functioning in the service of her pathological needs. But she was not given to repetition. She neither continued to produce similar figures nor did she play endlessly with the original two. Rather, they seemed to stimulate her toward the new exploits that characteristically follow successful sublimation. These works remained, however, limited in scope and the next important production again presented a puzzling mixture of the crudely sexual and the tender. Samantha's handling of her two idols nevertheless had an intense and solemn quality reminiscent of serious magical operations rather than play.

In her subsequent institutionalized childhood and adolescence that was dogged by repeated misfortunes (among

FIGURE 24. *Gregory:* Clay Figures (approx. 2″ each)

them her mother's death when Samantha was in her early teens) her artistic talent alternately served as a means of embodying delusional ideas and as a tenuous link to a healthier area of imagination. Figure 25, produced at age seventeen, expresses delusional confusion between people and animals (Samantha had never fully relinquished her identity as a dog). In Figure 26, drawn when she hopefully anticipated a move to a rural group home where she would be allowed to care for live animals, the effort to imagine a real mother dog and her puppies seems to prevail. Her

FIGURE 25. *Samantha:* Animals (pencil; 12″ x 30″)

FIGURE 26. *Samantha:* Mother Dog and Puppies (pencil; 18″ x 24″)

pathology seems to intrude to some extent. (The mother dog's penis-shaped right paw, for instance, is immediately noticeable.) Nevertheless, the drawing appears much less bizarre than Figure 25, and it testifies to a surprising capacity for observation and draftsmanship far above Samantha's level of functioning in other realms of life.

Our investigation of the boundaries of sublimation necessarily leads us into areas of great uncertainty. Our analysis of Samantha's pair of sculptures leaves us undecided as to their position between sublimation and purely symptomatic expression of emotional and sexual disturbance.

Since much of the art therapist's work occurs within these shadowy realms we cannot abandon our quest merely because we cannot hope to arrive at clear-cut answers. Rather, we must strive to recognize sublimation even when it manifests itself only fleetingly and abortively, and must be alert as well to signs of its breakdown.

We will conclude our collection of examples with a story that permits us to observe the intricacies of successful sublimation in great detail.

Sublimation Achieved

Sidney: Sidney, a bright boy aged ten and one-half, was admitted to a child psychiatric ward on petition of a home for dependent children where he had been placed at age eight, by court order because of his mother's abusive behavior. He had recently become severely regressed and disorganized. His symptoms included soiling, wetting, and self-destructive gestures.

Sidney was the only child of Mrs. F, a well-educated, large, powerful woman, who had physically abused her son throughout his childhood. A battle over toilet training, which was initiated at one year of age, had raged on for many years. Mrs. F's assaultive behavior had first come to the attention of the community when Sidney attended nursery school at age three. At this time, enraged because he had soiled himself, Mrs. F had broken his leg.

Also when her son was three years old she was divorced from Sidney's father. Mother and son then lived alone together until the mother's remarriage when Sidney was seven.

Sidney's episode of disintegration three and a half years later seemed to have been precipitated by his mother's impending second divorce. The prospect of a solitary mother with whom it might be possible to recreate the intimacy of the period between her two marriages must have been at once alluring and terrifying to the preadolescent. In this anxious and ambivalent state, Sidney had produced the very symptoms that had constituted the central conflict of his infancy, thereby making himself unacceptable both to his mother and to the home. He had, however, achieved the secondary gain of being referred to a place that was within his mother's easy reach.

At the children's ward, Sidney reintegrated quickly. There was no soiling or enuresis. His mother visited him regularly, and it seemed that these visits were good for them. The ward structure sheltered them from both his mother's rages and Sidney's compulsive provocations, and under these circumstances the two could begin to enjoy each other's company. Subsequently it was decided to refer Sidney to a residential treatment home where his mother could continue to visit regularly and where both of them could receive psychotherapeutic help. He remained on the ward for four months, improving steadily.

When he first came to art sessions, Sidney was a depressed lump of a boy, too despondent to exert himself. His first product was little more than an amorphous mass of brown clay that he called a hippopotamus. Head and body were barely differentiated and legs were not even suggested. Sidney never painted the sculpture but simply allowed it to dry as it was. He gave it to me as an ambivalent kind of present, letting me know that I could have this ugly thing because he did not care for it, but making sure at the same time that I would keep it safe. The same lumpy anality characterized his next work, a clay submarine.

Next Sidney embarked upon a more ambitious project: a lifesize painting of a sailor. He explained that his uncle was in the marines and that he planned to follow in the uncle's footsteps after finishing high school. The sailor, then, represented an unequivocal ego ideal; just as brown anality had characterized his sculptures, blue, the color of control, reigned supreme in the sailor painting.

Sidney drew the well-proportioned outlines of a slim sailor, in marked contrast to his own obese self, on a large sheet of wrapping paper. But when he painted the man's blue uniform standing against the blue sea, figure and background merged. The blue even spread onto the sailor's hands, so that only his pinkish face and his white cap could be clearly discerned in a sea of blue. Sidney was helplessly distressed, ready to abandon the project. I had to come to the rescue by helping him restore the lost boundaries. I mixed a lighter shade of blue for the background and a skin color for the sailor's hands. Subsequently Sidney returned to clay sculpturing, working more diligently and beginning to take pride in his products.

When he had been on the ward for nearly two months he entered the art room one day and informed me that he intended to make an ashtray for his mother. When I tried to dissuade him from such an uninteresting project, he categorically declared that the ashtray was very important for she smoked so much that she needed it badly. As a compromise I suggested that he make a sculpture of some animal that could then be hollowed out to serve as an ashtray.

Sidney thereupon began leafing through a book of animal photographs in search of a suitable subject. He hit upon a picture of a kangaroo and declared that he would make a female kangaroo whose pouch would be used as an ashtray. He went to work eagerly. He worked with such quiet absorption that I nearly forgot about his presence.

When I next looked at his sculpture, the pouch was filled with a baby kangaroo (Fig. 27) and Sidney was beaming. He never mentioned ashtrays again. Full of pride over his beautiful sculpture, he imagined how pleased and proud his mother would be when she saw it. He declared that he would make a whole series of clay animals and that his mother would have to get a special shelf made to display them together. In the subsequent two months he carried out this plan, making a total of six sculptures.

Following the kangaroo he assumed a proud and belligerent masculine stance as he carefully produced a crouching lion (Fig. 28). His sculpture regressed as he produced a huge and formless rabbit whose pronounced round cottontail was very like feces. But after he had completed his next sculpture, an elephant carrying a hunter who held a spear in his hand (Fig. 29), Sidney declared that neither the rabbit nor the earlier hippopotamus was worth keeping. Having successfully sculpted the elephant, an

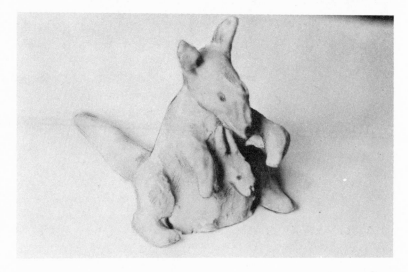

FIGURE 27. *Sidney:* Kangaroo with Baby (approx. 6″ high)

FIGURE 28. *Sidney:* Lion
(approx. 10″ long)

FIGURE 30. *Sidney:* Trophy
(approx. 8″ wide)

FIGURE 29. *Sidney:* Elephant and Rider (approx. 8″ high)

animal whose bigness is associated with benign strength and intelligence, in the act of serving a human master, Sidney seemed ready to discard the earlier images of degraded bulk. He decided to break them up to make more clay for himself and the group. From then on recycling clay became an important feature of Sidney's art therapy sessions. He was proud to be able to handle this difficult and seductively messy job in a controlled manner.

Sidney once more dealt with the issue of fatness and primitive aggressive behavior when he modeled a "trophy" that consisted of a rhinoceros head (Fig. 30). Here the well-defended, dangerous head is severed from the ungainly body and becomes the proud possession of the small, intelligent hunter. Inasmuch as the hunter, in acquiring the trophy, symbolically incorporates his prey's ferociousness, the mechanism remains a primitive identification with the aggressor.

A sculpture of a German shepherd dog (Fig.31) followed. The figure rather resembled a male kangaroo. As he made it, Sidney indulged in an extensive fantasy of being given such a dog when he was discharged to his mother's home. The idea was quite unrealistic and this may have prevented Sidney from being able to fully imagine the dog.

Last in the series was the upright figure of a sailor (Fig. 32), constructed laboriously around an armature which later had to be carefully removed for firing. With this sculpture, Sidney had come full cycle to his early ego ideal painted a little over three months before. It appears that this ideal was now no longer just a foreign element superimposed on an infantile personality but had become somewhat more integrated into Sidney's inner life.

It is interesting that Sidney left his sculptures unpainted after they had been fired in the hospital's kiln. He seemed to conceive of them as a definite unit and deliberately postponed giving them color until the group was completed and he was about to leave the ward. When he finally got around to it he did an excellent job, spending much

FIGURE 31. *Sidney:* German   FIGURE 32. *Sidney:* Sailor
Shepherd (approx. 6″ high)   (approx. 8″ high)

time mixing appropriate, realistic colors for each figure.

Even though there naturally were ups and downs in Sidney's productivity, he never wavered in his purpose. His choice of subject for each of the figures seemed to follow some inner necessity so that he seldom hesitated before embarking on a new project. His enthusiasm was nourished by the ward's admiration of his sculptures, but above all he was greatly encouraged by his mother's appreciation of his work. It seemed that Mrs. F could accept her son in the guise of a talented young artist even though she had not been able to put up with him when he was a messy baby. (I do not know whether or not she actually installed a shelf for the sculptures in her home.)

In the making of the kangaroo mother and baby and the subsequent sculptures, we can clearly perceive the process of sublimation in all its complexity. Sidney's earlier productions had been divided into the sculptures that embodied his infantile, degraded aspect and the painting given over to superego demands where his person is lost in a blue sea of control.

Originally the kangaroo was conceived in a context of anal concerns. It was to be a container of his mother's waste, and Sidney showed considerable hostility as he described her chain-smoking. When he selected a symbol of motherhood as his mother's ash container, the ashes in turn came to represent a worthless baby. As he restored a live, appealing baby to the empty pouch, Sidney broke the vicious circle of anal sadomasochistic give-and-take. The ashtray was entirely forgotten. Instead Sidney conceived of himself as the proud creator of a whole array of sculptures for which he could justly claim his mother's respectful admiration, and he achieved this aim within the following two months.

It is unlikely that Sidney would have been able to make such progress within so short a time if his childhood had been entirely destructive. We must assume that his mother had given him some measure of warmth and love—that pathology had distorted the relationship but had not entirely destroyed it. Without a foundation of positive real-life experiences Sidney could not have reintegrated so easily on the children's ward where he functioned on a preadolescent level. Neither would he have been able to create a convincing image of blissful, symbiotic union in the kangaroo group and by doing so gain impetus for making more sculptures.

The kangaroo group seems to have been conceived under the aegis of restoration without regression; its symbolic roots are rich and varied. As he transformed ashtray into external womb, Sidney restored the good mother he lost when her pathology interfered with their relationship. He restored as well his own blissful babyhood before toilet training began. By making something valuable and permanent from the malleable brown clay he both regained the anal gratification of which his severe and premature toilet training had deprived him and transcended primitive anal preoccupation. On the phallic level, placing the baby inside the mother kangaroo constituted fulfillment of Oedipal fantasies. Fulfillment, however, went hand in hand with renunciation of fantasies of direct instinctive gratification that had caused his recent episode of disintegration. It remained symbolic and there was no regression. Sidney comported himself as befitted an intelligent preadolescent, using his ego faculties to the hilt. He imaged his subjects well, handled the art materials competently, and planned ahead. The balance between gratification and renunciation characteristic of sublimation was reached.

Sidney's subsequent varied production and the energy with which he pursued it is further evidence of successful sublimation. When conflict is simply displaced the need for repetition persists. Sidney had no need to make more kangaroos. Rather, his work tells of an expanding personality free to express many aspects of his being. Although none of his later sculptures was as profoundly significant as the first one, being able to make these many sculptures was important. Through them Sidney established himself as a competent individual commanding dependable talents and skills. It was in keeping with his still-preadolescent state that the desire to please his mother remained an important incentive for his production.

Sidney's production in art therapy corresponded to positive changes in his life brought about through milieu therapy, individual therapy, and conjoint psychotherapeutic work with mother and son. Without such help there could have been no kangaroos. The intense gratification he experienced through his artwork gave Sidney additional energy for wrestling with his problems, helped him cement his gains and prepare for the future.

For Sidney's art therapy an abundant supply of clay was essential. His anal preoccupations would not have been worked through as successfully in the absence of this essential material. It was important that his early productions were accepted in spite of their infantile anal quality. Equally necessary was benign pressure toward more mature work. The anal productions expressed Sidney's feelings of worthlessness; therefore, unreserved acceptance of them could have served to confirm this degraded self-image. I had to steer a middle course, making it understood that I could accept him as he was but that I was confident that more and better were to come.

A period of four months of progress in art therapy, of course, gives no assurance that the faculty for sublimation can be maintained when therapy is discontinued. We can say no more than that at age ten years and eight months Sidney derived considerable benefit from an experience in art which partook of the process of sublimation, that he experienced the increase of energy and the feeling of elation which comes to the artist as he labors intensively and with full absorption on a work, a work that has profound personal meaning and that constitutes at the same time a gift to another person and in a wider sense to the world at large.

Our story also demonstrates that the relationship between sublimation and quality in art is far from simple. Sidney was only moderately gifted. Although he was fully justified in taking pride in his work, we must admit that none of his sculptures reach extraordinary heights of expressiveness or formal beauty. We would hardly expect Sidney to grow up to become a sculptor. We rather hope that his experience in art will serve as a model of healthy functioning that will sustain him even as he turns to other interests.

In an attempt at understanding the role of sublimation in the art and art therapy of children we have extended our quest beyond boundaries of the process itself. Searching for the origin of pleasure in sublimation, we even left humankind and investigated the behavior of the higher social animals and the proto-emotions foreshadowing human joy and grief that appear as individual bonds are established. Next we investigated the graphic productions of the very young and of the retarded. Dividing them into pleasurably invested repetitions and first attempts at sorting out opposites, we decided to count the former among precursors of sublimation and the latter among its earliest beginnings. We extended our investigations to the shadowy area where illusion blends into delusion in the art of children at the borderline of severe disintegration. Here we found both products entirely devoid of sublimation and work which showed vestiges of it—albeit distorted and limited by pathological processes.

Sidney's story finally afforded an intimate look into the process of sublimation as we defined it at the beginning of the chapter. However, even though his art reached unexpected heights as sublimation became possible for him, its objective esthetic level remained moderate.

To contemplate the ideal unity between artistic excellence and sublimation we must turn back to the miracles, Dwayne's *Self-Portrait* and Albert's *Autumn Tree*. The analysis of the outstanding work of five children presented in Chapter II has already taught us that we cannot assume any simplistic equation between excellence in art and the extent of sublimation in the artist's life as a whole. When sublimation is confined mainly to areas of artistic execution, esthetically outstanding work may be achieved even as emotional content remains profoundly disturbed and even as art serves to give substance to vengeful, cruel, and anxiety-ridden ideations, as exemplified by Remo's *Ghost House* and Harry's *Instruments of Execution*.

Whatever understanding we may have gained, we have not solved the mystery of the interrelationship between giftedness, sublimation, and emotional illness and health. We have, nevertheless, learned to recognize sublimation by a number of signs or rules of thumb: notable above all is the lessening of the need for repetition. Even the pleasurably invested repetitions characteristic of art activities that are forerunners of sublimation as exemplified by Elena's passion for repeating circular and radial shapes tends to disappear. No longer do compulsive, obsessive repetitions, indicating the presence of constricting mechanisms of defense, result in meager stereotyped production.[23] The child who can sublimate is free as well from the joyless impulse-ridden repetition of the psychopathic, as we have seen it in Morris's repetitious activities. Instead an appetite to *repeat the experience of sublimation* is born, so that the child is moved to produce different kinds of work or else variations on a number of recurring themes that retain their vitality as each variation presents a different aspect of the same subject.

The passionate hunger for the opportunity for sublimation, the despair when the desire is thwarted, and the intense joy and grief felt as sublimation succeeds or fails testify to its close linkage to the drives. Their need for gratification is not extinguished by any single sublimatory act. Neither intrapsychic conflict nor the conflict between man's drives and the demands of the environment permit of final solutions. Sublimation in art remains a continuous task, but one that never becomes stale or empty as does the repetition born of emotional deadlock. Rather, each new endeavor constitutes a fresh beginning leading to another partial solution so that, if all goes well, each new work becomes more powerful and interesting than the preceding one.

Cézanne's passionate struggle with Mont Ste.-Victoire could never come to a final solution. We can assume that some unending inner tension energized his efforts. Yet each painting constitutes an entirely fresh realization of some aspect of the mountain's appearance. Seen as a group the paintings reveal the infinite variety and depth of experience which any aspect of the natural world holds for us.

Turning from these exalted subjects to the simple, rudimentary, frequently inept productons of disturbed and handicapped children, we still find in the working of

23. For an extensive presentation of art in the service of defense, see Edith Kramer, *Art as Therapy with Children*, pp.121–156.

sublimation an increase of productive energy as well as a shift toward greater esthetic quality.

We see that the art therapist's attitude toward the concept of sublimation must fundamentally influence both practice and theoretical outlook. Art therapists who recognize in it a powerful source of energy will approach their task differently from those who perceive it as little more than the icing on the cake. While a general belief in the virtues of creativity may suffice to establish an atmosphere conducive to the inception of sublimation, if the concept remains amorphous the full fruition of sublimation may be prevented. A general mood of acceptance of all that is new, exciting, and joyful does not guarantee the clear perception that the child must make choices and must renounce certain pleasures. The profound inner reorganization that sublimation entails may be insufficiently understood, the playful element of art exalted above the passionate struggle for artistic realization.

The art therapist who sees in sublimation a process essential to health will be inclined to shield it from untimely interference, and this will influence the nature and timing of therapeutic intervention.

In work with the severely disturbed and the retarded, much depends on the art therapist's perception of the boundaries of sublimation and of the role of precursory activities. The theoretical orientation presented in this chapter encourages a search for vestiges of sublimation even where, in the full sense, it is out of reach.

As we recognize its powers we must guard against any starry-eyed belief in salvation through sublimation, and we must avoid oversimplification. We must remember that art and sublimation are not identical: art serves a great many purposes, both in the life of individuals and in the cultural and practical lives of peoples, all of them apt to become the art therapist's concern. Premature insistence on sublimation in the face of other pressing needs can be as destructive as failure to recognize its value.

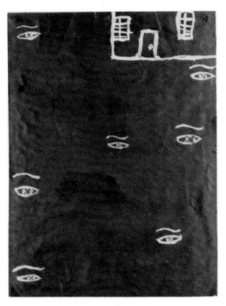

I. *Remo:* Ghost House

II. *Harry:* Guillotine

III. *Jesus:* Sunset Over the Bronx

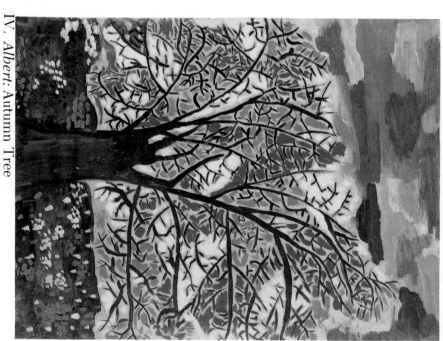

IV. *Albert:* Autumn Tree

V. *Mathew:* Muscle Man

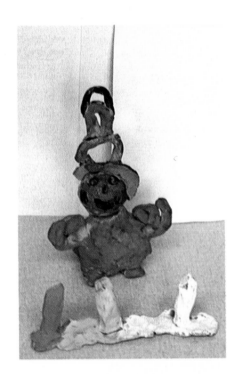

VI. *Howard:* Frederick Douglass

VII. *Rolf:* Tidal Wave

VIII. *Roberta:* Scribble

IX. *Tyrone:* Color Composition

X. *Joseph:* Storm

XI. *Carrol:* House I

XII. *Carrol:*
House II

XIII. *Jerry:* Forest Fire I

XIV. *Jerry:* Forest Fire II

XV. *Jerry:* Forest Fire III

XVI. *Jerry:* Forest Fire IV

PART TWO

*Notes on the Practice of
Art Therapy with
Children*

V

The Art Therapist's Functions

GENERAL PRINCIPLES

IN THE FIRST CHAPTER of this book we addressed ourselves to art therapy and childhood. We looked at the helping adult's relationship with the child as distinguished from his relationship with fellow adults in distress. We noted children's affinity to the arts and the extraordinary energy that is available to them for symbolic living; we considered children's incomplete systems of defense and their limited responsibility and how this allows for considerable truthfulness and vitality in their art. In the second chapter we contemplated the heights of evocative power and esthetic merit which the art of disturbed children occasionally attains. We devoted a third chapter to an investigation of the origin of play and to the distinction between play, playfulness, and art, and used these findings to clarify certain principles in handling play and playfulness in art therapy. In Chapter IV we discussed the complex and controversial concept of sublimation. We investigated social signaling among animals that seemed analogous to certain mechanisms which belong to the process of sublimation in man. We observed precursors of sublimation in the art of the very young and the retarded, investigated the boundaries of sublimation in the art of the severely disturbed, and concluded the chapter with an example of successful sublimation in a series of sculptures made by a disturbed eleven-year-old.

Having established these conceptual foundations we are ready to contemplate the many functions art therapists fulfill in the lives of troubled children and the position of art therapists within the therapeutic milieu, the therapeutic team, and the mental health professions in general. Of course, I cannot deal conclusively with these matters but can only present some ideas and illustrative examples.

Of the two words that together designate our profession I have in my previous writing been inclined to stress *art* above *therapy*. This emphasis stems in part from my strong personal commitment to the visual arts, and in part it comes about in response to the inclination of many of my fellow art therapists to neglect the art in art therapy or to take it for granted. In this chapter, I will address myself more consistently to the problem of therapy and to the many ways in which art and therapy intertwine in our work.

We must begin by distinguishing the adjective *therapeutic* from the noun *therapy*. Today anything in any way beneficial, that elevates the mind, quickens the spirit, or eases the body, is readily dignified with the adjective *therapeutic*. This inclination to stress the so-called therapeutic rather than mention the pleasant, useful, or helpful aspect of various educational, recreational, artistic, or public-spirited endeavors seems to be born of a certain irrational disdain for the practical and educational that pervades our cultural life. We deplore the global use of the adjective *therapeutic*. We must insist even more strongly that the noun *therapy* be not used so loosely.

We expect art therapy to be more than vaguely beneficial. From art therapists we expect systematic understanding of concepts of mental illness and health, of human development, and of the dynamic processes that govern psychic functioning. We expect them to have learned how to apply this knowledge in their own field and to continue to learn more about it throughout their professional lives. At a time when several concepts of personality structure and of therapeutic intervention compete we cannot categorically demand that art therapists adhere to one particular school of thought. This presentation will, however, rely on the concepts of Freudian psychoanalytic psychology because this is the foundation of my work and my thinking. Ideas from adjacent fields, including art therapy itself, broaden and complement my understanding.

Whatever their psychological orientation may be, art therapists must find ways of applying their theories within the context of predominately visual rather than verbal expression. At the onset we might say that just as verbal therapists have learned to listen with a third ear, art therapists learn to see art productions with a third eye. However, the analogy must be qualified as soon as it has been stated. Much confusion has arisen because the meaning of words and phrases that were invented within the framework of Freudian psychoanalytic treatment became blurred when these new terms were transplanted into related fields.

The metaphor "to listen with a third ear" was coined by Theodor Reik to characterize the psychoanalyst's attention to patients' utterances. The basic rule of free association—to suspend all normal inclination to select, suppress, or impose logic and order on ideas that come to mind—brings forth verbal productions that no sane person would ordinarily voice. The patient's elaboration on this outlandish material likewise is influenced by the peculiar character of the psychoanalytic situation. To find meaning in this kind of speech indeed requires a specially attuned and informed ear.

Beyond its importance in the treatment of neurotics the psychoanalyst's skill at discerning a multiplicity of meanings can be useful in numerous circumstances. The psychoanalytically informed therapist can comprehend utterances that are governed by primary-process thinking, such as the idiosyncratic talk of psychotics or young children's verbal fantasies as well as their play.

The same skill is also valuable in psychotherapeutic

interventions that address themselves in the main to the client's conscious and preconscious mind. Even when therapeutic goals are circumscribed and time is limited, psychoanalytic understanding makes it possible for therapists to listen to the derivatives of unconscious processes as well as to the client's more rational and circumstantial communications. They are able to pick up verbal and behavorial clues that allow insight into psychodynamic aspects of disturbed behavior that would elude the untutored observer.

Psychotherapists thus become adept at distinguishing banality, conscious and unconscious falsehood, or rationalization from genuine insight; at learning to listen to the voices of ego, id, and superego as they intermingle in the therapeutic interview; at learning to sense when to speak and when to be silent. Child therapists develop kindred skills in responding in words and action to the many ways in which children express themselves as they play, act, and talk. We think of skills such as these latter ones when we maintain that art therapists develop a *third eye* in perceiving meaning in line, color, and sculptural form. We have no right to compare ourselves to the psychoanalyst who listens to the patient's free associations, for no comparable material is apt to be brought forth in art therapy.

Even the widely used scribble technique is not really comparable to free association. Finding images in one's own scribbles more often than not brings forth latent ideas that would not have been readily accessible to a purposeful search for subject matter. The images may surprise and enlighten the scribbler, but this kind of illumination, however salutary it may be, stops short of unearthing deeply repressed content. Likewise the scribbler's comments on a scribble, on the ideas evoked by it or the meaning of the images discovered through it, differ essentially from free association. The scribbler may be moved to talk uninhibitedly and in the course of talking may be surprised, shocked, or enlightened by his spontaneous utterances. But the art therapy client does not submit to the rigors of free association, a discipline which the patient undergoing psychoanalysis acquires only slowly and painfully, for it contradicts the habits of a lifetime. The art therapist's suggestion to elaborate pictorially on the scribble, to make the discovered image more visible and comprehensible, brings the process under the ego's control and constitutes a process of synthesis rather than of analysis.

The art therapist's interchange with troubled individuals is centered squarely on the productive process in art. It is the art therapist's job to know when to offer what kind of materials, when to make suggestions or give active help, when to refrain from interfering. Art therapists also learn to perceive meaning in the seemingly incoherent and pointless pictorial productions of severely disturbed people.

In all realms pertaining to art and art materials the art therapist's skills surpass those of psychotherapists, who use art materials only incidentally. Conversely, art therapists, even though they develop considerable sagacity in the verbal interchange which naturally occurs in the course of art therapy, cannot be expected to match the psychotherapist's third ear or his knowledge about how to use words therapeutically.

Matters are, however, even more complicated. We cannot simply equate the art produced in art therapy with the words used in adult psychotherapy or the play and talk that replace purely verbal interchange in child therapy. Communication in psychotherapy is typically fluid and unformed, and attention is focused in the main on *content*. While art therapists encourage unconventional form as well as content in art, they are nevertheless intent on fostering *artistic eloquence.* As we have shown in the previous chapters, the depth and verity of the experience in art therapy is in many ways bound up with its *formal* qualities. Above all the individual's eloquent productions eloquently speak back to him both in the course of work and when he later contemplates it.

This dialogue between creator and creation has no exact

parallel in verbal psychotherapy. It can be likened only to what happens when the other arts—dance, music, drama, or poetry—are used in therapy. The order and structure with which artistic expression endows experience is of the utmost importance in all these therapies—a powerful aid in recognizing, sorting out, and mastering experience. To quote Susanne Langer: "The primary function of art is to objectify feeling so that we can contemplate and understand it. It is the formulation of so-called 'inward experience,' the 'inner life,' that is impossible to achieve by discursive thought, because its forms are incommensurable with the forms of language...."[1] Art therapists are therefore forever intent on helping individuals to become more coherent and more eloquent in their art. They are skilled in perceiving even the most hesitant moves in this direction and in finding ways of supporting the most rudimentary efforts.

Here again we must distinguish between adjective and noun, for while artistic pursuits may in themselves be *therapeutic*, it is only through the guidance of trained professionals that they become *therapy*. Even as we strive to enhance children's artistic eloquence we perform this task within the context of an informed appraisal of each child's general state of being.

Before pursuing these ideas further in theory we will illustrate the art therapist's work by a number of examples.

ON COMPLETING DEVELOPMENTAL TASKS

The following examples are about art therapy with physically ill children. I choose them because the urgency and drama of such children's predicaments bring certain aspects of the art therapist's function sharply into focus.

Children whose development has been interrupted or chronically impeded by physical illness typically face

1. Susanne Langer, *Philosophical Sketches*, p. 90.

certain difficulties. The most obvious ones belong directly to illness—pain, boredom, the trauma of hospitalization, helpless rage, and fear of dying. We know that illness is often consciously or unconsciously perceived as punishment for evil deeds or wishes so that the very intensity of suffering becomes a proof of blameworthiness and heightens irrational guilt feelings. Regression under the impact of physical helplessness and enforced dependency is also easily understood. Not as readily recognized are troubles engendered by the pressure of the vast, dammed-up energies for growth and change that belong to childhood.

As we have pointed out in Chapter I, the child who for whatever reason senses himself not meeting his inner developmental schedule feels mortally endangered even though he may be physically safe and sound. The sick child is doubly burdened—by the discomfort of illness and by the pressure of healthy needs for continued growth which are thwarted at every turn. The art therapist's most important function may be to help the physically ill child reach whatever stage of psychosexual and ego development he seems to be striving to attain, even while illness exerts its regressive pull. Symbolic living in art, which normally complements the child's actual life experiences, can also compensate for enforced deficiency of such experiences. Inasmuch as children remain emotionally healthy the vitality of childhood often makes it possible even for those who are dying to function to the very end as growing organisms bent on fulfilling their appointed developmental tasks.[2]

Daniela: Daniela[3] suffered from muscular dystrophy. At age ten she was confined to a wheelchair and her arms and hands had lost much of their strength. Tiny and emaciated,

2. For a general exposition of these problems, see Emma Plank, *Working with Children in Hospitals.*

3. The case material for this passage has been provided by Carol Smith-Daniels, A.T.R., former graduate student at the Master of Arts degree program in art therapy at George Washington University. It has been prepared with her cooperation.

she was nevertheless a remarkably vital and well-adjusted little girl. Her parents were divorced and she lived with her father, who took full responsibility for her care. She attended a special school for seriously ill and handicapped children, where an art teacher trained in working with handicapped children used the help of several art therapy students in meeting the children's creative needs.

When Christmas approached Daniela told her special art therapy student that she wanted to make a self-portrait in clay as a Christmas gift for her father. She had watched other children make large clay heads and knew just how to go about it. Since she was too weak to handle the clay effectively, she told the art therapy student exactly what to do—to get just the right amount of clay, roll it into a ball, flatten the ball into a pancake, make a round core of crushed newspaper, cover it well with the flattened clay, and set this roundish shape upon a cylindrical neck. Even though she was too weak to produce these shapes Daniela did not passively watch them being made. Instead she went through all the motions necessary to produce the basic shapes, keeping time with the student's actions. Next she carefully put her fingers onto the places where she intended to make the eyes and asked the student to help her push her fingers well into the clay. She made mouth, nose, and hair in the same manner, taking responsibility for all decisions but borrowing her helper's strength to carry them out. Later the same procedure was followed in painting the fired clay.

The student art therapist naturally was careful to allow Daniela all the autonomy she was capable of; therefore the completed self-portrait indeed represented Daniela's very self, made by her own efforts. As such it was a perfect gift by a little preadolescent girl to a kind and devoted father.

After this first common enterprise was successfully concluded Daniela continued to enjoy working with her adult helper. Most important was an image of a pregnant woman complete with breasts, vagina, and an unborn baby inside the womb. Daniela produced it in a mood of wonder and elation. She felt that this was a very private sculpture that concerned only women and girls like her student art therapist and herself. Because they were both women they needed to know all about the hidden, secret parts of women's bodies. The completed work became one of Daniela's most cherished possessions.

Since Daniela lived alone with a tender and caring father, it seems likely that an unconscious fantasy of bearing his child contributed to her enthusiasm for making the nude, pregnant woman. Her ability to absorb information and to concentrate on the productive work and, as well, her serene mood indicate that any such fantasies were adequately displaced and neutralized so that they could serve not as an impediment but as an incentive to maturation.

In the course of working with Daniela the student fulfilled several functions. First of all, she served as an auxiliary set of muscles. This helped the child maintain autonomy in the face of her debility. The therapist's readiness to *serve* rather than to teach opened the way for emotionally laden production. As she commanded an adult woman's physical and emotional support Daniela could venture a thorough investigation of the female body and its procreative powers. Interest in such investigation frequently gains impetus at the onset of puberty. Its tenor differs from the obsessive, voyeuristic curiosity of the Oedipal phase (ages three to six or seven).

While the displacements that characterize the sexual symbolism of latency may no longer fulfill the older child's developmental needs, the preadolescent girl is still unready for the full experience of the sexually exciting, seductive aspects of femininity. She is fortunate if she has an opportunity to approach the subject cautiously, using the moratorium of preadolescence to establish her sexual identity securely in preparation for the more radical physical and emotional changes to come.

As she gave sculptural form to her ideas of feminine

fecundity, Daniela fulfilled this developmental task of preadolescence. In the process the young student became an object of identification, standing for an image of sexually controlled, secure femininity. This was particularly important for Daniela who lived in a motherless home and whose own body could not offer her reassurance about the approaching rewards of womanhood. In addition to continuing to serve as auxiliary muscle power, the student became also an educator who supplied anatomical information.

Even though she was not destined to reach the age of puberty for which she was preparing herself, Daniela's emotional health depended on the continuous feeling of growth that stems from fulfillment of age-appropriate developmental tasks. The substantial sculptures confirmed the solidity of her developmental gains.

Howard: Our next example also tells of an emotionally healthy child. Howard[4] had grown up as a member of an intact and affectionate black middle-class family. In his twelfth year he developed an inoperable cancerous brain tumor. During a period of slowly increasing debility he attended the same day school as Daniela. He greatly enjoyed the art sessions and became a skillful painter. His most ambitious undertaking was a tempera portrait of Frederick Douglass (Pl. VI). It measured approximately twenty-four by thirty-six inches and he wrote the following poem about it:

> I choose the white for the peace
> I choose the blue for the love
> I choose the red for the soul
> I choose the black for the slavery
> I choose the brown for the freedom
> I choose the green for his work
> I choose the yellow for his death
> I choose the man Frederick Douglass for
> what he did to get freedom for the black people.

4. The material for this passage was provided by Betty Jo Clifford, art therapy supervisor for the Master of Arts degree program in art therapy of George Washington University. It was prepared with her cooperation.

Howard knew the main facts of his hero's life. I present a brief summary for the reader's information: Frederick Douglass (1817–1895) was born a slave, the son of a black woman and her white master. He was raised by his black grandmother until age five. While he lived in her cabin he had occasion to observe sadistic beatings inflicted by whites upon black women. He attained literacy in childhood. When he was later made to work as a farmhand he actively resisted physical punishment by his keepers. He escaped to the North at age twenty-one and became an eminently successful inspirational antislavery orator. His entire life remained devoted to the political and social emancipation of his people. He published three autobiographies which vividly evoke the brutal realities of slavery.[5]

In Howard's painting we see an almost skull-like face. Forehead, cheekbones, and chin are picked out in a luminous, light-tan color. The tan is superimposed on a dark-brown mass which is spread out so that it also surrounds the face. It is made to represent hair and beard by means of superimposed black brush strokes. The same brown also suggests a neck. Below the neck the brown disintegrates into several mysteriously erratic angular lines running across the torso. The figure wears a yellow tunic that is bounded by heavy brown outlines.

The most expressive element of the face is a pugnaciously determined mouth drawn in a single slashing black line; the painting conveys the impression of a thin-lipped, oldish man, quite different from Howard himself, whose own face is full-lipped, soft, and still childlike. The eyes somehow have expression even though Howard left the iris empty of pupils. He delineated the nose in a manner frequently adopted by children who have not quite managed to find a way of representing noses by shading.

5. *Narrative of My Life* (1845; Cambridge, Mass.: Harvard University Press, 1960), *My Bondage and My Freedom* (1855; New York: Dover Publications, 1969), and *Life and Times of Frederick Douglass* (1881; New York: Collier Books, 1962). For an excellent psychological study of Frederick Douglass and his autobiographies, see Stephen Weissman, "Frederick Douglass, Portrait of a Black Militant."

He has surrounded the figure with a bright warm red that to him signifies the soul, probably because of the color's vitality. Howard's illness manifested itself mainly by progressive numbing and paralysis of his faculties. The red may express an attempt at surrounding his body with warmth and vitality. An arch of cool blue seems to serve as boundary for the red. The "peaceful" white above extends upward to the paper's edge, never touching the figure directly. Howard has awarded green military honors to his hero whose work consisted of militant battle against slavery, but the black of slavery also appears on this medal. He painted Douglass's chest yellow, the color of death according to Howard's poem. While the brown skin color seems an appropriate symbol of racial liberation, we cannot escape the feeling that the brown lines meandering across the torso may signify destructive illness rather than freedom for enslaved Africans. We cannot, however, be sure exactly how much of their uncertain quality should be attributed to impaired perceptual faculties and declining manual control, how much to the expression of feeling. We also cannot fully penetrate the mystery of Howard's color symbolism or completely understand the relationship between poem and painting. The evocation of the color black, for instance, fits beautifully into the poem's rhythm, but it does not correspond to the role of black in the painting. There it is used mainly as the logical color to delineate the hero's features.

Howard's choice of a hero such as Frederick Douglass is typical for his age. By the time a boy is twelve years old the fantastic, flying superheroes of modern-day mythology begin to lose importance except as means of simple escape. Boys begin to measure their achievements more realistically against society's norms. They cast about for ego ideals that can embody their aspirations in a glorified but not entirely unrealistic manner.

In this sense Howard's celebration of Frederick Douglass corresponds to both his age and his membership in the black community. However, the choice appears to be determined also by his individual situation. He has selected a hero whose childhood and youth were mortally endangered just as his own life was in peril—a hero who was exposed to extreme cruelty and overcame nearly insurmountable obstacles, but who lived a long and productive life in spite of all. Frederick Douglass's early sufferings became an incentive for persistent, passionate exertion in the cause of his race and this ultimately brought him lasting fame. For Howard, who was to die before reaching manhood, identification with a man whose fame outlasted his life provided a sense of vicarious achievement and immortality. The hero's virtue in the face of suffering may also have helped Howard cope with his inevitable anger at the irrational guilt which illness inevitably arouses and with his need for redemption.

Identification, however, was not in the service of escape and denial. Howard's poem ends with the word *death*. The painting's dominant color is yellow, his professed symbol of death. Frederick Douglass's face looks like a death's head. It seems further that the insidiously creeping illness has found unconscious representation in the tortuous brown lines traveling across the hero's chest. Red, even though Howard stresses its vital, warm significance, is nevertheless also the color of blood and of anger and we are reminded of the accounts of sadistic whippings in Douglass's autobiography.

Howard's painting thus represents both an ego ideal and part of his real self. He completes the developmental tasks of internalizing a viable ego ideal that can help him attain maturity. He avoids any massive denial of his actual condition, a denial which would have necessitated his splitting his self into an acceptable and a rejected part. Because the painting contributed to preserving his inner unity the act of painting it did not mean a flight into fantasy. It could feel entirely real to Howard. We can safely conclude that Howard achieved sublimation as he painted Frederick Douglass's image.

It is interesting that after having completed the painting

of his hero Howard was ready to look closely enough at his own person to do a self-portrait with the aid of a mirror. This was again in keeping with his developmental stage. Younger children are easily satisfied with schematic representations that can stand for specific people or for themselves if only some characteristic properties such as eye or hair color or particular garments or adornments are added. Preadolescents, on the other hand, begin to scrutinize individual features and attempt realistic likenesses. I have also frequently observed that creating the image of an ego ideal that is at an optimal distance from the actual self (glorified but not entirely out of reach) often prepares the way for attempting unadorned and undisguised self-portraits.

By the time Howard was ready to paint his self-portrait he was rapidly losing his capacity for manual coordination. The portrait had to become a joint undertaking between himself and an art therapy student assigned to help him with it.[6] He consistently roused himself, however, to contribute to it, mainly by mixing skin colors and applying them as best he could. Since the student was an excellent portraitist this final undertaking became deeply satisfying to Howard and to his family. In this instance the student art therapist could perform the therapeutic function toward the child in her care only because of her sound art training and continued immersion in her own art. Again we see artistic experience enabling a child to continue his psychological growth even while his physical life is cut short.

Dorothy: My third example[7] is concerned with a fifteen-year-old mildly retarded and emotionally disturbed girl suffering from spina bifida.[8] Somewhat overweight but

6. Nancy Hiller, at that time enrolled in the Master of Arts degree program in art therapy at George Washington University.

7. The material for this passage was furnished by Linda Eidelberg, A.T.R., art therapist at New York University Medical Center, Institute of Rehabilitation Medicine. It has been prepared with her cooperation.

8. Spina bifida is a birth defect of the spine resulting in permanent damage to the nervous system of the lower parts of the body. Because of the absence of

attractive looking and well developed, Dorothy had entered the hospital at her own request to undergo a Bricker operation. Dorothy had decided on the operation because menstruation in combination with her leaking bladder cause her great discomfort. Also, she no longer wanted to submit to the indignity of wearing diapers and of being catheterized by her mother.

After the surgery had been performed successfully, Dorothy remained at the hospital in order to be taught to walk. Despite unusually well-developed muscle power she had hitherto preferred to crawl on the floor or propel herself in a wheelchair. When she was first made to walk she constantly fell and often hurt herself. On the one hand she was eager to attain greater autonomy; the operation had been undertaken on her urgent request. She also longed for sexual conquests and was striving to attain full teenage status. At the same time she seemed mortally afraid to leave the safety of babyhood and assume an upright gait. Her fear had a realistic basis inasmuch as her urgent sexual needs, her mental retardation, and her overactive fantasy life left her unable to cope with the dangers the adolescent actually encounters in New York City.

Being forever confined to a wheelchair or crawling the floor, however, would have further impeded whatever emotional and intellectual development she was capable of. Therefore, every effort was made to induce Dorothy to walk. Psychotherapy was tried and soon abandoned because of her lack of insight and inability to respond to verbal communication. A regime of behavior modification also proved futile. Neither rewards nor withheld privileges, praise nor disapproval affected her gait. During this period

---

sphincter sensation, people suffering from it are permanently incontinent. Bowel elimination is usually regulated by medication. Urine can be released either by periodic catheterization, or else a "Bricker" operation can be performed. This permits the urine to collect in a bag outside the body and children can learn to take care of their needs without outside help. Spina bifida also impairs sensations in the legs so that these children must laboriously be taught to walk.

of deadlock in her rehabilitation Dorothy began attending art therapy sessions.

Her first attempts started with grandiose plans of painting "masterpieces" followed by complete blocking when she attempted to do so. Her efforts were further complicated by her fear of soiling herself with the paint. Figure 33 is a good example of her early work. We see high above an empty foreground an expanse of solid blue sky into which a small sun has been painted at the upper left corner. In this same corner but slightly below the sky are two round shapes, one of them solid black and next to it a smaller red one. At the bottom right-hand corner of the page we see Dorothy's initials neatly done in red.

She could not be induced to relieve the stark emptiness of her work by making any additions. The picture was painted laboriously with a tiny brush, even though larger brushes were offered. Beyond the painting's meagerness, we are impressed by the secretive quality of the imagery and by an arragement which places these red and black balls that seem to be full of condensed meaning high above the ground, beyond the reach of a fifteen-year-old who spends much of her time on the floor.

A turning point came during a session which began with Dorothy's painting another tight red ball high in the sky; she called it a sunset. At the time she was openly angry at a fellow patient who had rejected her amorous advances. When the art therapist pointed out that her red sun looked just as angry as she felt, Dorothy abandoned the painting and set out to mix a new color to represent her anger. She no longer used red, possibly because she intuitively felt that the color would excite her beyond endurance. Instead she produced an olive green that reminded her of "weedy crabgrass." Armed with a large brush she made sweeping strokes rising upward from the bottom of the twelve- by eighteen-inch paper. She succeeded admirably in producing an image of tall, windswept wild grasses (Fig. 34).

Dorothy was enormously proud of her picture. She also

FIGURE 33. *Dorothy:* Sky with Black and Red Balls (12″ x 18″)

FIGURE 34. *Dorothy:* Crabgrass I (12″ x 18″)

commented that the grass reminded her of a grassy beach which she had visited with her sister. According to her it was a dangerous area where girls got raped.

A major step had been taken. Sexual excitement and frustration had initially found expression in a highly controlled, balled-up red shape that gave her neither relief nor satisfaction. The same emotions were now conveyed through an image that could serve as an appropriate equivalent for her wild and driven state. Although the fantasies which accompanied her painting remained undisguisedly sexual and sadomasochistic, the act of painting was not disrupted by their intensity. It seemed that sufficient defense was provided by the mechanism of displacing the wild abandon of the sexual deeds that she imagined being enacted on the beach onto the sheltering grass which hides those deeds from view. The displacement permitted her to express her emotions symbolically in art without losing control of her actions.

Dorothy did the crabgrass painting sitting in a wheelchair at a table. She painted her next version of the same subject matter on the floor. The session had begun with a futile attempt at producing, with the art therapist's help, a realistic self-portrait. This became an impossible struggle and finally Dorothy declared that the project was hopeless. She decided that instead she wanted to paint a large house and that she would need a lot of space and paint for it. When the art therapist invited her to work on the floor she accepted the suggestion readily. Painting with utter abandon and sweeping strokes, oblivious of paint spattering her apron, hands, and face, she produced a larger version of her first grass picture (Fig. 35).

While she painted she spoke about being a wild, free woman who could travel all over the world, meet lots of boys, and finally return home to her mother. Of the finished painting she declared that the crabgrass had grown so wildly that it had eaten up the house and all the people in it.

The painting is more disorganized than her first grassy

picture and she herself appeared to be in a state of greater regression. Nevertheless, in the midst of it all Dorothy attained independent locomotion for the first time. Needing more paint and clean water, she managed to raise herself off the floor, dragged herself to sink and table, helped herself to the materials, and returned to her painting, holding onto the furniture on her way. This occurred even though, or more probably because, the art therapist had readily helped her in every way so that she could paint her picture in comfort rather than exerting any pressure for her to act independently.

The fantasies which accompanied Dorothy's painting were more globally destructive than those of the first crabgrass picture. No longer did boys merely do injury to girls' vaginas; wild weeds now indiscriminantly swallowed whole houses and people. The grass, formerly a sheltering screen for forbidden pleasures, now became the agent of wholesale destruction.

FIGURE 35. *Dorothy:* Crabgrass II (18" x 24")

The theme of destruction was continued in the following session when for the first time Dorothy used reds and browns as she again painted on the floor (Fig. 36). This time she spoke of autumn leaves being burnt up in a fire and tossed about by the wind. She said that the fire was hidden behind the masses of brown and purplish color at the painting's center, and she later superimposed bright-red slashes onto these dark masses to better indicate the flames. She titled the picture *The Torn Burnt Leaves of Charlene*, using not the name given her at birth but the new name she had acquired at her confirmation, the one which symbolized entering a more adult and responsible state of life. Again she used her muscular powers well, helping herself to water and paint and later helping effectively in cleanup and in setting up the room for the next group.

Her gains in mobility extended beyond the art therapy room. She soon surprised the physiotherapists and her mother with her progress. Since the hospital was geared mainly toward physical rehabilitation, Dorothy was soon discharged. There was no time to observe her art beyond the stage of liberation and abandon which we have seen. Reintegration had not as yet become apparent in her art but was evident in her more mature behavior toward the physiotherapists and her fellow patients.

Dorothy's story brings two separate problems into focus: first, the predicament of a child with a birth defect who, through medical intervention, was faced with entirely new physical experiences that had to be integrated; and second, the situation of an art therapist who functioned as a member of a therapeutic team that focused predominantly on physical rather than emotional rehabilitation.

To take up the art therapist's problem first, we note that, working with seriously ill children, she naturally was expected at all times to subordinate her actions to medical exigencies. She had to learn to give much physical aid and to use her ingenuity in helping children circumvent physical

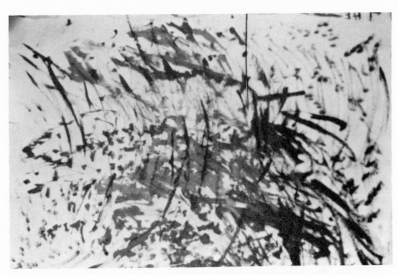

FIGURE 36. *Dorothy:* The Torn Burnt Leaves of Charlene (24″ x 30″)

handicaps. Since the work achieved under her guidance had symbolic rather than practical significance, she was in a sense out of step with the team's main concerns and worked in comparative isolation. The art room constituted a unique area wherein emotional problems became the focus of a trained adult's attention. This very uniqueness made art important.

Our example shows the art therapist coping admirably with the situation. She uses the physical properties of paint and brushes effectively to convey to the child both a sense of freedom and an understanding of the possibility of control. This allows Dorothy to experience aspects of her personality in safety that ordinarily either remain repressed or erupt destructively. Since the therapist's psychoanalytic knowledge was well integrated into her therapeutic approach, she was able to respond quickly and intuitively to the messages contained in both Dorothy's behavior and her art. Without such an echo on the part of the adult the therapeutic impact of expressive activities rarely reaches its full force. Yet the therapist spoke little and the suggestion that Dorothy's red shape might signify her anger was the only interpretation that was made.

Dorothy's task of integrating the consequences of her operation was complex. On the positive side there was the entirely new experience of being clean, free from sores and from smelling bad, of being thus more acceptable to the environment. Because the excessive anxiety over cleanliness which burdens children who have never been able to achieve command over elimination was now greatly reduced, Dorothy could complete the developmental tasks belonging to the anal phase, even though full control over elimination remained physically impossible. She began by experiencing the anal pleasures of messing and smearing that were originally denied to her. By refusing to be coerced or bribed into walking she also took on the stubborn attitude characteristic of the anal phase. Parallel with her attainment of a degree of autonomy over her own body, she took responsibility toward the environment by cleaning up after having enjoyed the abandon of freely using paints.

But besides reaping the rewards of her operation Dorothy also had to come to terms with its limitations. Any chronically ill child consciously or unconsciously entertains unrealistic hopes for magically complete recovery and these fantasies are heightened when medical intervention does indeed promise some relief. Realistic explanations can afford some preparation for disappointments but they cannot be expected to eliminate magical hopes entirely. When Dorothy titled her painting *The Torn Burnt Leaves of Charlene*, using the name given to her upon entering the adult community, she gave form to her sense of permanent, tragically irreparable injury. She expressed this sense of loss concurrently with the feeling of abandon and sexual excitement which pervades her three paintings.

That she could say so much without using words links Dorothy to Daniela and Howard. Art can acquire special value for children who must face such destinies as these three had to face. Truth can be expressed in a manner that has intense reality and profoundly touches the core of the child's being and yet circumvents the stark finality of the spoken word. This is important not only because it would be intolerably cruel to say these things to the child. Words would also tend to mobilize the child's healthy defenses of denial and isolation. For to be able to strive for maturity, the stark finality of chronic illness must be denied even while the child learns to cope with the limitations imposed by it. Factually truthful information might either not be heard at all or be taken in intellectually, leaving the emotional life untouched.

Situations can arise when terrible facts must be explicitly stated, e.g., in order to disperse an atmosphere of nameless dread. However, in order for a child to continue to function as a living and growing organism some truth must be kept at just the right distance—close enough so that there will be no splitting of the personality into an acceptable part and another hidden and rejected one, yet sufficiently disguised, displaced, and distanced to prevent causing massive despair. Particularly when children command the help of a courageous and skilled art therapist their art can become a safe container of otherwise unbearable truth.

In this context we must also consider the adult's inner adjustment for these difficult tasks. In work with children who are severely ill or seriously handicapped it becomes essential to find a viable balance between healthy denial and acceptance of the inevitable. Blatantly false optimism about their fate would lead therapists to make, either explicitly or implicitly, unrealistic demands on the children in their care. The children would then be burdened with the responsibility of upholding a fiction established not for their own good but for the adult's protection.

However, to elicit healthy functioning one must address oneself to whatever health or vitality a child maintains. To work with dedication and spirit rather than under a cloud of depression, to avoid perceiving seriously ill children as not quite human, therapists must learn to see beyond their diminished and distorted appearance to the healthy and growing organisms these children ought to have been. To perceive their health one must to some extent deny their illness. We should be alert to the distinction between such healthy denial and its destructive counterpart in the therapist as well as in parents' and families' adjustment to their sick and handicapped children.

For example, when I work with blind children or adults, I find that it is important for me to look at them while we talk even though they would not notice it if I looked elsewhere. For me as for any sighted person, allowing myself to lose eye contact during a serious conversation signifies inattention at best, at worst a way of making the partner disappear. The autistic child's unfocused gaze that seems to look through people, perceive them, and at the same time fail to acknowledge their existence epitomizes this absence of contact. To prevent myself from reducing the blind person to someone who need not be fully acknowledged as an equal partner I must deny the blindness while we are talking. I must at the same time take into consideration the partner's sightless state and choose my words so that we will communicate without undue misunderstandings.

Our three examples show art therapists serving children in many capacities: as their auxiliary muscles, as sources of factual information, as instructors in artistic techniques, as providers of sanctuary for beneficial regression and for experimenting with new attitudes toward the self and the environment, as recipients of confidences and fantasies, and last but not least, as objects of identification. (Our examples have not presented us with any vivid examples of transference phenomena. We will discuss this aspect of the art therapist's role later on.)

For the work that has been described, psychoanalytic

understanding of child development was indispensable, as was familiarity with child development in art. The manner in which this understanding was used, however, was largely determined by the circumstance that these children were working very seriously with pencil, paint, and clay.

FIRST AID THROUGH ART THERAPY

My next example presents a rare instance where art materials were not an integral part of the therapeutic process. Rather, they became means of therapeutic intervention simply because the therapeutic work happened to fall to an art therapist.

Peter: Seven-year-old Peter was the youngest of six siblings in a close-knit, intact family. He had a history of autistically tinged withdrawal at age three from which he spontaneously recovered, attaining normal speech and capacity for warm relationships within his family circle. However, he had been troubled by paralyzing shyness amounting to mutism at school. I saw him first in an evaluatory art therapy session that was part of an extensive diagnostic procedure undertaken in preparation for treatment at an outpatient clinic.

Because he was extremely distressed at the idea of separating from her, his mother was invited to accompany Peter to the art room. Even in her presence he remained at first frozen into immobility, sitting rigidly in his chair, his hands tightly clenched in a paroxysm of shyness. Since Peter made no move to approach the art materials on his own, I demonstrated how they can be used and tried to inspire him by making a little clay turtle—an easy thing to make that might symbolize his need to withdraw and feel protected. Peter, however, did not respond to my overtures except by following my movements with his eyes in rapt attention. After a while he discovered that the office chair he sat in had wheels so that he could, almost effortlessly, wheel himself toward the table which held the art materials and again withdraw from it. He tried it out repeatedly. When I commented that he seemed to like this wonderful chair, I was rewarded with a smile. I thereupon made a clay model of his chair complete with wheels, and also made a boy to sit in it. Peter seemed to be fascinated. To make more explicit the connection between Peter's person and these clay objects, I set out to paint chair and boy in the appropriate colors, carefully matching the colors of the real chair and of Peter's hair, skin, and clothing. At this point Peter began a kind of silent peek-a-boo game where he alternately showed and hid from me his hands, feet, shoes, socks, jacket, and shirt. I responded by making it a guessing game. As I painted each object I asked out loud, "I wonder what color I must make the hair, shoes, socks," and so on, much as one would play with a three-year-old. Peter finally uttered the single word "red" when I asked about the color of his socks as he stuck out his feet for inspection and then quickly hid them under his chair.

Although he was very interested in everything I did Peter still did not venture to touch the paint or the clay. I therefore set out to make a clay woman and tried to induce Peter to decide whom it should represent. Although he was unable to voice his desire, he was evidently delighted when I decided for him that the figure should be his mother. Again I matched the clay figure's hair, hat, clothes, and accessories to his mother's. At last Peter ventured to mix the color of his mother's coat and to paint it. Finally, he actually fashioned his mother's pocketbook, painted it, and hung it over the figure's arm. By this time Peter was talking freely.

Finally I suggested that we make something that was not in the room, maybe something from Peter's home, something I could know nothing about, so that he would have to tell me what it was like. With some prompting from his mother, I learned that Peter had a pet cat and a pet dog. He undertook to make a clay image of his dog, Roger. He achieved it with a little help from me, trembling with excitement, which reached its height as he attached the tail.

At the end of the session mother and son left the art room triumphantly. Peter was tenderly carrying his clay figures to show them to his brother and sisters and was evidently taking special pride in the clay dog he made himself.

Within the compass of a session Peter seemed to have recapitulated several stages on the road from symbiosis to individuation. At first he observed the world much as does an infant in his baby carriage, fascinated but unable to participate actively. Next he established autonomy by practicing coming close and withdrawing again of his own free will. However, he did not give up the safety of the chair that seemed to have become his very own territory. Next he established object constancy as he played peek-a-boo with me. He acted much like a playful infant who alternately hides his face from view and triumphantly shows it again, who covers his own eyes causing his partner to disappear from his sight and again joyfully discovers the constancy of the world as he uncovers his eyes, perceives his partner, and is perceived by her.

Since Peter was seven years old rather than two the play could be enacted in a more complex manner that included symbolic representation. It included the real Peter on his chair as well as his clay image on the clay chair. I became the one who had to discover Peter's identity as he playfully helped me find his several parts and attributes, so that I could make the right image. His mother's identity was established in a similar manner and now Peter was able to contribute actively in creating it. It is interesting that he became particularly active in fashioning a detachable attribute, her pocketbook. We perceive intimations of the transitional object, but Peter did not elaborate on it. Speech became fluent as he perceived himself as well as his mother present both in the flesh and once more in clay. Only after mother and son had both been firmly established as constant and separate could Peter venture to evoke something that was absent. Roger, the pet dog, was conjured up by his master. We can assume that this was symbolic self-representation, for Roger had the enviable life of a permanently dependent and cherished pet.

Treatment for Peter would probably have been most successful if his relationship to his mother could have been worked through in subsequent joint sessions for mother and son. Unfortunately, this could not be arranged. As a stopgap, Peter, who had made good contact with me, was assigned to attend an art therapy group which met once a week at the clinic.

He arrived for his first session despondent and mute, accompanied by his grandmother because his mother was sick with the flu. However, he perked up when I suggested that we make mommy in her room in bed. Using a shoebox to represent her room, he managed to construct a bed and bedside table, placed his mother's figure in the bed, and decided to have her read a book. Finally he triumphantly placed Mumbo, the family cat, under the bed. His joyful pride in this clay image left no doubt that this again was a self-representation. Indeed, he would no doubt have much preferred to have been there in Mumbo's place, but it was encouraging that he was nevertheless able to take pleasure in making the cat.

In subsequent sessions, Peter's need to conjure up his mother and family pets slowly diminished. He joined with another seven-year-old in constructing clay cars. Later on he painted a series of pictures where he represented himself as the owner of a big red car taking his family for rides. As he learned to handle himself more successfully in the art therapy group his schoolwork improved. He began to speak up in class and play with his schoolmates.

For the moment the family was reassured and art therapy was therefore soon discontinued. However, it seemed likely that Peter would require more help in the future. The emotional difficulties which led to his selective mutism had been only superficially dealt with and were likely to impede his further development.

Art therapy provided much-needed first aid for Peter. His right to approach and withdraw at will had been confirmed; his person and his boundaries became libidinized in a piece-by-piece evocation of his body parts and the clothes that covered them. His mother's identity as distinct from his own was confirmed in a similar way. Having practiced imagining his mother first within the shelter of her presence, he learned to also evoke her image in her absence. Evidently none of this was beyond his reach since change took place so quickly. Since an intense, emphatic experience had sufficed to unhook Peter for the moment and set him on the road to increasing autonomy, we can conclude that Peter's development had not been arrested at the phase of symbiotic dependency on his mother. Rather, he had regressed to it. His great interest in detachable things such as the pocketbook and the dog's tail and his curious peeking indicate phallic concerns. We can assume that Peter's phallic anxieties which in themselves were to be expected of a six-year-old had been heightened beyond his endurance when he had to stand up for himself at school without his mother's protection. Regressing under the impact of these anxieties to earlier fixations, he gave the impression of a much more immature child. (We recall that he also had regressed briefly at the onset of the phallic phase at age three.)

During our session, I helped him deal with sexual symbols that were neutralized and distanced and therefore less threatening—for instance, a clay pocketbook belonging to his mother's clay image. All this afforded relief. The road back from his regressed state could be traversed swiftly but not by a single leap. Earlier ways of functioning had to be touched upon along the way.

The manner in which help was given was largely determined by my happening to be available and happening to be an art therapist. The message that needed to be conveyed to Peter probably would have come across equally well with the aid of toys, puppets, or other facilitating props had another kind of therapist happened to be in charge. Familiarity with the psychoanalytic theory of symbiosis and individuation as presented by Margaret Mahler and her collaborators had been essential,[9] as was familiarity with the typical problems of the phallic phase; a corresponding understanding of the therapeutic use of art materials was not needed in this case.

It is evident that art therapists should be competent to perform psychotherapeutic first aid as exemplified in Peter's case, and should be willing to undertake it. They lose perspective, however, when they perceive work of this kind as more desirable or as of a higher order than work wherein their competence as *art* therapists is more fully used.

ART THERAPY IN GROUPS

We have up to now presented examples of art therapy with individual children. Severely psychotic or acutely traumatized children usually need privacy and an adult's undivided attention. Severely physically ill or handicapped children often need a whole adult to help them manage the physical aspects of working with art materials. The profoundly retarded, functioning below a three- to four-year-old level, are usually developmentally unready to profit from companionship with other children.

However, a great many disturbed children who have reached latency or preadolescence become more productive in the company of their peers. Therefore we must now consider art therapists working with groups. No adult's empathy or encouragement can engender quite the same mutual inspiration, understanding, and creative fervor that characterize such groups of children when they are functioning at their best. This heightened intensity compensates the therapist for the hardship of keeping the peace

9. Margaret Mahler, *On Human Symbiosis and the Vicissitudes of Individuation;* Margaret Mahler, Fred Pine, and Anni Bergman, *The Psychological Birth of the Human Infant.*

and serving the needs of quarrelsome, competitive, and impulsive boys and girls. Ideally, any art therapy program serving a community of children should command sufficient personnel to strike the right balance between individual sessions and sessions held in groups composed of children who can be expected to profit from each other's company. I will describe two art therapy sessions to illustrate this point.

The sessions occurred in the child psychiatric ward of a city hospital that also functioned as teaching hospital for a medical school.[10] The ward comprises fifteen beds for children between three and twelve years old. Their disturbances vary, and include autism, childhood schizophrenia, delinquency, and severe neurosis. The majority are considered borderline cases, not acutely psychotic but in need of intensive psychiatric care and close supervision.

As this is a teaching hospital all the children are given a fair amount of attention from the psychiatrists in training. Their parents also receive more emotional support and psychiatric help than would be offered in an ordinary city hospital. However, both children and parents are likely to suffer repeated separations as the young professionals' training requires them to spend time in different psychiatric units. Efforts are made to avoid such separations for those children who have been selected for long-term treatment.

The nursing staff, on the other hand, is fairly steady and among the nurses and nurses' aides are highly skilled, dedicated, and experienced people. The Board of Education maintains an elementary school on the ward, and a nursery school run by the hospital takes care of the educational needs of the younger or more immature children. The services of recreational workers, social workers, and group workers are also available. Team

10. The following material was first presented in somewhat different form in the *American Journal of Art Therapy*, 11, No. 3 (1972). The hospital referred to is Jacobi Hospital, teaching hospital for Albert Einstein Medical College, both in the Bronx, New York.

meetings, rounds, and case conferences maintain communication among the many workers, including the art therapist.

Art therapy sessions are conducted in a room exclusively reserved for this activity. It is adequately furnished with tables, closets for art materials, shelves for storing finished and unfinished sculpture, and racks for drying pictures and storing portfolios. There is no shortage of art materials, which are purposely kept simple. Available are excellent ceramic clay mixed with fine grog, gallons of poster paint, charcoal, colored chalks, crayons, a roll of three-foot-wide brown wrapping paper, reams of manila paper (both eighteen by twenty-four and twelve by eighteen inches), and bristle brushes in several sizes. There are muffin tins of twelve cups each for mixing colors.

Work with clay is done on the reverse side of oilcloth pads. Heavy cardboard tubes are used as rolling pins. The necessary assortment of sticks and modeling tools is at hand. There is a wedging board, and a kiln is available on another ward.

I am on the ward twice a week. Part of my work is done after supper, at a time when the excitement of school, doctors' and parents' visits, and other pressures has abated. I try to see each child each time I am on the ward and to schedule my time so that there is occasion for unwinding as sessions draw to a close, or for seeing a child alone at the end of the day if this should be necessary.

Children are seen in small groups, the size being determined by the situations. There may be three, four, five, or at the most six children present at one time.

Sessions are scheduled to last at least one full hour, and are often extended to an hour and a quarter or an hour and a half. This differs from the strategy frequently used in work with children whose attention span is short and whose frustration tolerance is low, to change activities at the first sign of flagging enthusiasm. This policy reduces the likelihood of chaotic sessions but it defeats educational and therapeutic purposes. We hope to help the children reach the reserves of creative energy that become available when difficulties are *overcome* rather than *circumvented*. Thus the children's most fruitful work is more often than not done on the second wind.[11]

Sessions tend to present a complex pattern, beginning with enthusiasm that is often followed by upset and partial disintegration which, if all goes well, is redeemed by a second period of integration in which creative work is resumed with renewed intensity. Naturally the schedule is flexible. Children who indeed cannot tolerate a whole period are scheduled to attend only part of a session, and it is also possible to dismiss a child ahead of time if his behavior becomes entirely intolerable.

Art sessions are not conducted according to any preconceived plan. Rather, the simple art materials at hand are available for the children to make of them what they choose. I try to let the children know that I have no ax to grind, that I am not trying to find out about them or to coerce them into doing something I have planned for reasons of my own, that I want to know each one of them well in order to help them make what they want to make. I am there to help them find out what they can do when they are able to muster all their energy in the service of a creative task of their own choosing. However, I do convey the idea that art sessions are a time for work, not play, and that I prefer personal expression to stereotyped repetition.

---

11. Maria Montessori observed this phenomenon systematically (see her *Spontaneous Activity in Education*). In classrooms conducted according to her method, teachers observed a regular curve of goal-directed activity and quiescence. The children regularly began the day with a spurt of exploratory activities in which they tried to master a number of tasks quickly. This was followed by a period of "false fatigue" when children became restless and disorganized. If they were left to themselves disorganization soon gave way to more concentrated and more clearly focused renewed efforts. "Only when this second period had run its course did the children reach a state of genuine calm when they spontaneously detached themselves from their internal concentration. ...If at the period of *false fatigue* an inexperienced teacher...intervenes calling the children to her, and making them rest, etc., their restlessness persists and the subsequent work is not undertaken" (p. 99).

To put it in theoretical language, I offer myself to the children as an auxiliary ego, ready to support them in an adventure that entails taking risks and of which neither they nor I can predict the ultimate outcome.

Naturally this basic attitude may be modified if the situation demands it. There are times when I must give more explicit directions—for example, if total freedom frightens a particular child too much. A chaotic situation may require temporary rigid structuring or a particular task may be so difficult that it is necessary to tell a child exactly what to do.

The Empire State Building

On the afternoon I will now describe, four children are present: Alfred, Emil, Steven, and Raffael.

Alfred, eleven years old, has been diagnosed as suffering from childhood schizophrenia. He has developed an elaborate system of obsessive-compulsive defense, and his activities in the art room are usually limited to drawings of electrical circuits or scientific equipment and to making clay models of transistor radios and the like. After being on the ward for several months he had been discharged to his mother's care. Now, after six months on the outside, he has been readmitted. He is deadly pale, profoundly shaken, feels trapped and doomed.

Alfred has come to the art room mainly as a place of refuge. He becomes engaged in making "designs." Carefully he places blobs of poster paint on pieces of paper and folds and reopens them, thus producing colorful, bilateral configurations reminiscent of Rorschach cards. He signs and dates each of these products, but he is not ready to elaborate on the designs by working them over, to try to see images in them, or to tell stories about them. The activity remains sterile and repetitious. Feeling that I cannot expect much of Alfred today and that efforts to draw him out would only make him unhappier, I leave him to his devices.

Emil is a depressed little boy of eleven. He is well liked by the other children and seems on the whole to be intact, although burdened with many worries. He has been on the ward only for observation and is due for discharge in the next few days. He is inclined to imitate the work of children he admires. Therefore, he wants to make a clay horse before he leaves. (Horses have become very popular on the ward since one of the oldest boys made a large male horse complete with erect penis.)

Steven, also eleven years old, is a newcomer. His left arm has been amputated six inches from the shoulder. I have seen him only once before, in an individual session where I was impressed with his dexterity in working the clay with his only hand. With very little help from me he had produced a well-integrated horse and rider. I have also been surprised by the other children's ready acceptance of him. As far as I can observe no one is horror-struck or disgusted by the missing arm. Beyond these observations I know nothing of Steven.

Raffael, the youngest of the four, is an eight-and-a-half-year-old Puerto Rican boy. He has been on the ward for more than a year and we are old friends. He was admitted because of swings between destructive and withdrawn behavior that had reached intolerable intensity after his discharge from the pediatric ward where he had been treated for burns. One of six siblings living with their mother on welfare, he had been burnt while alone in the kitchen at breakfast time. Somehow his pajama sleeve caught fire and he was rescued by his mother who herself sustained minor injuries as she doused the flames.

During his illness Raffael's mother visited him at the hospital daily but seemed much shaken by her son's disfigurement and barely able to conceal her physical revulsion. It seemed as if his injuries had compounded for her a previously formed conception of Raffael as the family scapegoat, "a runt, a hunchback, a crazy person." This view of him is in no way realistic. Raffael is small for his age but well proportioned; he moves gracefully, is endowed with considerable charm, and is well liked both by children and staff. His scars have healed well, leaving only minor traces of the accident.

Competent and ambitious, Raffael runs with the oldest boys on the ward, all somewhat older and bigger than he is. He succeeds, with considerable effort, in being accepted by them as an equal.

Upon entering the art room Raffael turns to the large clay horse that started the vogue for making horses. It was made by Jesus, the leader of the group, and was too large to be fired in the hospital's kiln. Jesus had given it to Raffael as a present. It had originally been adorned with a large penis, but this had broken off in the course of time. Raffael had tried unsuccessfully to repair it with glue and masking tape. Now he declares that he will smash up the horse to make new clay. Thereupon Emil intervenes, begging Raffael not to destroy the horse but rather to give it to him. Raffael is not moved. I intervene, using two contradictory lines of argument. While I plead with Raffael to let the horse live and to let Emil have it, I try to persuade Emil that it would be better anyway for him to make his own horse. I am not very successful with either of the two boys.

The matter is taken out of my hands by Steven who organizes and leads a communal, controlled destruction of the horse in which all three boys join with glee (Alfred pays no attention to these goings-on but continues making his designs). The horse is reduced to hunks of dry clay which the boys gather into an empty can. Emil then gets ready to construct a clay horse of his own. Steven puts water in the can with the broken-up horse and then starts wedging clay that has been soaking for some time in another container. Raffael declares that now he wants to make designs just like Alfred.

I tell Raffael that I am letting Alfred make designs because he is sad and upset and in no condition to work hard. Of him, Raffael, I expect a lot more. Anyone can make designs, they just happen—even a baby can make them. I want *him* to make a picture where *he* decides what's going to happen, where *he* is the boss. I know that he can do it, for I know all the good work he has done before.

So encouraged, Raffael agrees to paint a picture of his own. He asks for a large sheet of brown mural paper, charcoal, and a tray of poster paint. I tape a three- by five-foot piece of brown paper against the wall and hand him his paint. Then I turn my attention to Emil and his horse. A little later I look in Raffael's direction and see that he is about to tear down his paper. It is empty except for a tiny structure at the bottom of the page painted in gray and subsequently scratched out. I stop Raffael from tearing down his paper and ask whether he had meant to paint the Empire State Building. (This magnificent structure is such a favorite with New York City children that one learns to recognize it in the most unlikely configurations.) Yes, he admits, but it is too small. We contemplate the size of the paper and decide first to draw a sidewalk and then to try again, using the whole height of the paper. Raffael manages to draw a fairly large structure but it is fat and squat rather than thin and tall and he is getting quite desperate.

Having egged Raffael on to the adventure, it would be entirely wrong to abandon him to failure now. I pick up the charcoal and, beginning from the bottom up, I draw the left side of the Empire State Building in the schematic style in which most of New York's children seem to draw this popular symbol. As I reach the top Raffael suddenly understands, takes the charcoal out of my hand, completes the right side of the building, adds curtained windows, and then adds all the other buildings in the picture. He contemplates his work and then declares that now he needs an open manhole on the street such as one can see sometimes when men are working underground. Between the two of us we draw a manhole and a Con Ed sign with two flags (Fig. 37).[12]

12. Consolidated Edison is the electrical utility company serving New York City.

At this point, Raffael has an audience: both Emil and Steven are watching developments on the mural. Turning to them Raffael explains that now he will make an underground passageway and a monster who lives underground and he will make a house for the monster to live in. He draws the house (Fig. 38) and seems enormously pleased with his idea. Then he draws cars, trees, a playground, and a sun (which looks a great deal like himself).

At this point the art session ends because it is time for supper. In the subsequent session Raffael draws a street, two persons, trees, and birds, and embellishes the whole with colored chalks. The Empire State Building, colored a brilliant pink-red and outlined in turquoise, dominates the picture.

Raffael is eager to show his work to all available children and adults, but he is not ready to tell stories about it. Later on he proudly shows the mural to his psychotherapist, but when the doctor asks him to tell him more about this monster he only reiterates what he has said before: the monster is just there; he has always been there; he will stay there in his underground house; there is no more to tell

FIGURE 37. *Raffael:* The Empire State Building (3′ x 5′)

about him. Subsequently Raffael often speaks about *The Empire State Building* as a "masterpiece," but not as a work needing further explanation.

We can now try to imagine what the art therapy session may have meant for each of the four boys. We must of course always remember that we are now dealing with conjectures. We may be incorrect in some of our surmises and naturally much may have happened that will never be known to us.

As far as one could tell, the activity had been consolatory for Alfred. For an hour he had been a little less lost and unhappy than during the rest of the day. He remains an outsider throughout the session.

The other three boys have a good deal in common. They are absorbed in the phallic aspirations typical for their age, striving for acceptance in their peer group, for leadership, for achievement.

Emil had been distressed at the beginning of the session, disturbed by the violence of Raffael's attack on the horse and anxious lest he would never be able to make a horse of his own. When, under Steven's leadership, he joined in the

FIGURE 38. *Raffael:* The Empire State Building, detail

orderly destruction of Jesus's horse and when subsequently he produced a horse himself (I somehow managed in between helping Raffael to see to it that Emil finished his sculpture), the destructive act was redeemed and Emil's fear of violence was alleviated.

Emil's clay horse was adequate but not remarkable. It appeared that Emil had no passionate inner need to create a horse—rather, he needed to show that he could make what everyone else in his group had made. Thus Emil's fears of violence were lessened, his self-esteem heightened, but the session had neither made great demands on him nor had it brought him unusual pain or pleasure.

Steven produced no art but he did exert leadership of a quality that was (as I later learned) entirely characteristic of him. Being himself in the throes of the struggle for hierarchical position he was far better able than I to sense how best to solve the problem of Jesus's horse. He found a way to remove the object that had become an irritant to the group in such a manner that all the boys shared in the guilt and no one profited unduly by usurping the absent leader's power or by appropriating his possessions.

Steven was in the process of establishing a position of leadership which he was to retain throughout his residence on the ward. During this time Steven's influence oscillated between organizing well-planned delinquent escapades and keeping the group functioning in a constructive, rational manner. We can say that the art session brought forth the benign aspect of his leadership.

Raffael's experiences were more complex and more intense than those of the other three boys. It is not possible to fathom all that went into his initial destructive attack on Jesus's horse. The passion with which he picked up a hammer to smash the clay figure gave the impression of a theatrical gesture, a make-believe ferocity vented on an expendable object. Yet such threatening gestures, which Raffael made quite frequently and always harmlessly on the ward, were reminiscent of his actions at home where he had threatened his family and the family's possessions with a hammer. At home, however, he had acted in dead earnest. Although he had never seriously injured anyone, he had at times wreaked considerable havoc on property.

It is also noteworthy that destruction was directed against the work of the biggest, most sexually mature boy of his group. We can surmise that rage against this often high-handed ruler of the ward was vented in the act. Smashing the horse seemed, however, above all an act of liberation, for as long as Raffael continued scavenging and begging from the older boys he surely would not learn to work independently.

After breaking up the horse Raffael was at first inclined to regress; he wanted to make designs like Alfred. However, his energy could readily be mobilized for ambitious, constructive work. When I encouraged Raffael and showed my confidence in his powers, he was ready to tackle a three- by five-foot mural. Having just destroyed a horse adorned with a huge (but broken) penis he set out to paint a picture of the biggest, most magnificently erect thing in his world, and at first he failed totally. Instead of the desired tall, monumental building, a miniature structure appeared at the very bottom of his paper. Raffael was confronted with the discrepancy between his high aspirations and his actual feeling of insignificance. No wonder he wanted to destroy his picture.

Was I mistaken, then, in having encouraged Raffael to try to paint a picture where *he* would be "the boss"? (We must remember that I did not suggest the subject matter. The Empire State Building was his own choice.)

Subsequent events prove that my confidence in his abilities was not entirely unrealistic, for when I gave him a little help, Raffael's performance improved very quickly. Had he felt as profoundly insignificant, as castrated as his first drawing seemed to indicate, it would have been impossible for me to restore his self-confidence simply by drawing part of the building for him. His picture would have been doomed to failure no matter what I might have done (short of doing the whole job for him).

His quick recovery of enthusiasm and inventive powers once I had proved my readiness actively to help him erect his building shows that he had not entirely internalized his mother's distorted perception of him. Even though his mother perceived him as a misshapen, disfigured runt, there must have been some core of inner strength, some sanctuary where Raffael felt inviolate. Thus another motherly woman's perception of him as manly, competent, and whole could move him to creative action.

The complete picture can be viewed as an excellent self-portrait. We see a not particularly gifted, somewhat immature child, his world rather impoverished and disjointed. He is haunted by some underlying, nameless trouble, but he has aspiration and vitality and he seems capable of functioning adequately in many areas of daily life.

Looking only at its formal qualities, how would we rate Raffael's picture? If we apply the categories presented in the Introduction (p. xxviii), we can say that the work includes elements of pictogram, of stereotyped production, and of formed expression.[13] The area containing the monster is mainly pictogram. The drawing is weak and indistinct. The hidden menace of the monster is not visually expressed; its meaning can be understood only through Raffael's spoken comment. Yet the monster part of the picture is very important psychologically.

The playground, street, trees, people, and cars are presented in a perfunctory, stereotyped manner, perhaps with the exception of the birds (which have a certain power) and of the sun–face, which is not at all stereotyped and indeed constitutes an unconscious but accurate self-portrait.

The pleasure of giving expressive form, one of the

13. For a more extensive discussion of these categories, see my "The Problem of Quality in Art," in *Art as Therapy with Children*, pp. 55–63.

hallmarks of sublimation, can be felt mainly in the gaily colored skycrapers. We have, however, other evidence that Raffael had experienced the process of sublimation. At the beginning there was some expression of aggressive sexuality in the raw, and this was followed by the wish to regress to the infantile pleasures of smearing and messing with paint. But Raffael renounced these pleasures in favor of constructive, ego-syntonic action. Direct concern with the penis was displaced onto a universal phallic symbol. As he thus gratified his phallic aspirations, victoriously overcoming his feeling of insignificance, he gained access to repressed and menacing emotional content. Sublimation faltered; he was unable to give full expression to this material. He turned instead to more conventional, emotionally more neutral subject matter.

Raffael's finished work fails to attain the inner consistency and evocative power characteristic of artwork embodying complete sublimation, but he has come close enough to sublimation to experience the special kind of pleasure that belongs to it. We can hope that this experience will pave the way to kindred experiences in the future.

Portraits

My next story tells about a very different group of children. They are Jane, Paula, Gregory, and Hal.

Jane, an eleven-year-old white girl, has suffered much from being shifted back and forth between her mother and father. The parents separated when Jane was two and a half years old, and since this time there has been a pattern of her mother's forcing her father to take charge of Jane and her older brother whenever their behavior becomes difficult, only to take them back as soon as they adjusted to life with him. At the time of Jane's admission the father has finally obtained legal custody of his two children, but the ingrained pattern of moving back and forth between the two parents has not changed.

Jane's emotional turmoil is aggravated by minor organic perceptual difficulties which make it impossible for her to learn to read by conventional academic methods and make her a behavior problem in school. However, she excels in all crafts and has talent for art.

On the ward we find that in her better moments Jane can cope with emotional turbulence by submerging herself totally in some constructive activity, becoming oblivious to the world around her. However, when her anxiety reaches too high a pitch she becomes hyperactive, drowning her troubles in loud gibberish and wild gyrations.

Jane's voice is harsh, staccato, and unmodulated. She is inclined to be extremely bossy and prefers the company of the younger children whom she can easily dominate. She is nevertheless much loved by the little ones, for even though she orders them around and screams at them, she also pays a lot of attention to them, defends them fiercely against the ward's bullies, and does not herself mistreat them physically. In the art room Jane is usually quiet, busy, often helpful, but always bossy.

Paula, twelve years old, is a large, overweight black child, who wears thick eyeglasses. She had been admitted because of recurrent states of withdrawal of nearly catatonic quality. These are usually preceded by periods of agitation when she becomes aggressive. In the times between these pathological states she seems amiable and emotionally flat. She is the oldest of the six children of an unwed, thirty-year-old mother. She has experienced the advent of several men in the home who have fathered her brothers and sisters. There is an extensive history of mental illness and violence in the family.

Paula's art oscillates between outright psychotic productions—sheets of paper covered with her name or with black or dark-purple paint—and noncommittal, defensive periods. During the latter she covers paper with squares and stripes of pastel shades of pink, blue, or violet, or manufactures clay ashtrays or cups. Between these extremes there are times when her work becomes more communicative. She then makes faces and figures in clay and tells stories about them. These tales usually center around mutilation, blood, sex, and death, and they are all told in a flat, amiable manner.

In spite of her severe disturbance, Paula is well liked by her peers. She can be pleasant, cooperative, and generous. The girls in particular protect her during her periods of acute illness.

Gregory, an eleven-year-old Puerto Rican boy, was diagnosed as suffering from childhood schizophrenia. He lives within an elaborate system of avoidances, rituals, and fantasies. He had been treated as an invalid by his family throughout his life and had obtained considerable secondary gain by tyrannizing everyone with his obsessions and rituals. He seems helpless in everyday matters, but he is intelligent and reads and writes well. When crossed or perturbed he stands rigidly, screaming at the top of his lungs. When this fails to bring results he is apt to become irrationally violent. However, in the course of his residence on the ward he has learned to adopt a diplomatic, conciliatory attitude in most of his dealings with the other children. He therefore gets along well with Jane, who enjoys bossing him around.

Gregory loves to draw and to work with clay. A recurrent topic of his drawings is magical changes of size, particularly the miniaturizing of various imaginary personalities. This preoccupation also finds expression in his production in clay, which consists mainly of smallish lumps reminiscent of fecal matter and adorned with faces and tiny arms and feet. I have used his work (Fig. 24, p. 18) as an example of repetitive psychotically tinged productions.

Hal is a nine-year-old Puerto Rican boy who on first impression appears to be a bright, attractive, somewhat overtalkative and clinging child. Upon closer acquaintance there emerges an extremely disoriented, confused, and unformed being, beset by suspicions and fears, who maintains himself mainly by clinging to and attempting to control any adult he comes in contact with. Information on the history of his illness is scanty. A pathological interplay between constitutional factors in the child and the mother's inclination to establish a symbiotic kind of relationship with her difficult and demanding son seems to dominate the disturbance.

Up to now Hal has produced next to nothing in art, even though he always comes to his session. His time and attention are exclusively focused on observing everyone in the room and attempting to control me and the other children. He will go to any length to be allowed to hold my keys and if he gains possession his time is taken up in locking and unlocking doors and closets, controlling all comings and goings, and accompanying these activities with a stream of talk. His behavior would be entirely intolerable if it were not for the frantic quality of it all, which communicates the underlying anxiety and disorientation he is holding at bay.

Hal has been placed with Jane, Gregory, and Paula because he is too immature and confused to tolerate any group in which there is a phallic type of competition for leadership. The four children are in the main self-absorbed individuals pursuing their own aims. Jane is bossy but not really a leader. Thus Hal has somehow managed to survive in this setting.

On the day I am about to describe Hal greets me with the news that this is his last day on the ward. Tomorrow he will be transferred to another hospital. Hal is scheduled for admission to a long-term treatment program at a children's hospital in the vicinity. He has been prepared for it for quite a while, and we have already spent some time packing his ceramic work into boxes in preparation for the move.

Today his first concern is with his work in progress. Would I deliver to him all the clay sculptures that would still be too soft for packing and the paintings that would still be wet? I assure him that I will deliver all precious objects left behind. This calms him a little. He is nevertheless quite agitated, his voice very high-pitched, his movements jerky. I foresee a very difficult session.

At first Hal manages to control himself by controlling Paula. He declares tht he will teach her how to make a cup out of clay and begins demonstrating each step to her. Paula submits amiably and each child produces a cup.

Jane meanwhile has cut a large piece of brown wrapping paper, tacked it on the wall, and pushed Gregory against it in order to trace his body. She then paints his portrait, using the tracing and working very hard at matching his skin color and the color of his clothes (Fig. 39).

I have no idea what prompted her to this action. No such tracing has been done lately and no pictures of this kind are currently displayed in the art room or on the ward. Gregory, having submitted docilely to Jane's wishes, returns to his usual little clay figures and for the rest of the session remains preoccupied with his own work.

Meanwhile, Paula and Hal have both completed their cups and Paula is getting tired of being ordered about by him. As he loses control over her, Hal's agitation mounts. He digs up large lumps of clay and bangs them with both fists, declaring that he is killing me. He makes abortive attempts to give the lumps human form (the better to kill them) but seems unable to master his feelings sufficiently to arrive at any recognizable shape.

His hostility infects Paula and both children spend some time symbolically killing me by banging the clay. Paula subsides after a little while and is inclined to return to the manufacture of more clay cups. When I point out that she has made plenty of them already and that I know that she can make more interesting things, she fashions a little girl's head, torso, and skirt. I suggest that she give the girl a pair of legs. "No," she says in her flat, pleasant voice, "the girl got no legs, she was run over by a car and it was so bad they had to cut them off."

Hal meanwhile continues to kill me, rocking the table with his wild drumming and shouting at the top of his voice. I suggest to him that he may be angry because he is leaving. Maybe he would prefer me to be dead because I am not coming with him, or maybe he would rather see me dead than think of me working with other children.

This attempt at interpretation does not reduce Hal's hostility but his activity becomes more defined. He now rolls out a clay sausage and declares that this is a cobra and that I am this cobra full of poison. He pretends that the cobra is biting him and that he must quickly suck the poison out of the wound and spit it out. The fantasy excites him so much that he begins to spit violently on the floor. I foresee that he will soon spit in my face. Jane is getting quite upset by Hal's behavior and threatens to beat him up. The atmosphere becomes explosive, and it looks as if I might have to evict Hal forcibly from the art room.

At this juncture Hal notices Jane's painting of Gregory, which is nearly finished. It is quite a remarkable piece of portraiture. Jane succeeded in capturing Gregory's stiff posture and defensive smile. Hal declares that he will now make a tracing of me. His whole manner changes. He purposefully measures out a length of wrapping paper and, climbing on a table, tacks it against the wall at such a height that he can trace me while I stand on a chair. He places a chair against the paper, orders me to stand on it, and, having thus literally pushed me against the wall, he proceeds to outline my body methodically, taking care to trace my hands, fingers, legs, and feet accurately (Fig. 40). This accomplished, he permits me to climb down.

He completes the picture by drawing my face, hair, and blue smock. He looks at his work critically, notices that the left arm is raised higher than the right one, and that the fingers of my right hand are not as evenly spread out as those of my left, but he concludes very reasonably that such irregularities are only natural, for people never stand quite stiff, but move about. He sets up a tray of paint, and with

FIGURE 39. *Jane:* Portrait of Gregory (3' x 5')

FIGURE 40. *Hal:* Portrait of the Art Therapist (3' x 6')

FIGURE 41. *Jane:* Portrait of the Art Therapist (3' x 5')

FIGURE 42. *Paula:* Self-Portrait (3' x 5')

some assistance from me mixes a skin color. He then proceeds to paint peacefully, and even though his control is to be shaken a few times before the picture is finished he manages in the end to produce a well-organized, complete painting.

Now Jane, who has observed Hal's procedure, declares that she too will trace me. She quickly tacks up a piece of paper and traces my outline, singing at the top of her voice, "I am your father, your mother, your sister, and your brother."

Working very fast, she achieves a good likeness as she did before in Gregory's portrait (Fig. 41). At this point Paula declares that she too wants to be traced, and Jane does the tracing for her. Paula does not, however, want Jane to do her portrait. Instead she herself uses the tracing as the basis for a self-portrait (Fig. 42).

Paula's performance is much more disorganized than that of the other children. She begins by painting a white blouse similar to the one she is wearing, but perseverates and also paints the hands white. Then she paints the skirt dark blue. When Jane points out to her that she has painted hands and blouse the same color, she changes the hands to gray and uses the same gray color on the face. She then swiftly paints the face, complete with large eyeglasses. She ends up by attacking the picture with swirling strokes of black paint. However she stops short of entirely destroying her work, and this is, for Paula, quite a victory, for most of her self-representations end up as an unrecognizable black mess.

At this point the session ends. Hal has not finished his picture, and because it is his last day I promise him that he can come back after supper and finish it.

I explain to the group scheduled for art therapy after supper that Hal has special permission to stay on because it is his last day and he is very anxious to finish his picture. The children accept this and Hal enters on his very best behavior and immediately goes to work.

Among the group now present are two seven-year-old boys, Martin and Alfonso, who are friends and are facing an impending separation, for Alfonso too is scheduled for admission to the Children's Hospital in the near future.

Seeing Hal's portrait of me, Martin decides to make a similar one of Alfonso. Alfonso, on the other hand, busies himself making a present for Martin, a clay bird sitting on top of a birdhouse. Thus separation continues as a main theme even in this new group. I will not, however, describe the evening session in detail. It passes without major mishaps or important events. Hal maintains his self-control and manages to finish his picture. I promise that I will deliver it to him very soon.

At the end of the session Hal stays with me to close up and is permitted to hold the keys and unlock and lock doors. When I am about to put on my coat he grabs it, wraps himself in it, and rolls on the table like a little baby but then gives it up without a real struggle.

When I deliver his painting to him three weeks later, Hal is pleased but it is evident that his conflicting feelings have by now been transferred to his woman counselor at the Children's Hospital. She is greatly impressed with Hal's picture as he has not yet done anything comparable during his residence there.

This does not surprise me, for the painting is unique among Hal's earlier productions. Never before had he given artwork his undivided attention. Never had he worked with so little help and prodding. Never before had he painted or modeled a whole human being.

If we compare our second example with the first, we find a few similarities and a great many differences. In each case one child remains an outsider, quite untouched by the session's dramatic events (Alfred and Gregory). Each story has its hero, a child who ultimately gains the most from the session (Raffael and Hal). In each story one child plays a decisive part in helping the therapeutic process along

(Steven and Jane), and in each session another child has an uneventful, benign experience (Emil and Paula).

The central theme of the first session is the struggle against feelings of insignificance and castration, with its counterpart, the striving toward masculine achievement. When Raffael draws the monster he touches upon more infantile, more deeply repressed material, but these ideas emerge within the context of his phallic strivings. My role is an active one throughout the session. I discourage regression, encourage independent action, come to the rescue, admire achievement.

The second session revolves around problems of individuation, of separating the self from the object and of learning to perceive it as a distinct entity. My role was much more passive. At first it was limited to withstanding the onslaught of Hal's aggression. Later I made myself available for Hal's and later Jane's benign control and possession of my person. The main therapeutic agent of the session was the child Jane, who set an example that helped Hal come to terms with the conflicts aroused by impending separation.

The difference in my role stems from the different quality of the relationship which the children had established with me. Raffael perceived me as an old friend, quite distinct both from himself and from other people in his life, particularly from his mother. Transference phenomena entered the relationship (we will discuss these at greater length further on). However, in the main ours was a working alliance geared toward productivity and growth. In a less intense way, the same alliance also prevailed in my relationship to Emil and to Steven.

Hal's relationship with me was much more infantile and amorphous. He barely distinguished me from himself or from any of the other adults on the ward. All relationships were still cast in the image of the symbiotic tie to his mother. Jane had achieved more individuation, but she was afraid to form ties to anyone whose actions she could not control. Paula's relationships were shallow, her sense of self too severely impaired to sustain any personal involvement. Gregory was unavailable for anything that would deflect his attention from his fantasies.

Thus I could not offer myself to these children in any specific role. Rather, I had to be available for whatever kind of relationship they brought forth, only maintaining enough authority to curb excessive destructiveness.

If we look at each child's experiences in turn, we find that Gregory remained quite untouched by the drama. He was probably thankful that Jane, instead of ordering him about as usual, confined herself to tracing his outline. The portrait itself made little impression on him. He was above all intent on returning to his habitual preoccupations.

Paula was to some extent drawn into the activities of Hal and Jane. Since she was on an even keel this particular day, her responses were amiable and flat. Her story about the little girl whose legs were amputated, although indicative of her pathology, was in no way unusual for her. When Jane and Hal drew outlines she also wanted to be traced. However, she did not attempt to draw the portrait of another person but tried to define herself. Her self-portrait was a little more successful than any of her previous attempts. Although she finally attacked it she did not entirely obliterate it. Thus there were some slight gains for Paula.

Both Hal's and Jane's experiences were more intense. In Hal's case the events of the session demonstrated how unusual pressures need not necessarily lead to increased pathology. They can also mobilize hitherto untapped reserves of energy for mastery and integration. We have encountered a similar process in Eduardo's story (Chapter IV).

Hal began the session by using habitual defenses, warding off anxiety by controlling Paula and by usurping my role as teacher and disciplinarian. (The mechanism whereby Hal took on my role cannot be termed identification, but is rather a primitive forerunner of it.) As soon as this mechanism failed because Paula no longer complied, his conflicts erupted in full force. He perceived me as a deadly power that existed outside himself and that had also invaded and poisoned him. Thus he needed to kill me and simultaneously to rid himself of that part of me which he had incorporated. Hal's behavior disintegrated, and we perceive, transferred onto my person all that is most pathological in his relationship to his mother and to all women. The session threatened to end disastrously, but then Hal perceived Jane's portrait of Gregory and everything changed.

It is interesting that Jane attained a new level of integrative functioning during a session when Hal's disturbance reached its highest pitch. We have no way of ascertaining whether this was coincidence or whether Hal's distress mobilized her to unusually constructive action.

Whatever the reason may have been, Jane, who was in the habit of treating Gregory as a possession she could dominate entirely, chose this moment to perceive him as a person. While her gesture of pushing him against the wall in order to trace him still contained some aggression, her subsequent attempt to create his likeness was serene, without malice, and within the limitations of her age and talent, quite successful.

Her success was probably crucial for Hal, for it demonstrated to him that a child like himself could do such a thing and do it well. Just like Jane, Hal discharged some aggression in the act of pushing me against the wall to trace me. From then on, however, his perception of my person lost its aggressive and delusional quality. The image of the poisonous cobra was no longer in evidence. Instead, Hal produced a painting that could represent his art teacher as he knew her. Noteworthy was his sensible comment that it was quite all right that my arms and hands were not extended in perfect symmetry, because people do move. (Hal was obsessively perfectionistic and as a rule could tolerate no asymmetry.)

We recall that Hal's example in turn inspired Jane too to do my portrait.

It is interesting to see how the same action can have different meanings to different children. Painting my portrait helped Hal to detach his own person from me and to detach my actual self from fantasies he had transferred onto me. When Jane, on the other hand, traced my outline she brought forth a new fantasy as she sang: "I am your father, your mother, your sister, and your brother."

The two children's needs were diametrically opposed. Hal was inclined to fuse symbiotically with any woman who became important to him. Being one with her, he could neither perceive her nor establish a relationship with her. He needed to detach himself and to perceive his partner more objectively. Jane, on the contrary, held herself aloof from all close relationships. She habitually treated me as dispenser of art materials, keeper of peace, and occasional source of information concerning the handling of clay or paint—nothing more. When she drew my portrait I seemed to have become a person, someone close, something like a relative, and so she sang. Her excitement, however, remained within acceptable bounds, and the painting was completed without mishap. We can conjecture that the portrait had made it possible for Jane to allow herself to feel close to me without feeling endangered or engulfed.

We see that for both children the gain hinged on finding a symbolic object that could contain their feelings and on creating an image of it, partly through the primitive method of tracing, partly by more mature observation and action. The ambivalence that had burdened their relationship to the person whose image they created was thereby greatly reduced.

We cannot fathom all the mechanisms that contributed to this change. Finding an acceptable way of possessing another person, indeed obtaining her cooperation in this act, certainly was one factor. Furthermore, possessing the person in this symbolic way entailed none of the dangers of actual possession.

For Hal, who was about to leave the ward, a problem that commonly arises upon separation might have contributed both to his initial disturbed behavior and to the dramatic change later on. When a loved object is lost, the inclination arises to make up for the loss by internalizing the object. However, since any departure is unconsciously experienced as an aggressive act, hostility against the object is generated. Thus there is danger that the negative cathexis will be internalized along with the object. In such an event the psychic organization is indeed severely burdened.

Although Hal's cobra fantasy was in keeping with his developmental arrest at the symbiotic phase, the impending separation may have helped bring it out so forcefully. Conceivably, painting my portrait rescued him from having to deal with the separation in a more primitive and damaging way, by killing me in fantasy and being forced to take me along with him as a poisonous presence.

I have frequently observed that creating portraits can be helpful in mastering ambivalent relationships. In particular, drawing portraits and having one's portrait made can help mitigate the conflict and pain of separation.

Just as in Raffael's *Empire State Building,* we can observe in this session the dawning of sublimation. At the start, primitive aggressive and sexual impulses are held at bay by various mechanisms of defense. As these defenses give way under the pressure of mounting affect, there is a moment when regression and disorganization threaten to win out. However, as the children find more mature means of gratifying their instinctive needs, aggression and sexual excitement abate, and energy becomes available for objective observation, rational thinking, constructive action, and other ego functions. Jane attained a moment of sublimation as she relinquished her struggle to maintain control over recalcitrant companions and contented herself with possession of their portraits. These were indisputably hers, for she had achieved these likenesses by observing her subjects closely and using all her faculties to produce their likeness.

We observe that sublimation, or at least behavior that contained elements of sublimation, became possible for Hal at a moment when his habitual mechanisms of defense were inadequate. A similar moment of crisis, when ordinary defenses were powerless and disorganization threatened, also occurred when Raffael made *The Empire State Building*.

Although this degree of stress is not an indispensable condition for sublimation, it does frequently develop under just such a circumstance. We may then ask whether the art therapist should actively attempt to encourage children to lower their defenses.

We must remember that the art materials and the invitation to use them freely already invite suspension of obsessive-compulsive defenses. In treating children with such precarious ego organization as those I have described, it would not be advisable to go any further. These children's controls break down all too easily. Should we show ourselves too eager to dismantle their protective armor, we would risk becoming suspect in the children's eyes, allies of the dark powers that threaten them all the time. It suffices if we do not allow the need to maintain order and discipline make us too afraid of turmoil and of the primitive, affect-laden behavior that often accompanies positive change.

Our illustrative examples can scarcely be taken as typical. If therapy consisted mainly of successful, highly revealing sessions, treatment would be infinitely quicker and cheaper. In art therapy as in every form of therapeutic endeavor, much that occurs is inconclusive, much is banal, many sessions are at best moderately successful, some are disastrous. Once in a great while something happens that has the character of a minor miracle, and such sessions are again followed by setbacks, by emptiness, by failures that seem to invalidate the miracle.

When one attempts to demonstrate the workings of a method, however, one necessarily chooses illustrative material that shows some measure of success and contains some drama. Thus I have selected two stories that demonstrate the infinite variety of our work and the surprises it holds. This—the element of surprise—is, I believe, the hallmark of the exceptional both in art and in art therapy. No matter how carefully it has been planned and prepared for, every good work of art and every memorable art therapy session brings something unexpected.

Theoretical analysis must naturally follow events. In the turmoil of the session there is no time for reflection. One must act, hoping that training, experience, intuition, and luck will converge to make one's acts beneficial rather than detrimental to the children in one's charge.

TRANSFERENCE AND THE THERAPEUTIC ALLIANCE

The Concepts

The drama of the two sessions I have described owes much of its intensity to the transference mechanisms[14] that colored Raffael's and Hal's, and to a lesser extent Jane's, behavior. Thus we can use the same case material as a basis for detailed discussion of the transference phenomenon and its role in art therapy. Already we can infer that within the therapeutic relationship characteristic of art therapy, transference does not ordinarily assume a central position comparable to its role in psychotherapy. If it were so

14. Transference is "the displacement of feelings and behavior, originally experienced with significant figures of one's childhood, to individuals in one's current relationships. This *unconscious* process thus brings about a repetition not consciously perceived, of attitudes, *fantasies*, and emotions of love, hate, anger, etc., under many different circumstances." From Burness E. Moore and Bernard O. Fine, eds., *A Glossary of Psychoanalytic Terms and Concepts* (New York: American Psychoanalytic Association, 1968).

central, we could not have discussed case material at such great length throughout the better part of this book without frequently referring to transference.

As we observe the complexities of the therapeutic relationship we must clearly distinguish between these main aspects: (1) interactions that are dominated by the unconsciously determined, irrational, exaggerated, and shifting emotions of positive and negative transference; (2) the fund of trust and hope that underlies the therapeutic alliance—an alliance that must endure independent of the ups and downs of transference if treatment is to be successful; (3) actual events and the interplay of personalities that may arouse justified positive or negative feelings that cannot be ascribed to transference.

In appraising this third kind of response the clients' inclination to ascribe their transference reactions to objective causes has its counterpart in therapists' propensity to perceive negative feelings caused by their own actual human frailties or by their thoughtlessness as arising from the client's negative transference.

At this point we must question whether we are justified in using terms such as *transference, countertransference,* and *therapeutic alliance,* which have been originally defined within the framework of Freudian psychoanalytic treatment, to describe interactions occurring in art therapy. Are we not watering down or distorting the meaning of these words?

Since transference is a universal phenomenon that may occur in any relationship and since it is bound to make its appearance between art therapists and clients, coining a different term would only be confusing. We must, however, be cautious to distinguish clearly between transference phenomena outside of psychoanalysis—such as we are apt to encounter in our work—and transference as it develops in the course of psychoanalytic treatment. We must not confound the limited ways of dealing with transference that are open to us with the methods developed clinically to capitalize on processes of transference in psychoanalysis. The examples to be presented have been selected to illustrate methods appropriate to art therapy.

Before we turn to our case materials, we will briefly describe what the term *transference* implies in classical psychoanalytic treatment where the phenomenon was first observed and conceptualized. According to Robert Waelder,

> an *analytic situation* is a situation of artificial, partial, and controlled regression for the purpose of a study of inner conflicts. In an analytic situation, the balance between the inner forces— between the conscious and the unconscious, between purposive, goal-directed, activities and impulses acting upon us—is altered artificially in favor of the unconscious and the impulsive. Such a change is necessary to make it possible for those aspects of the personality which are ordinarily prevented from direct expression to manifest themselves more clearly, while at the same time being able to see the inhibitory responses which are stimulated into increased activity by the very emergence of otherwise checked impulses. . . .
>
> Psychoanalytic technique consists of three groups of measures:
>
> 1. procedures necessary to establish and to maintain an "analytic situation," i.e., a setup designed for the search into the repressed;
>
> 2. the handling of resistance and transference; and
>
> 3. ways and means of how to introduce the patient into the insights gained by the analyst or the hypotheses formed by him, so as to assure it as far as possible that the analysand will understand them accurately and completely and face up to them.[15]

It is important for us to remember that "*Transference* is not simply the attribution to new objects of characteristics of old ones but the attempt to re-establish and relive, with whatever object will permit it, an infantile situation much longed for because it was once either greatly enjoyed or greatly missed."[16]

Thus psychoanalytic treatment purposely establishes a situation in which transference phenomena are allowed to

15. Robert Waelder, *Basic Theory of Psychoanalysis*, p. 237.

16. Waelder, *Basic Theory of Psychoanalysis*, p. 253.

attain extraordinary intensity. The patient may find himself harboring irrational, at times incomprehensible, childish feelings and ideas directed toward the analyst. These feelings carry conviction even when the patient understands that they belong to his early childhood and were originally directed toward the important persons in his past and that they are only transferred onto the analyst. Thus it becomes possible to observe in the transference a new edition of ancient conflicts at close quarters.

However, bringing the past into the present in this manner can be salutary only if the patient can manage to maintain sufficient judgment not to lose sight of the distinctions between the analytic situation and real life. Or more precisely, with the analyst's help he must recognize the artificial quality of transference and distance himself from it time and again. The patient's ability to regain perspective must be sufficiently dependable to protect analyst and patient from harm. To quote Waelder once more:

> In psychoanalytic treatment transference constitutes, on the other hand, a source of information about the most potent childhood desires and attitudes. The latter aspect would make it advisable to permit the transference to develop fully, without interference—which in some instances may lead to manifestations which one might call quasi-psychotic—while the former aspect would suggest to interfere with it, through confrontation with reality and through interpretation. Transference is properly "handled" if the analyst can extract a maximum of information from it without permitting it to harm the analysis.[17]

Ultimately, transference must be dissolved, and the analyst's inflated image must regain its realistic proportions.[18]

The intensity which transference phenomena are allowed to attain in psychoanalytic treatment imposes extensive restraints on the analyst. The patient's inclination to

17. Waelder, *Basic Theory of Psychoanalysis*, p. 241.

18. For a lucid exposition of psychoanalytic treatment, see Rudolph Wittenberg, *Common Sense About Psychoanalysis* (New York: Funk & Wagnalls, 1968).

confound transference reactions and reality is so great that if the analyst offers or takes any action that impinges on the patient's actual life, confusion is almost certain to result. Therefore the analyst must keep a very careful watch on his words and deeds.

Because it must endure in spite of the extraordinary frustrations and perplexities that psychoanalysis entails,the therapeutic alliance between analyst and patient must be a very solid one.

In describing the relationships that develop in art therapy we must refer to transference because transference is a universal phenomenon. Should we also adopt the term *therapeutic alliance*?[19] We cannot claim here that we are speaking about any universal phenomenon.

Possibly the term *working relationship* would describe the art therapist's function more accurately and modestly, but I am inclined to use the term *therapeutic alliance*. Adults and children inevitably sense the therapeutic personality and the therapeutic attitude in us even when we keep our focus strictly on the productive process. Whether we want them to or not, troubled people will form therapeutic alliances with us. We can only hope to understand the psychodynamic processes that contribute to building this alliance and to prove ourselves adequate to its demands.

All patterns of relationship have roots in early childhood. We conceive of *transference* phenomena as descendants of drive-dominated, ambivalently invested early childhood relationships. The prototype of the *therapeutic alliance*, on the other hand, may well lie in the area of relaxed tension between mother and child essential to

19. "Transference should be carefully differentiated from the *therapeutic alliance*, a conscious aspect of the relationship between analyst and patient. In this, each implicitly agrees and understands their working together to help the analysand mature through insight, progressive understanding, and control....A strong therapeutic alliance is often essential to the continuation of analysis during periods of strong negative transference." From Moore and Fine, *A Glossary of Psychoanalytic Terms and Concepts.*

healthy development. Winnicott describes it as a neutral space protected by mother's quiet availability wherein the child can safely undergo id experiences (we have discussed this specific phenomenon briefly in Chapter IV, p. 101).

The situation Winnicott postulates depends on the one hand on the mother's being in a state of serenity which enables her to make her protective presence felt without communicating to her child any libidinal or aggressive arousal of her own. On the other hand, the child must be in a state of equilibrium, free from acute pressures that would necessitate urgent attempts to gain the mother's attention. Winnicott assumes that during such periods of calm the small child can experience impulses and fantasies arising from the id without being overwhelmed by them. Instead, the child's ego is able to integrate the influx and gain energy in the process.

Such states cannot and should not last indefinitely. Both mother and child must experience new upsurges of libidinal and aggressive impulses. Even the best mother cannot always remain dispassionate and nonintrusive or refrain from gratifying any of her own needs in her relationship with her child.

In the artificial partnership between client and therapist, on the other hand, the expectation that the therapist will indeed maintain an attitude of benign attention and restraint comparable to Winnicott's serene mother is justified. The patient should have every reason to be confident that any intervention on the therapist's part will be undertaken strictly in the patient's interest and not to further the therapist's own wishes.

The patient, on the other hand, will attain the state Winnicott ascribes to the child only on rare occasions. These will be moments of illumination when therapeutic work is being integrated and attains a sense of full reality. More of the patient's time will be taken up with unloading ambivalent feelings and conflicts onto the therapist. However, chances of successful therapy are greater when the

patient's past also includes experiences that are analogous
to the therapeutic alliance.

Concerning the therapeutic alliance with children, we
must remember that, unlike adults, children rarely come to
psychotherapy with the professed intention of getting well.
They hardly ever approach a therapeutic art session with
such ideas. Whatever alliance they establish with us is
nourished in the main by children's need to find adults who
can help them grow up, their need to find objects of
identification outside the immediate family, and their
hunger for constructive symbolic experiences (we have
discussed this at great length in Chapter I).

As they venture into the wider world children need to
find that it offers them a measure of protection and nurture.
Because of this normal childish dependency, behavior that
we could ascribe to transference if it came from an adult
because of its childlike demandingness may well be an
aspect of a child's therapeutic alliance, for the child
rightfully expects the adult's help. Raffael's story exemplifies this well, for even when his behavior toward me was
not determined by transference, he remained dependent in
a childlike way.

As to transference, we must not forget that even though
past and current conflicts and emotions are reflected in
children's transference responses, their passionate emotions
continue to revolve in the main around the interchange with
their mother, father, siblings, and other important figures
within their families, and this influences the quality of their
transference to adults in authority.[20]

Raffael: Raffael's story admirably exemplifies the interplay between transference and therapeutic alliance. When
my exhortation to renounce regression and paint a picture
where he was the boss brought forth an upsurge of
ambition followed by an involuntary expression of his
extreme feelings of phallic insignificance, this seemed to be
more than just a symptom of his basic insecurity (he

20. See Anna Freud, *The Psychoanalytic Treatment of Children.*

ordinarily functioned much more adequately). It rather seemed to be a transference response to the woman who made impossible demands, raised vain hopes only to make one feel one's impotence all the more. This was typical of Raffael's experience with his mother. His hope of impressing her and winning her love was kept alive by her seductive warmth but just as continuously dashed by her profoundly disparaging attitude toward him.

Inasmuch as transference determined his feelings, he would rather destroy his artistic attempts than admit to his helplessness or allow himself to trust in a woman's willingness or ability to help him. When my reassuring actions reestablished me as a person distinct from his mother, the trust that had formed between Raffael and me gained ascendance over the transference. His functioning thereupon improved dramatically.

At age eight and a half Raffael was ready to displace much of the energy of primitive phallic strivings onto various kinds of achievement. He needed to be assured that adult women would rejoice in manifestations of his budding masculinity, providing they were expressed in age-appropriate symbolic form. Raffael's impulsive mother was unable to give him such reassurance. A woman who was content to see him intent on constructive work and controlled self-expression rather than on passionate demonstrations of devotion to her was a new kind of person in his life. When I helped him erect his magnificently tall and well-shaped building I presented him with a model of relationships between children and adults that was new to him. The experience, one of many similar ones, made alternate ways of functioning possible. Even though the gains may have remained limited to behavior outside the family circle, we can speak of a corrective experience of limited scope.

As he completed his picture to his own satisfaction, therapeutic alliance gained ascendance over transference phenomena. The drama was concluded in serenity. If, on the contrary, negative transference had simply given way to its primitive counterpart, Raffael's success at painting his picture would inevitably have been followed by irrational demands for rewards on a personal level. He would have cast me once more in the role of the seductive mother and the experience would inevitably have ended in disappointment.

In my work with him these issues of course appeared and reappeared frequently, and partial solutions had to be found time and again. Each incident brought him closer to the point where he would be able to function more independently without the need for excessive support from mother figures.

Hal: Transference interfered with Raffael's functioning. For him progress meant unraveling the confusion of feelings caused by it. For Hal the appearance of transference mechanisms signaled improvement.

Habitually Hal functioned by indiscriminately merging with others. Thus when I became a cobra in his eyes, my person, his own self, and the coil of clay in his hands became fused for the time being. This fusion was patterned on his symbiotic relationship to his mother, but was not actually transferred from her person onto mine. His habitual ways of functioning were not sufficiently differentiated for such complex transactions.

Only as he found a way of stabilizing my image, gained control over it, and thereby delivered himself of the poisonous introject, can we rightly speak of transference. He now used my person to practice new and less destructive ways of relating to a woman—ways he ought to have established years ago in relating to his mother. With the appearance of transference we also perceive intimations of the therapeutic alliance. Even when he pushed me against the wall in a preemptory manner, as he made the portrait, he was fully confident of my ready cooperation. He sensed that I knew that this action would help him stabilize his perception of my person as benign and distinct from himself. Had he attempted to enact a similar symbolic separation between himself and the person of his mother he could not have been equally certain of her acceding to his wishes or of her approval.

Jane: Transference mechanisms served yet another purpose for Jane. When she sang of being my father and mother (which was true in a symbolic sense, for she was parent to my portrait) she transferred a fantasy about family life onto me. All would be well for her if only she could become the controlling parent rather than being pushed around by her father and mother. She tried out this solution with me, someone who was certain neither to victimize her nor to become her victim.

The reversal of roles permitted her to experience more intimacy than she usually allowed herself. Since she had sublimated her aggressively possessive impulses by producing portraits the experience need not end with a letdown when she had to relinquish control over my person in the flesh. She was still in possession of the portrait and had also in the course of the session discovered her talent for portraiture. These gains would outlast the session.

Our examples have shown us much about transference that is applicable to many forms of therapy. We see that art therapy, as with any kind of therapeutic interchange, must frequently elicit transference responses. We have also seen that in art therapy transference phenomena become agents of beneficial change only if they are experienced within the framework of a therapeutic alliance; this too applies to therapy in general. Whenever transference phenomena unroll automatically and compulsively, any therapist will strive to bring them into the fold of some viable therapeutic relationship. Common to all forms of therapy also is inevitable disenchantment as expectations arising from both negative and positive transference feelings must be disappointed. Ultimately the therapist must be recognized as having neither the power nor the wish to do the evil that negative transference ascribes to him and as equally unable to give the love or perform the miracles positive transference expects of him.

When therapy focuses on the therapeutic relationship per se, as it does in most psychoanalytically oriented forms of psychotherapy, the transference phenomenon becomes the main instrument for observing the child's patterns of feeling and relating. Through transference the child's past modes of relating as well as the current emotional constellations between child and family are brought into the sessions. More often than not the child's transference becomes the focal point of treatment.

When interchange between therapist and child is focused on sculptural and pictorial production, transference phenomena rarely attain such all-pervasive importance. If children are to make the most of their creative powers in the service of inner integration and as a means of coming to terms with past and present conflicts and misfortunes, transference phenomena must remain within bounds. Otherwise their overriding urgency would interfere with the productive process.

The necessity of keeping transference under control is immediately apparent in situations that are geared to achieving objective tasks, such as academic learning. Teachers who work with emotionally disturbed children must understand the phenomenon well. Even though many of them do not apply psychoanalytic terminology to their actions they must indeed continuously strive to uphold their identity and their specific function against the pull of violent transference manifestations.

All learning would cease if the teacher were sucked into the seething cauldron of a multitude of disturbed children's transference passions. However, any relationship that can inspire the willingness to learn must necessarily partake of transference. Teachers must find ways of navigating in such a manner that the energy freed via transference can be sublimated into learning. They must rely in the main on establishing solid therapeutic alliances with the children in their care.

Even less than academic teachers can art therapists hope to circumvent transference phenomena. We must encourage children to make artworks that are emotionally charged, but we too must resist the children's inclination to enact their transference conflicts in personal interchange to the detriment of their art. Ultimately, their passions should find expression in their work rather than in their behavior toward us. For instance, in our two examples the children's emotionally laden interchange with me culminated in the making of one large cityscape and two lifesize portraits.

Countertransference and Empathy

We cannot conclude our discussion of the transference phenomenon without also considering its counterpart, the therapist's countertransference. On principle the adult's inclination to transfer unconscious personal concerns onto the relationship with the child is detrimental to therapy. Therapists' perceptions are blurred when they impose on the child feelings stemming from their own childhood experience. Under the impact of countertransference, responses to the child are likely to become charged with inappropriate urgency. Even though countertransference, like transference, makes enormous energy available, this energy cannot be used in the child's best interest. It serves rather to fulfill the therapist's own unconscious needs.[21]

The close relationship between the benign process of empathy and the harmful workings of countertransference complicates the problem. To respond with profound understanding to the unconscious aspects of the children's art and of their behavior, art therapists must allow unconscious messages to find an echo in their own unconscious minds. They must be prepared to permit

21. For a dramatic example of the dangers of countertransference in art therapy, see Edith Kramer, *Art as Therapy with Children*, pp. 38–43.

themselves moments of tentative identification or of merging with the child that are quickly relinquished and transformed into empathy.[22] Ideally, empathy should be free from countertransference distortions. However, the unconscious, being irrational, responds strongly to the irrational in others. As unresolved childhood conflicts are touched upon the therapist's empathy may imperceptibly blend into countertransference, so that far from being relinquished, tentative identifications gather momentum until the art therapist's own childish image blots out the patient's person. The irrational love and aggression of countertransference may awaken illusions of therapeutic omnipotence or stimulate unreasonable guilt or anger.

We see that constant vigilance against one's inclination to countertransference is imperative. With time each of us learns to recognize situations that particularly invite uncontrolled countertransference responses. One strives to avoid them whenever possible and tries to keep up one's guard if forced to work under their pressures.

Acting out impulses aroused by countertransference can only be detrimental to therapy. However, observing one's own inclination toward such acting-out can sometimes yield valuable information about the meaning of a child's behavior. Providing the therapist has attained profound self-knowledge through psychoanalysis or intensive psychotherapy so that he knows his typical countertransference responses well, it is possible to draw inferences about the situation which brought them on.

This method of gaining understanding is fraught with danger. Under these circumstances the therapist's unconscious is not the ideal clear mirror reflecting the child's unconscious but rather a distorting mirror that yields information indirectly as the therapist recognizes the inner causes of the distortions.[23]

22. For an excellent exposition of this mechanism, see Christine Olden, "On Adult Empathy with Children," and "Notes on the Development of Empathy."

23. For an excellent presentation of these and other complexities, see Annie Reich, *Psychoanalytic Contributions: On Counter-Transference; Further Remarks*

The Absent Leader's Possessions: In the session where Raffael painted *The Empire State Building,* I handled his phallic strivings well but dealt less competently with the problem of destroying Jesus's horse. Focusing exclusively on it as a piece of sculpture that ought to be preserved, I was unable (or unready) to perceive its symbolic meaning as the absent leader's possession. My profound exasperation with school-aged children's endless wrangling over hierarchical position contrasted with my patience in the face of other behavior problems.

I know that this typical reaction of mine is fed by an irrational feeling of helplessness stemming from my own childhood. As an only child I had no experience with sibling rivalry at home and was unprepared for the rivalry among peers when I encountered it at school. My incomprehension of the passion aroused by the struggle for position within the various hierarchies that formed themselves among my schoolmates has left its imprint. I am still inclined to respond with incomprehension and exasperation to children who act in this manner. In this particular situation my willingness to let Steven handle the impasse saved the day. As long as I maintained my position as ultimate authority figure, I could be reasonably sure that his influence would remain benign. He would deal more competently with the problem than I could hope to do as long as I was in the throes of countertransference.

My knowledge of my prospensity to respond with countertransference under this specific kind of pressure did not give me the wisdom to handle the situation well myself. It did, however, help me sense the intrinsic rightness of Steven's solution even though—or just because—it contradicted my own inclinations.

Naturally, I do not wish to convey the impression that these considerations went through my conscious mind

---

on Counter-Transference (New York: International Universities Press, 1960); and *Empathy and Counter-Transference* (New York: International Universities Press, 1973).

while I conducted this session. My attention was, on the contrary, entirely taken up with the task at hand and my responses were intuitive. This probably facilitated the smooth synchronization of the session's multiple transactions.

It is generally not advisable to allow self-observation to siphon off attention that should be focused on the children. To observe one's countertransference reaction can itself become a narcissistically invested preoccupation that constitutes yet another aspect of countertransference. When the self replaces the child as focus of attention, the therapist once more unloads his own concerns onto the child. Whatever self-understanding may come to the therapist must never be attained at the child's expense.

The Problem of Power

One of the chief problems of the transference phenomenon stems from its incalculable power. Arising from the unconscious, transference commands primeval forces that are impervious to rational intervention. The therapeutic alliance implies above all that transference feelings, both of love and hate, are accepted as a sacred trust not to be abused or used in the therapist's own interest. It also implies the obligation that the therapist's countertransference shall not be allowed to harm the patient. On the basis of this solid ground for trust the client's irrational feelings, whether distrust and hate or admiration and love, can be safely enacted. The following story exemplifies this.

The Art Therapist as a Witch: During a stormy art therapy session a boy had incurred an infinitesimal cut on his finger. On the ward the matter was thoroughly discussed with all children who had been present. A group of three girls arrived from an outing after the excitement had died down. Among them was ten-year-old Rachel, whose mother was dangerously violent. When the three children heard of the cut finger Rachel decided that I was a witch and that the three of them would never again dare to be alone with me in the art room, for I might kill them. To publicize their feelings, all three of them stormed into the art room where I was alone. They urgently asked to be given paint and paper to make posters and proceeded to write on them, "Miss Kramer you are a witch" in blood-red letters. They confidently asked for help in spelling and decorating these declarations.

The inconsistency of the girls' behavior did not mean that their feelings were insincere. It showed rather two distinct levels of functioning—the irrational transference in which the mother's dangerous violence was transferred onto me and the concomitant therapeutic alliance in the light of which the children knew that I would help them in whatever they had to do to help themselves. Painting the posters helped bind Rachel's very genuine anxiety. It was my function as their art therapist to help them paint posters and so they never doubted that I would fulfill my duty.

Transference love and transference hate make the child vulnerable on two fronts—his irrational hate makes him anxious and prone to unfounded feelings of being persecuted and punished, and since it is not always easy for those who have become the object of transference hate to refrain from anger or retaliation, the child's actual experiences may confirm his worst expectations. Transference love, on the other hand, lends itself to exploitation. Therapists must resist the temptation to gain short-lived therapeutic successes or to acquire devoted helpers by means of positive transference. However, children sometimes feel that they have been exploited when they have not been. Their feeling itself can be a symptom of transference distortion. Expectations born of transference love are notoriously exaggerated and unrealistic. Thus the child may feel betrayed even though we neither made false promises nor blackmailed him into undertaking exaggerated labors of love.

Gifts of Love: A group of preadolescent boys attended art therapy sessions conducted by two young women. For a period of several weeks the boys developed a pattern of being extraordinarily cooperative and well behaved throughout the session. They rarely asked for help and spent much time making rather trite and pretty presents for the art therapists, their classroom teachers, the nurses, and even for each other. Toward the end of each session they regularly went through an endless game of teasingly stealing art materials. This game usually culminated in passionate, seemingly irrational accusations against the two women of being mean, stingy, and unjust. There was no reasoning with the boys, for evidently their gifts of love and their good behavior could not be rewarded according to the demands of transference love.

To discourage continued dramatizations of transference tragedies the sessions' duration had to be strictly limited until the boys had come to terms with the actual situation. They also had to be discouraged from being so unnaturally good and from making so many presents. Rather, they were encouraged to ask for help in their artwork so that they could feel loved and nurtured in a manner that was appropriate to art therapy. This kind of impasse is not unusual and it cannot be avoided entirely. If we recognize its origin we usually can manage to get it under control.

Even though we are as a rule cautious not to encourage the development of transference love, we must occasionally resort to using it as an opening wedge. Particularly when a child has had no opportunity at all for experiencing the pleasure of doing constructive work we may have to lure him into such ventures by mobilizing the powers of transference. If we decide to do this we must be braced to endure the consequences, for the volatile, irrational behavior characteristic of transference will inevitably follow. If we are lucky a therapeutic alliance and some capacity for sublimation will develop as the child becomes engaged in artwork, and we will be able to wean the child from the transference entanglement.

The Coat of Many Colors: Ten-year-old Alfredo was a neglected and rejected Puerto Rican child who compensated for emotional starvation at home by incessant indiscriminate bids for attention from any woman in his orbit. This preoccupation made it impossible for him to concentrate on art—only the emotional appeal of color could hold his attention for any length of time. Even so, he could not use color effectively; he could only become deeply engrossed in mixing beautiful colors. His paintings never went beyond loosely conceived designs that he kept changing. As he added color after color his paintings were again and again reduced to oozy messes.

By mobilizing his narcissistic love of adornment and his great need to make himself attractive to others, I eventually managed to get him interested in painting a picture of a dandy wearing a stylishly multicolored jacket. In this way Alfredo could use all the beautiful colors he had mixed, at the same time having to stay within the boundaries set by his own drawing. By giving him a great deal of attention and praise, I managed to keep him at work on this picture for several sessions.

However, at the close of each session he regularly enacted a drama of separation. Using a whole gamut of behavior from eager helpfulness to teasing to open defiance, he did everything in his power to prolong his stay. The intensity of this battle mounted with each session. When none of his maneuvers succeeded in keeping me with him beyond the allotted time he took to turning his aggression violently against his own work, which was at this time nearing completion.

Short of forcibly removing the picture in its unfinished state, there seemed to be no way of preventing its ultimate destruction. It would have been impossible to watch his every move all the time. My only recourse seemed to lie in making the painting's fate a personal issue between us. As he once more made a move to tear it up, I stopped him bodily and vigorously berated him for hurting my feelings.

At first Alfredo was entirely at a loss to understand what

I meant. How could he have hurt me when he had not hit me, had not even touched me? I emphatically pointed out that I had helped him make the picture and that its destruction was therefore a personal injury to me.

It took quite a while for Alfredo to make the connection. In his pragmatic world people got hurt only if they themselves or their personal property were attacked. A painting that ultimately would belong to him, not me, did not fit into this scheme. Once he had understood me, however, he refrained from further attempts to tear up his work.

The scene between Alfredo and me was transacted on a high emotional key; it was more like an argument between two people of volatile Spanish temperament than the usual restrained therapeutic interchange. This made it easier for Alfredo to understand my behavior but at the same time it fed into his transference response, for my behavior inevitably reminded him of his mother.

The incident was a corrective experience. Alfredo had had little if any reason to believe that a beloved adult could value any of his productions enough to feel hurt at their destruction. Gaining an emotional reward by displacing energy from direct acting-out to more sublimated work was also a new experience for him. The incident is thus reminiscent of Raffael's murals, but my transaction with Alfredo occurred within the context of transference, rather than that of therapeutic alliance. Alfredo's gains remained, therefore, precarious, dependent on the vagaries of his transference emotions. Separation would be likely to precipitate regression unless our relationship could shift toward the more serene realm of therapeutic alliance.

After our dramatic interchange, Alfredo himself seemed to feel the need for a cooling-off period. When he had completed his dandy bedecked with extravagantly colorful clothes he retreated into painting a white snowman, a rather empty and childish production.

This was followed by a protracted weaning process. I

increasingly encouraged Alfredo, who had learned so much about painting from me, to help the other children in their work. He was proud to become my assistant, advising the others, helping them, and at times taking it upon himself to administer harsh discipline. Competing with his peers, cooperating with them on various projects, or winning their admiration increasingly took precedence over his intense demands on me. Identification with me supplanted demands for direct nurturance and love. Identification in turn stimulated maturational processes that helped him establish a more secure position among his peers. There was reason for cautious hope that the gains initiated under the impact of transference might outlast our immediate contact.

We noted at the beginning of our investigation of transference in childhood that children have a healthy need and a right to form identifications outside the family. While certain (usually short-lived) identifications may repeat pathogenic patterns within the family, truly new identifications are continuously being established. For better or for worse, all adults serve as models of behavior for the children in their care. Alfredo's *transference* to me had to be dissolved after it had fulfilled its function as an opening wedge for initiating the productive process. His *identification* with me as a competent artist ready to share her skills with children could become a healthy addition to his repertoire of models for functioning.

DISPLACEMENT AND DISTANCING

A Family of Horses: Throughout our investigation we have taken for granted that it is good for children to find subject matter that serves both as a link to reality and as a symbolic container of their libidinal and aggressive strivings. The horse family of Rachel, Joanna, and Gertrude (Figs. 43, 44, and 45) presents an excellent example of a successful struggle against considerable odds for benign displacement. The horse family came into being on the same child psychiatric ward that was the setting of the two group art therapy sessions already described in detail.

Ten-year-old Rachel was petite, black, and competent. Life with a dangerously violent and rejecting mother and a number of aggressive stepfathers had made her suspicious, belligerent, and unable to get along with anybody. At the same time she gave the impression of being precociously mature—almost a miniature woman—and of being a little infant still seeking the gratifications of early childhood.

Joanna was eleven years old, tall, black, physically pubescent, and of limited intelligence. She had a history of severe emotional disturbance from early childhood on. For years she had successfully insisted on sleeping between her parents, interfering seriously with their sex life. She had remained an only child.

Ten-and-a-half-year-old Gertrude was small, blond, blue eyed, and pretty, intellectually brilliant and artistically talented. Her disturbance seemed to be rooted in a pathological relationship with her paranoid schizophrenic mother that had features of a folie à deux. The three girls fought incessantly, the two black ones frequently ganging up against the white one. Gertrude retaliated both by showing off her superior talents and by frightening them with fantastic tales of rape, pregnancy, abortion, and infanticide.

The three girls were hard pressed, being a minority on a ward full of boys. Between the girls' fear and their compulsively provocative sexuality and the boys' aggressive and anxious responses, the nurses had their hands full keeping order between the sexes.

The boys had recently been much engaged in sculpting clay horses (I have described the drama of the disposal of the leader's horse in the passage on *The Empire State Building.*) Gertrude became possessed of the ambition to sculpt such a horse. She tried again and again, but each time Rachel and Joanna managed to destroy her horse before it

FIGURE 43. *Gertrude:* Stallion (approx. 14″ high)

FIGURE 44. *Joanna:* Mare (approx. 13″ high)

FIGURE 45. *Rachel:* Foal (approx. 8″ high)

was completed. Gertrude persisted, however, and eventually succeeded in inspiring the two to join her in making a family of horses. For more than a month the three girls met twice a week in relative concord to produce their family, Gertrude making the stallion (Fig. 43), Joanna the mare (Fig. 44), and Rachel the foal (Fig. 45). Gertrude's ambition setting the pace, the three horses grew inordinately large (the completed stallion was approximately twelve inches high and fourteen inches long). They were constructed in sections over an armature of crushed newspaper so that it would be possible to fire them in the hospital's kiln. To make them strong enough to support the heavy bodies, each leg had to be fashioned separately and allowed to dry to a leathery consistency before being joined to the body. As long as they were unattached to any bodies, the shape and size of these legs made them greatly reminiscent of lifesize penises. Preparing a hole for each leg in the horse's underside, serrating the surfaces that had to be joined, and using clay slip to attach the legs securely greatly suggested intercourse. In the course of making the three horses, twelve legs turned into twelve penises, twelve holes dug into the horses' bellies became vaginas, while the clay slip turned to semen. Holding the clay legs in their hands the girls enacted possession of the coveted penis as well as the act of penetration.

Again and again the clay pieces had to be reestablished as legs and bodies belonging to their sculptures. To try to forbid the sexual play or to suppress the girls' excitement would have been useless. Rather, they had to be continuously reminded of their purpose and brought back to the technical problem of constructing large clay sculptures. Even as the sculptures' monumental size contributed to sexual arousal, their very bulk and weight helped keep the girls to their task.

Eventually, to their immense pride and the whole staff's amazement, the horse family emerged intact, was fired and painted, and now needed a permanent abode. The three girls felt that their horse family should not be broken up when they were discharged to their separate homes. After much soul-searching they entrusted the group to the school's principal, consoling themselves for their loss with the idea that the family would be safe, cherished and admired forever.

Spurred by their success they decided to embark on another similar project. They chose a family of cheetahs as their next subject. This was a deliberate attempt at coming to terms with their racial differences. They decided that the spotted cheetahs could represent white or black people equally well. They also changed jobs. Rachel undertook making the male and Gertrude made the baby, while Joanna again made the mother animal.

On the whole the girls worked more calmly. Rachel and Gertrude gave their cheetahs crouching positions that offered less stimulus to sexual fantasies. Joanna refrained from giving the mother cheetah any nipples. The change from the phallic horses to animals that are identified with femininity also seemed to be in keeping with their need to unwind after the excitement of creating the horses. Eventually the cheetah family joined the family of horses in the principal's office. Shortly thereafter the three girls were discharged to their parents.

Returning to the history of the making of the three horses, it was interesting to observe how differently each of the three girls coped with her task. Joanna, who was the most severely disturbed of the three, had the greatest difficulty in resisting the pull toward uncontrolled sexual acting-out. Only the pressure of her companions reinforced by my authority helped keep her at work. Her mare (Fig. 44), with its rounded chest, round muzzle, and decorative black mane, conveys a feeling of femininity.

Joanna was eager to give her horse nipples for suckling the foal; she conceived of them as a kind of cow's udder. But even though she tried repeatedly to arrive at a round, breastlike shape, somehow the udder again and again took on a strangely penislike appearance that testified to her sexual confusion. Her difficulty demonstrates how excessive sexual stimulation reinforces rather than corrects the fantasies and misconceptions born of the incomplete sexual organization of childhood. The very girl who had the amplest opportunity to observe both father's and mother's sexual organs and their functioning remained entirely unable to distinguish between nipple and penis in her sculpture.

Gertrude gave her stallion no penis. However, she had great difficulty keeping her horse's head in any kind of reasonable proportion to its body. The sculpture's total appearance with its exaggeratedly large head, conveys a feeling of intense phallic thrust. Its dramatic black-and-white coloring reinforces the impression of aggressive masculinity (Fig. 43).

Rachel's decision to make the foal (Fig. 45) expressed her need for nurturance as well as her greater sexual restraint. She had less trouble than her companions in keeping sexual excitement at bay. Her baby horse is not quite as impressive a piece of sculpture as the other two horses, but it is more realistic and has a more horselike head. The whole venture's success depended on the calming influence of her more rational and controlled personality.

In the art of both boys and girls horses frequently serve as symbols of sexual power. During the period in which the girls' three horses came into existence both sexes were engaged in sculpturing horses, and this preoccupation exerted a civilizing influence on the whole child psychiatric ward.

For the boys the idea of a strong but essentially tame or tamable creature that also requires care and feeding was more salutary than their habitual concentration on mechanical symbols such as cars, airplanes, rockets, or on invulnerable superheroes.

For the girls the horses were even more important. In general we find girls less inclined than boys to invest mechanical objects with sexual significance. Since their bodies provide no model of dramatic erection and detumescence, girls are not as readily fascinated by objects that can be made to start and stop at their owner's will. Large animals that can be induced to lend their strength to the people astride their backs seem on the other hand to be particularly suited to express the little girl's fantasy of possessing a penis or of gaining possession of a whole man's powers and so partaking of his masculinity. Providing that the aggressively possessive aspect of the fantasy is modified in due time, an interest in horses can become a benign container for a girl's masculine strivings. Such an interest may help the girl grow into a woman who takes healthy pleasure in actively mastering the world.

We find our girls involved in just such a task but greatly impeded by their precarious mental state. Hovering at the border of disintegration, they have not achieved reliable repressions or dependable mechanisms of defense. Art therapy had to focus on helping them detach their interest from obsessive preoccupation with sexual organs and the act of intercourse. Their emotional energy needed to be redirected toward the libidinal investment of the whole body and of relationships that can outlast sexual contact. In the struggle toward this new level of functioning, displacing emotional investment onto symbols that remained at a safe distance from mankind was helpful.

To experiment with new attitudes the girls needed to be by themselves. Even though they had invited the boys to their art sessions on previous occasions, they jealously guarded their privacy while building their horses. In this their intuitions served them well. They would not have been able to contain their sexual excitement or displace, and in part sublimate, their penis envy in the presence of those who aroused these feelings to their highest pitch.

In the completed animal families, interest still revolves,

as it must, around the theme of procreation, but emphasis has shifted from intercourse to family life. In the course of making their horses the girls gained assurance that somehow out of the wild excitement and aggression of sexuality benign and stable family relationships could emerge. Since their own childhood provided them with insufficient evidence of such an ideal state their confidence remained precarious. The serenity of a horse's family could not easily be transferred onto humans.

In conclusion we can say that the girls achieved sublimation. Pathology intruded, distorting the mare's nipples, making the stallion's head too big for its body, and subduing the foal's vitality. None of the girls could have attained sublimation unaided and their gains remained precarious. Nevertheless, they experienced the specific kind of joy and the increase of creative energy that are the hallmarks of the process.

Our story exemplifies the problems of working with borderline children as contrasted with those we encounter when we work with neurotic ones. In art therapy with neurotic children—those who are burdened with excessive repressions and laboring under overly rigid mechanisms of defense—we often welcome temporary regression. Suppose, for instance, that I had been working with a group of *neurotic* preadolescent girls who had displaced their infantile penis envy and aggressive sexual fantasies onto a craze for horses. They would probably have started out by obsessively constructing horse after horse in art therapy. My efforts would have been directed to helping them relinquish their unproductive repetition and turn to more varied subject matter, preferably to humans.

In such a situation I might have welcomed an episode of primitive acting-out comparable to those which continuously disrupted my work with Rachel, Joanna, and Gertrude. A temporary lifting of the repression that isolated these hypothetical neurotic girls' infantile passions from their more mature selves could have been beneficial. The episode might have led to some discussion of their past jealousies and childish misconceptions. I could have relied on their egos' capacity to integrate such experiences and to maintain adequate controls during sessions.

For our three girls the therapeutic goal was quite different. Neurotic rigidity was not their problem. There would have been no point in encouraging them to relinquish defenses for they had never developed any reliable defense mechanisms. Rather, they needed to be helped to achieve, belatedly, a capacity for distancing themselves from their infantile sexuality and for benign displacement. They needed help in learning to enjoy the world of symbols and imagination to which they had remained strangers. By opening the door to symbolic living for them we could hope that they would begin to develop viable defenses and reach some measure of emotional stability.

VI

The Art Materials in Art Therapy

OUR LAST STORY in Chapter V exemplifies the importance of art materials in our work. The dramatic events described could never have happened if good-quality ceramic clay had not been abundantly available or if a kiln for firing the horses had been lacking. If we had followed the common practice of indiscriminately glazing children's sculptures, the full emotional significance of each of the horses could not have found expression. It was essential that each girl select and mix the exact color she wished her horse to be, and to do this she had to use tempera paint rather than any mysteriously changing clay body or glaze that reveals its true color only after firing.

Having stressed the unity of form and content from the outset, we must now investigate the many ways in which art materials influence children's work.

PRE-ART MATERIAL

By Laurie Wilson

Children become interested in malleable matter and movable objects before they are ready to create visual symbols with them. Experimenting with sand, mud, water, with sticks and stones, leaves and grasses, furniture and kitchen utensils, prepares the child for the complexities of art. Where natural materials such as these are not available, nursery schools and parents offer substitutes such as finger paint, shaving cream, soapsuds, play dough, objects that can be pasted or glued to a surface, and building blocks.

Some children, however, are too disturbed or handicapped to respond readily to the attraction of the usual pre-art materials. A retarded child may have become so isolated and withdrawn that even these commonplace things appear frightening or unfamiliar. An autistic or psychotic child may be so rigidly attached to specific objects or behavior that he appears to be indifferent to all stimuli. A physically ill or disabled child may have been so protected that he has had little opportunity to explore materials. Because for various reasons they have been deprived of natural opportunities to learn about the world and their place in it, such children must be offered an even greater range of materials and experiences in the art room than is normally necessary.

Severely retarded children and some psychotic ones who are afraid of the unfamiliar are best approached through pleasant, familiar experiences that can ultimately lead to drawing, painting, and sculpting. Choosing from a range of experiences offering different tactile and kinesthetic sensations, the art therapist must select those most suited to the needs of any particular child. Thus a child who does not respond to the gentle touch of a feather or soft cloth on the hand or arm might nevertheless enjoy playing with warm soapy water, an experience obviously reminiscent of the infant's bath—a very early pleasurable tactile sensation that usually follows close upon contact with the mother's body. Beginning with fingertips in the water or a few drops placed gingerly on the child's hand one can move gradually to immerse the child's whole hand and lower arm and then introduce cups, funnels, and floating toys to provide opportunities for more complex behavior.

As they lift and pour water and play with floating objects, children make many important discoveries about the physical properties of the world and develop motor control and eye–hand coordination—they learn about concepts such as full and empty, light and heavy, dry and wet, and so on. We must keep in mind that the ultimate goal of all such activities is to make children able to use art materials from which lasting symbolic objects can be made, and indeed the excitement and pleasure that often accompany these early explorations reappear later when the child uses art materials to continue and extend his investigations.

Ideally, one follows a progression beginning with the simple and familiar. For instance, the sequence might lead from water play to play with tinted water. Next would come finger paint, and this would lead to painting with brushes and tempera.

Each step toward paint or clay may be broken into smaller components. The introduction to finger paint may begin with various finger exercises or pat-a-cake games followed by water play during which the child is encouraged to place his wet hand or finger on a piece of paper. Once the child is accustomed to the feel and look of wet paper, either tinted water or a small amount of finger paint may be introduced. The introduction to clay might begin with play in a sandbox where one accustoms the child to the feel of dry sand by pouring a little of it on his fingers and hands. Next the art therapist might help him poke holes in the sand or bury his hand in it. This may be followed by play with cups and funnels of dry and wet sand that culminates in making sand cakes. Once the child is accustomed to molding and manipulating wet sand, play dough or clay can be introduced.

These activities may be accompanied by comments about the effects of the child's initially random or kinesthetically experienced acts. "Look at the spot you put on the paper" or "Look at the mark you made in the sand"— whether the words are understood or not, the tone of voice must convey enthusiasm and support for the child's efforts.

Autistically withdrawn children may be approached through their preferred objects and activities, again beginning with the familiar and moving slowly to the new. For example, a boy who constantly twirls a string before his eyes may be coaxed into taking an interest in string and yarn of different colors and textures. He may then become ready to tear strips of paper or cloth and may eventually learn to enjoy making collages from these materials. Like the retarded, these children need continuous encouragement and praise for any signs of autonomous behavior and any movement toward more flexible or more mature ego functioning. One must expect persistent avoidance of the unfamiliar and slow, uneven progress. Even when the child has become able to work productively with some art media, new materials often will not be accepted until they, in turn, have been introduced through playful manipulation.

Physically disabled children are less likely to fear contact with unfamiliar materials than are retarded ones. With sufficient encouragement and support they usually greet with enthusiasm the opportunity to explore the world. We need to offer them special pre-art materials mainly when deprivations imposed by illness have impeded maturation so that these children, too, are not ready to use art materials without a period of playful preparation.

Our task consists in the main of circumventing physical difficulties. We must find ways to provide experiences that may seem out of reach or must find materials that can be handled in spite of a child's handicaps, so that each child can reach whatever level of artistic production he may be capable of. Examples of work with physically ill and disabled children were given in Chapter V.

LINE: MOVEMENT AND ORDER

The capacity to use line to create symbolic meaning develops before clay and paint can be used for anything besides playful manipulation. Our exploration of the development of young children's drawing from undirected scribbling to the production of controlled configurations (Chapter V) has shown us the double affinity of line: on the one hand to movement and on the other to intellectual processes concerned with establishing boundaries and creating order.

We have seen that pleasure in creating regular gestalten for their own sake and pleasure in representational drawing usually run parallel. Mastering regular shapes such as circles, triangles, squares, and somewhat later the five-pointed star, and combining them in various designs are in themselves a delight; it also helps children to build up schemata that can be adapted to describing the real world.[1]

Because lines define boundaries quickly and unequivocally, the child who wants to represent an object clearly or tells a story fast will be inclined to turn to pencil or crayon rather than to paint or clay.

Experience tells us that children who are engaged in drawing tend to become quietly absorbed. Excitement mounts when we offer color. Nevertheless, drawing is not all sober description. Since line expresses movement it also conveys mood. Children's drawings and paintings abound with billowing and spiraling smoke, sharply zigzagging lightning, exhaust issuing in short staccato strokes from motorcycles or rockets, softly or wildly waving water, undulating hills, and so on.

In school-age children's drawings and paintings, such expressive lines usually appear in conjunction with more static representations. The excitement of motion may, however, override other concerns. We know this well from boys' war pictures where a tangle of lines denoting the path traveled by bullets and bombs, by falling and exploding objects, or by running soldiers is often all that can be seen when the picture is finished.

1. For the detailed study of these and related processes, see Rudolph Arnheim, "Art and Visual Perception 1969," in *Visual Thinking 1969* (Berkeley: University of California Press, 1969).

Rolf: The making of *The Tidal Wave* (Pl. VII) exemplifies a progression from drawing that is solely a record of self-perpetuating movement to a more controlled, descriptive use of line.

Rolf, a mildly retarded teenager, was hospitalized for short-term treatment because of agitated, disorganized, and delinquent behavior. I met him first when he was slowly emerging from an acutely psychotic state.

He spent his first art therapy sessions covering sheet after sheet of paper with wildly spiraling lines. When long strips of paper were readily available he spiraled over them from end to end. When paper was scarce he covered and recovered the same sheet innumerable times. For several weeks there was no stopping him.

A change occurred during a session which began like all the preceding ones with Rolf covering a longish sheet of paper with spirals. He had chosen a box of colored chalks and had used one color after another, seemingly at random. The paper, however, was taking on a decidedly blue-green hue. The tangle of superimposed spirals through which the color had come into being was still discernible, so that the page conveyed a feeling of agitation.

At this point I managed to induce Rolf to take notice of what he had done so far. He said that his paper looked blue and green like the sea. I suggested that he could use what he had produced as a background. If he would now switch to poster paint, its strong colors would stand out well on top of the colored chalk.

Thereupon Rolf picked up a thin brush, dipped it into a jar of bright-red tempera paint, and deliberately drew a thin zigzag line across the expanse of the paper. This, he explained, was a tidal wave. It would swallow the world. In the end he added a rudimentary figure in black paint, to stand for the drowned people. He seemed calm and he was proud of his picture.

A few days later Rolf was discharged to his parents' care. He had rediscovered a taste for art which he had earlier enjoyed at school. His joining an outpatient art therapy group was recommended.

Even though we are primarily interested in the function of line in general rather than in a particular case history, we cannot leave Rolf without briefly discussing the role of art therapy in his short-term treatment.

My relationship to him was established when he was severely agitated and glad to give vent to his state of mind by means of his spirals. As medication and the beneficial influence of a structured environment took effect, his condition improved. In this improved state he was able to superimpose a single controlled line upon his driven scribbles and thereby to tell a story. Even though the story told of impending catastrophe, his drawing seemed to have helped him to distance himself from both his agitation and his fantasies.

The incident was brief, its effect fleeting. The distinction between reality and fantasy probably remained blurred. Yet there had been some neutralization and containment.

Short-term treatment can rarely do more than bring about moderately improved functioning. It must perforce concentrate heavily on shoring up defenses. If under these conditions art therapy enables the patient even in a limited way to deal with some of his troubles symbolically, to gain distance, to neutralize some of his drive energy, much has been achieved. It would be unrealistic to expect more.

Returning to Rolf's picture, we can see that only the complementary color red could have given his zigzag line sufficient impact to stand out against the agitated blue-green background. Nevertheless, the picture's message is linked to line and movement rather than to color.

COLOR

Even though, as we have just seen, color can add excitement to a line, color comes into its own only when it expands over space. Line demands that the viewer make some effort. We speak of following a line with our eyes. When we see a surface upon which lines have been drawn in any way that is not hopelessly confusing, we feel compelled to seek for some order and meaning in them.

Color makes no comparable demands on us. It impresses us even if we remain passively receptive. To exert its influence color need not take on any definite shape. Indeed, color cannot be fully confined within boundaries. Colors change the areas they cover, make them expand or contract, approach or recede. Further, colors influence each other so vigorously that they seem constantly to overstep any rigid boundaries, establishing interrelationships with all the colors in their vicinity.[2]

As children work with colors they are subject to sensations that actively emanate from the art material. They can learn to anticipate these sensations and make deliberate changes in them as they choose and mix colors and organize them into pictures. They are nevertheless working with substances that have a life of their own, quite unlike the drawing materials that are more fully under the control of the hand that wields them.[3]

Tempera Paint

Because learning to modulate colors is essential to perceiving and making use of their power, we strive to offer children tempera paints and the opportunity to mix them whenever this is at all feasible. Even the richest assortment of felt pens or colored crayons or pastels affords primarily the opportunity to choose colors, not to create

2. For an excellent exposition of these phenomena, see E. H. Gombrich, *Art and Illusion*, Chapter IX.

3. In general, our observations of the dichotomy of line and color in art tally with findings arrived at in the systematic study of responses to the Rorschach series of black-and-white and colored inkblots.

them. Only tempera paints enable children to see colors change mysteriously while they are being mixed.[4]

However, poster paint affords such experiences only to children who are able to gain some measure of physical control over it. Very young or very impulse-ridden or retarded children may be unable to handle paint effectively. Some of them may nevertheless be able to respond to the appeal of color. Dry materials such as felt pens, wax crayons, or colored papers are then appropriate.

But we should not be too ready to confine children to materials that are easy for us and them to manage. Handicapped children such as Dorothy (p. 148) and Howard (p. 144) would have been deprived of intense creative experiences had not their therapists been ready to provide them with poster paint even though arranging for it required work and ingenuity. With patient instruction many mildly retarded children can learn to handle tempera beautifully. Specific techniques may be needed to enable children suffering from minimal brain dysfunction to use color successfully.[5]

Crayons

Roberta: Roberta[6] could never have used fluid paints in an organized manner. She was a severely retarded twenty-one-year-old woman with an IQ of 24. Her repertoire of lines was limited to short strokes, but she was sensitive to the appeal of colored crayons. She worked with both hands moving in and out from a center, starting at the bottom of

4. For an excellent exposition of the reasons for offering tempera paints and of practical methods of using them with children's groups, see Sandra Pine, "Fostering Growth Through Art, Art Therapy, and Art in Psychotherapy," pp. 60–94.

5. For an excellent exposition of such methods, see Susan E. Gonick Barris, "Art for Children With Minimal Brain Dysfunction."

6. Case material for this section was provided by Anne Hausman, art therapist at the Brooklyn Developmental Center, Brooklyn, N.Y.

the paper and working her way upward and outward. Plate VIII is one of her innumerable similar (but never quite identical) productions.

She could only be induced to make her designs if an ample choice of variously colored crayons was offered. To the casual observer it appeared that she selected them at random. She kept her eyes halfway averted from her hands as she reached for crayons in a manner that is typical for many retardates. Nevertheless, her behavior indicated that she knew what she was doing. She scribbled hard with her crayons, never stopping until the colors stood out brightly on the paper. She changed colors deliberately and on each of her designs regularly used a black crayon last. With this black she scribbled over some of her bright colors but never entirely obliterated the colored effect. Roberta knew when each picture was finished and stopped of her own accord. She never destroyed her designs by perseverating. For an individual of her limited mental capacities, the control she exerted in making colored patterns was remarkable.

Tyrone: Plate IX expresses a spirit of colorful excitement which seems, in spite of its greater complexity, akin to that of Roberta's scribbles. It was one of a series of similar productions made by three-and-a-half-year-old Tyrone, a child who was very precocious intellectually and whose father was an artist.

Tyrone produced these configurations in the span of a few weeks during which crayons were his overriding passion. Working on his hands and knees he covered sheet after sheet, pushing his crayons vigorously back and forth in short strokes that were reminiscent of Roberta's. During this time he did not draw even though he was already capable of quite advanced representational work.

Tyrone's color compositions were infinitely more varied and beautiful than Roberta's simple productions. But the intense immersion in color that emanates from both Roberta's and Tyrone's work is similar. For both of them the experience hinged on the opportunity to use a rich assortment of vividly colored crayons. Poster paint would have been useless to Roberta as well to Tyrone—for the one because he was still too young to be able to control them to his own satisfaction, for the other because she would never reach the maturity necessary to handle them effectively. Tyrone soon reached a stage where his capacity for organized drawing and his gift for color were combined in many felicitous ways. Roberta remained confined to her scribbles.

COLOR AND INTELLECT

Even at three and a half years Tyrone's intelligence surpassed twenty-one-year-old Roberta's by far. The similarity of their color productions demonstrates the relative independence from intellectual functioning of the faculty to respond to color and to combine and apply colors with esthetic discrimination. Therefore it is particularly important in working with retardates to offer them materials that enable them to develop any latent gift for using color expressively.[7]

The relationship between line and intellect is radically different. To draw complex configurations requires intelligence. We would not expect any mentally deficient individual to be able to change directions and take aim five times, as he must in order to draw a five-pointed star, let alone comprehend the complexities of overlapping or of linear perspective. Whenever we find age-adequate functioning in this area in an individual whose behavior otherwise impresses us as severely mentally retarded and whose psychological tests also indicate a low intelligence

7. For additional material on color sensitivity among the retarded, see "Therapeutic Art Programs Around the World: Art and Applied Art by Mentally Defective Children," in Elinor Ulman and Penny Dachinger, eds., *Art Therapy in Theory and Practice*, pp. 208–212; and Max Klager, *Jane C. Symbolisches Denken in Bildern und Sprache*.

quotient, we can safely conclude that the person's intelligence is considerably higher than it appears—that the child cannot use his intellect for reasons other than organically determined mental deficiency. (Naturally such assumptions cannot be reversed—the absence of ability to draw complex configurations does not by itself allow us to conclude that intellectual potential is limited.)

We cannot, however, assume underlying potential intelligence when we find that an individual whose intellectual functioning seems grossly inadequate has a gift for handling color beautifully. On the other hand, when such a person impresses us as emotionally blunted, we have reasons to think that his inner life may be more vivid and differentiated than his behavior indicates. (This proposition also cannot be reversed.)

We must distinguish the gift for modulating colors and achieving esthetically valid color combinations from the ability to comprehend the logical principles involved in mixing colors. A seven-year-old who after only a few experiments concludes that adding white paint must always make any color lighter is exercising his intellect, but his paintings might nevertheless remain uninspired. It might take another child years to arrive at any generalizations about mixing colors, yet he might produce exquisite color mixtures and harmonies in his painting. Joseph is an example.

Joseph: Ten-year-old Joseph's beautifully colored, strangely immobile *Storm* (Pl. X) exemplifies a mildly retarded child's capacity to mix and combine colors.

Joseph had been admitted to the children's psychiatric ward for observation because of frequent periods of apathy and disorientation that suggested quite possibly petit mal. In the course of several months on the ward it became possible to establish effective medication to control the brief lapses when he became somnolent and confused. He was discharged to his mother, who was also under medical care for petit mal.

On the ward Joseph appeared passive, amiable, and emotionally flat. An intelligence test revealed an IQ of 72. He soon developed a liking for art and became particularly engrossed in mixing color. From the beginning he was able to exert control and judgment; he rarely reverted to smearing. Many subtle shades similar to those of *Storm* emerged under his hands, but even though Joseph felt very proud of the beautiful colors he created, he did not use them to paint pictures. Instead he made himself into the ward's color expert, readily mixing colors for his friends as needed.

For himself Joseph used his colors mainly to paint his many clay coffins. They were identical brick-shaped, thick-walled boxes with heavy lids. Inside, Joseph placed rudimentary, faceless clay figures representing various members of his family. The boxes were neatly painted inside and out in one or several of his special colors, and then the lids were always tightly closed. He often took some of these coffins along on home visits as presents to his family. When I asked whether his people were upset at seeing him bring home all these coffins, he calmly stated, "They don't mind what I do." Joseph's social worker confirmed that the family indeed seemed sublimely indifferent to Joseph's actions and to their meaning.

Shortly before his discharge from the hospital, Joseph began to use his colors to paint so-called abstract designs, as he had been taught to do at school by making random scribbles and filling in with color the various loops and odd shapes produced.

One of the dullest and most mechanical practices perpetrated in the name of art, such scribbles sadly cover acres of wall space in innumerable classrooms where helpless teachers encourge busywork to control unruly masses of emotionally empty and recalcitrant children. I have discussed the use and misuse of scribble at great length in my book *Art as Therapy with Children*.

At first these pictures remained trite and confused, in

spite of the beautiful colors Joseph had mixed for them. When he set out to do the picture which was to become *Storm* he began it as usual by drawing random lines across the paper in many directions. I expected yet another dull stereotype. To my surprise, Joseph left many spaces empty and when I asked why, he explained that he was painting a storm. The answer seemed odd, but looking more closely I saw that he had indeed produced a strangely haunting storm, and the empty areas were an essential part of the image. The storm's vastness is established by the small, faceless figure caught in hollow emptiness at the bottom of the page on the right. With arms outstretched toward the left and his feet pointing the opposite way, he seems lost. Somehow the flatly painted, clearly circumscribed multi-colored areas combine to convey a sense of some powerful indefinable event—a storm—sweeping over the trapped little figure. It seems to be coming relentlessly from the left directly downward to the right, with no end in sight. The sense of more to come is conveyed by the narrow colorful areas at the left border, defining a convex empty space. The two isolated bright-red areas, one of them appearing at the upper left, the other disappearing toward the lower right, contribute to a feeling of blindingly colorful masses moving on. Yet this sense of movement coexists with an impression of frozen immobility emanating from the rigidly geometric shapes.

Joseph was an inarticulate child. No explanation could be gleaned from him concerning the experiences which might have stimulated his singular painting. But it is interesting that Joseph painted his storm at a period when his mental lapses had subsided through medication. We could speculate that the picture might symbolize his experience of petit mal, a color-suffused brainstorm that leaves him disoriented and diminished.

We are on firmer ground when we consider the formal element of Joseph's painting and the manner in which it was made. While organicity usually impairs form perception, it often leaves color perception intact. Filling in with subtle color shapes simple enough to be within their perceptual capacities frequently constitutes a deeply gratifying experience for organically impaired children. As he painted his picture, Joseph exercised his perceptual faculties to their fullest extent and circumvented his handicaps.

Intellect is not the only factor that determines the individual's emphasis on color or line. Drawing and painting make different demands and offer different rewards; therefore, the balance between them varies also in the work of intellectually well-endowed people. Impulsive people with easy access to their feelings (for example, Alfredo, p. 209) are often attracted to color but find it hard to organize their pictures. Children whose controls depend in the main on intellectual functioning often love to draw but feel uneasy when they are exposed to the emotional stimulation of paint. Other children again handle both line and color with confidence and achieve equilibrium between color and linear organization. When such a balance is reached, color may still dominate as in Remo's *Ghost House* (Pl. I) or Albert's *Autumn Tree* (Pl. IV), or linear organization may dominate as in Harry's *Instruments of Execution* (Figs. 2, 3, and 4). Finally, importance of line and color may be more evenly balanced, as in Jesus's *Sunset over the Bronx* (Pl. III).

COLOR AND EMOTION

The various warm and cold hues of Roberta's and Tyrone's productions make us feel the vitality of color, but beyond a feeling of excitement no specific moods are established. While we need not doubt that color can express mood, attempts to link specific colors to specific moods have often led to questionable generalizations. We must not forget that the meaning various cultures assign to specific colors differs widely. Also, specific life experiences may determine a person's feelings about certain colors or color combinations so that they are at variance with more conventionally accepted meanings.

There are nevertheless a number of experiences so universal that we can assume that they must have some bearing on the emotions which certain colors or families of colors are apt to arouse. However, even those universal experiences are many-sided.

Black—absence of light—holds the terrors of the unknown and of loss of orientation. Awakening at night the small child cries for reassurance which it would not need in the light of day. The terrifying experience of losing consciousness is often accompanied by the sensation of blacking out. However, the absence of light can also be soothing. Night invites rest and benign withdrawal from life's demands. To be deprived of darkness for protracted periods causes severe suffering.

The black of Remo's painting (Pl. I) expresses night's sinister qualities. When Mary painted a picture of her dream of Santa bringing all the presents she had wished for, she chose a black piece of paper to stand for nighttime. On it she painted herself as well as Santa and many presents. Her bright colors shone out vividly against the dark background. The picture conveyed the mystery of night and of dreams. But the dream had provided benign wish fulfillment and the painting did not convey fear of the dark.

The liquid issuing from our wounds is red and extremes of anger, exertion, or fear can cause us literally to see red. These experiences must contribute to our response to the color red. But we look upon red not only as the color of carnage or of extreme passion, but also as the color of vitality and warmth. We respond with pleasure to the sight of healthy, rosy cheeks. The sight of red and orange flames is as old as mankind. It carries connotations of reassuring warmth and comfort as well as the terror of raging fires. We perceive the red and orange colors of Albert's *Autumn Tree* (Pl. IV) as exuberant but not at all aggressive. The red glow in Jesus's dark-blue sky (Pl. III) impresses us as beautiful but somewhat menacing. We were in doubt about the emotional quality of the red in Howard's painting (Pl. VI); it seemed to convey vitality bordering on rage.

Excrement is brown. Most of the colors of our own body are warm ones. These experiences may make us inclined to perceive warm colors as related to the visceral and sensual aspects of life.

Good weather means blue skies; we see more blue and green when we turn away from preoccupaton with our own bodies and look into the world. This must have some bearing on the sense of calm that we associate with these cool colors.

When Anton painted a blue and green *Heaven* (Fig. 19, p. 106) and a brown and black *Hell* (Fig. 20, p. 106) he used cold colors to express benign control and warm ones to express the passionate and sinister aspects of life. (Unfortunately our illustrations are in black and white.)

White gives a maximum of light but offers none of the various sensations that radiate from colors. Sudden loss or disappointment makes us turn pale and we speak of a face being drained of color. All this may be involved when cultures associate white with the absence of any distinguishing quality. The innocent and pure are clothed in white, but so are ghosts, and we speak of a blank expression.

When we turn from universal experiences to those that depend on specific environments matters become even more complicated. A poem by a thirteen-year-old Israeli girl exemplifies this:

> I had a paint box—
> Each color glowing with delight;
> I had a paint box with colors
> Warm and cool and bright.
> I had no red for wounds and blood,
> I had no black for an orphaned child,
> I had no white for the face of death,
> I had no yellow for burning sand.
> I had orange for joy and life,

I had green for buds and blooms,
I had blue for clear bright skies,
I had pink for dreams and rest.
I sat down
And painted
Peace.[8]

We all can empathize readily with her color symbols except for the destructive meaning she ascribes to yellow. Those of us who live in a temperate climate have no experience of burning sand. For us yellow belongs above all to the good sun. However, we recall that Howard chose yellow to stand for Frederick Douglass's death (Pl. VI). The Nazi regime forced the doomed Jewish people to wear a yellow Star of David (this may have influenced the Israeli child's color symbolism). It seems that even in the Western world the color [yellow] is apt to have not only positive but also destructive meaning. We can only speculate on the reasons for this duality. Two observations may be significant: first, the color's vulnerability. Although pure yellow is the most brilliant of all colors, even minute admixtures of any other color suffice to transform it into a different hue. Second, there is the relationship of yellow to the sun. For all of us the glow of the midday sun is immediately associated with undiluted yellow. Psychologists conceive of the ubiquitous yellow sun in children's pictures as a symbol of parental power. We can imagine that the ambiguous connotation of yellow may be linked to ambivalent feelings toward the parents.

Cultural or political factors may exclusively determine the meaning of certain colors. When a black child colors sheets of paper in red, green, and black, or finds a way of introducing these three colors into all of his paintings, we will not probe for profound personal reasons. Rather, we conclude that he is using these colors to establish his identity as a member of the black community. By the same

8. From Ellen Davidson, "How does a child paint Peace?" *Features from Jerusalem*; Consulate General of Israel Information Department.

token we will not search for roots in his individual history when a Catholic child painting a madonna adorns her with a blue mantle. We would be more apt to search for personal motivation if he departed from convention by using some other color.

As we contemplate the world's manifold complexities it seems as if the few universal experiences we have singled out must be entirely insufficient to explain the emotional meaning of particular colors. Applying general associations to individual productions, especially when we deal with the artwork of people who are open to cultural influences, would indeed lead to gross oversimplifications. However, the colors used by individuals whose inner turmoil isolates them from the larger world often seem to be decisively determined by fundamental experiences and general associations such as those we have described. To a lesser extent this also applies to the color choices of children below school age.[9]

A few simple observations imply the possibility of quantification. My own records show that the consumption of the colors blue and green exceeds the demand for red, orange, and black among children of school age who are on the whole reality oriented. This is true not only of normal or normally neurotic children, but also of aggressive and delinquent ones and those who suffer from severe behavior disorders.

On child psychiatric wards, on the other hand, the demand for red, orange, and black usually exceeds the consumption of blue and green.[10] (Here I speak of green for the sake of simplicity. I ordinarily do not offer green paint

9. For an extensive study of colors used by preschool children, see R. H. Alschuler and L. W. Hattwick, *Painting and Personality*.

10. Colleagues working with similar children's groups have confirmed my observations. Art therapists working with adults have observed a high demand for black and red paint among their psychotic patients but I know of no investigation concerning patterns of color consumption among different adult populations. On the other hand, art therapists who work with adolescents report a high demand for red and orange among both disturbed and normal populations.

but provide yellow and blue for mixing. A jar of commercially supplied green—an unfortunately dominating and unnatural color—is kept in reserve for those children who cannot do without this familiar shade.)

Classroom teachers who work with disturbed children agree that only an inexperienced teacher would venture to offer red finger paint in such classrooms without leading up to it gradually. Blue and green can usually be handled safely; brown invites anal jokes and smearing. Red will turn into a disastrous bloodbath in a matter of minutes.

Fragmentation and Control

Carrol: The linkage of color and mood becomes dramatically apparent in the art of borderline children whose fluctuating state of mind frequently finds expression in their color choices.

Ten-and-a-half-year-old Carrol was admitted to the child psychiatric ward of a city hospital because of severe disorganization, temper tantrums, and intermittent auditory and visual hallucinations.

His first painting after admission (Pl. XI) was exceedingly fragmented. He began it by drawing a simple but adequate schema of a house complete with two windows and a door but lacking the obligatory chimney. Except for one window which remained intact, this linear organization was lost as he began using color. He divided the surface of the house into arbitrary, irregular shapes, each painted a different color. Remarkable above all was the incomplete roof and a diamond-shaped area painted white which conveyed the impression of a hole in the wall of the house. Carrol completed the picture by adding one red and one blue square at the two bottom corners of the paper. The fragmentation and arbitrary use of color was reminiscent of productions by adult schizophrenics.[11]

11. For extensive studies on color disintegration and integration, see the writings of Ernst and Edith Zierer.

After a few weeks on the ward Carrol's agitation had somewhat subsided. He tried hard to control his tantrums, and his art productions became more coherent. Color and state of mind remained closely linked. The dramatic transformation of his house (see Pl. XII) illustrates this interrelationship.

Carrol began this picture by establishing a green expanse of grass at the bottom of his paper. Upon it he planted the bright-red outline of a house with a pointed roof. Next he added two windows and a door, also outlined in red paint.

While Carrol was painting, eleven-year-old Geraldine who was working at an adjacent table began to tease and taunt him relentlessly. An explosion seemed imminent. Carrol, however, controlled his temper. He went to the table where paints and brushes were kept in readiness and picked up a small jar of thick white paint. He then proceeded to cover the tan-colored manila paper upon which he had outlined the house thickly with white paint and went on to cover with white the areas inside his outlined house as well. He worked hard at preventing the white from turning pink where it touched the red outline of the house and covered more heavily with white whatever pink emerged in spite of his efforts. He then overlaid the red outlines with solid black and filled in the windows and the door with brown. Finally he superimposed bright orange over the expanse of green grass beneath the house and on this orange area wrote his name in yellow paint.

The character of the painting had changed radically. Carrol's heroic effort at keeping his temper had drained his house of vitality, reduced it to a ghostlike, transparent shell standing black and stark against blank whiteness. The warm red had been pushed underground but there it had been transformed into a violent hue, made even more blinding by Carrol's yellow name. The grass had disappeared as if scorched by all the suppressed violence.

Carrol's precarious victory over his temper was achieved

at a high cost, but the effort was still worthwhile. For him to be able to create an image that symbolized an emotional process rather than to act upon an impulse was a step forward. The effort brought rewards. Carrol was able to talk about how angry he had been at Geraldine and how hard it had been to keep on with his work. We rejoiced over his victory and commiserated with him about how hard it is to keep one's temper.

It is interesting that even when he was not being provoked, strips of red paint often appeared at the very bottom of Carrol's pictures beneath the green grass or brown earth he had painted. The red did not obliterate these other colors but remained below them. The organization recalls the division between hell, earth, and heaven as it is depicted in medieval art. Affect welling up from within seems frequently to find expression at the bottom of pictures (we will present another example of this).

Outside Pressures

example.

Emil: When pressures come from outside, on the other hand, the sky often takes on ominous qualities. When eight-year-old Emil's older sister was dying of an incurable disease, their mother protected herself against her grief by forbidding any talk about his sister's illness at home or at school. Emil obeyed to the letter, but the skies of all his paintings turned either red or orange or else black and purple.

Pervasive Moods

When a child is swayed by some all-pervasive mood or preoccupation, this often finds expression in background colors that set the tone for the entire picture.

We have seen white spread over the background of Carrol's picture and from there invade the surface of his house. We also recall how a blue background not only merged with the blue uniform of Sidney's *Sailor* but also even spread over the sailor's hands (p. 122).

Changing Vistas

Geraldine: After her psychiatric evaluation had been completed, ten-year-old Geraldine was kept on a child psychiatric ward awaiting decisions about her immediate future. She would either be discharged to her mother who had been ailing for years and who might soon be undergoing serious surgery, or else be sent to the rural South to live with her aunt whom she knew and loved well. While the decision about her fate was pending, she began to construct a dollhouse from a corrugated cardboard box. When it seemed likely that she would have to return to a stressful life with her mother overshadowed by the threat of illness and death, she painted the outside of the dollhouse red. For the interior walls she used ultramarine blue straight from the jar, which made for a somber effect, appearing almost black. Against this darkness the floors, painted solid red, stood out brilliantly. When it later became certain that she would be living with her aunt, she changed the interior walls of the dollhouse to light blue and painted its red floors pink and superimposed on the red of the outside walls an overlay of black, crisscrossing lines that suggested bricks. She seemed to be preparing herself for an environment that would control her explosiveness and provide her with more peaceful living conditions than she had experienced with her mother.

Forest Fire: A Tragedy in Four Acts

Jerry: We conclude our investigation of the emotional meaning of color with an analysis of four paintings depicting the outbreak and control of a forest fire, a complex series executed with verve and skill. It was painted by Jerry, a bright, talented eleven-year-old black boy. He had been admitted to the Wiltwyck School by court orders because of delinquent acts, truancy, and aggressive behavior. His troubles had erupted after the family had moved from the rural South to Manhattan when he was nine years old.

Begin

Jerry had accepted the court's decision with detached acquiescence. Conceiving of his life at school as serving time, he managed to keep his cool and held himself aloof from emotional involvement with peers or staff. He liked art from the beginning but his production had in the main served narcissistic aggrandizement. He was adept at painting elaborately dressed exotic figures. Even when he painted a prisoner he had managed to turn the striped prisoners' garb into an elegant costume.[12]

The emotional intensity of the *Forest Fire* series came as a surprise. At the outset Jerry had declared that this would be a story with several chapters. For his first installment Jerry chose a twenty-four- by thirty-six-inch sheet of construction paper colored a tannish yellow. He was to select a different-colored paper of the same size for each of the three subsequent chapters.

The setting is the same in all four pictures. There are gray cone-shaped mountains in the distance and green pine trees in the foreground, among them one brown tree stump. The fire fighter's red helicopter appears in the sky.

Jerry's loose brush strokes leave the colored paper visible throughout each picture. The color of each sheet of contruction paper therefore sets the tone for each of the four paintings.

In painting number one (Pl. XIII) we see Smokey the Bear standing upright, his paws raised in a gesture of supplication. A fire fighter is floating down in his parachute

12. For a discussion of Jerry's prisoner, see Edith Kramer, *Art Therapy in a Children's Community*, pp. 71–75.

and it looks as if he is about to land right in Smokey's arms. Jerry explained that Smokey had given the alarm. He seems gravely threatened by flames shooting as high as his chest on either side of him, but Jerry has not made them engulf his body. There may also be hope for a rabbit at the left bottom corner that seems about to jump out of the picture. The skunk at the right might be moving too slowly to reach safety. The trees are still green. The red of the flames on the ground is repeated in the large red body of the helicopter above. The yellow construction paper imparts an eerily menacing atmosphere to the entire scene.

In picture number two (Pl. XIV) the situation has become more desperate. Jerry chose a bright-orange sheet of paper to paint on and the scene is suffused with its glow. The conflagration has spread. Flames are leaping as high as the treetops. Skunk and rabbit have disappeared. We see Smokey only indistinctly, half hidden by leaves at the picture's very left. Jerry explained that Smokey is fighting the fire among the lower bushes. The fire fighter in his white asbestos suit and mask is walking toward the right. He has turned his back on Smokey and is busy spraying a pine tree. Two more fire fighters are descending from far above. Their helicopter can be seen very far away in the upper right corner. Only a solitary stag adorned with a pair of magnificent antlers has reached absolute safety. Jerry has provided him with a ledge of solid rock high on the central mountain.

By the time Jerry completed his second painting his project had aroused considerable interest throughout the school. Everybody wanted to know the story's outcome. Above all the boys wondered whether Smokey would be saved. But Jerry was not telling. They had to wait for chapter three.

Jerry set the stage for tragedy when he selected a gray piece of paper for his third picture (Pl. XV). The scene has changed radically. The fire is under control. The blue sky has turned a solid gray. The distant mountans are barely visible against it. Their snow-white peaks have disappeared. Before it came under control the fire seems to have reached the trees, for we still see streaks of red flame on all of them. The downward movement of Jerry's brush strokes conveys more the impression of dripping blood than of leaping flames. However, in spite of the fire the trees still have their green needles. The ground is still smoldering brightly and from it three black columns of smoke are spiraling dramatically skyward. Jerry has given depth to the picture by letting a tree stand in front of the column of smoke at the right.

Stretched out flat on the ground Smokey lies dead. His belly is on fire. At his head the central column of smoke is rising. At his feet a fire fighter stands directing his fire extinguisher onto the outstretched body in a vain attempt to save him. We see a white substance issuing from his instrument. Another fire fighter is aiming his spray gun upward at a burning tree. Above the scene hangs the helicopter, huge and red, the brightest area of color in the picture.

The majority of the boys who had been waiting for the story's outcome were dismayed to see Smokey die. Jerry seemed rather pleased with himself, both for having staged the tragic ending and for having aroused so much curiosity and sorrow among his peers.

Smokey's death, however, was not the end of the story. For his final painting (Pl. XVI) Jerry chose green paper. We see the world again verdant, the sky is blue, the trees are restored. However, a thin layer of smoldering fire still covers the ground.

The scene is empty of wildlife. Instead, a new object has been added. At the left where Smokey had struggled among the undergrowth in chapter two (Pl. XIV) a lookout cabin has been built. Sitting higher than the trees, the brown cabin dominates the landscape. It is rather precariously perched on three stilts that do not quite touch ground. A ladder leading up to it also seems to be suspended in midair. Jerry said that the fire fighters would be taking turns staying in the cabin, but we cannot see anyone and the cabin has no windows.

The red helicopter has turned around and now points homeward. A ladder must have been let down while it hovered above the cabin, allowing the men to reenter their craft. We see the last man still suspended on the ladder while the helicopter is already in midair. Located in the picture's center and painted in bright colors, the dramatic departure dominates the scene.

Jerry was in somewhat of a hurry to be done with his last painting. His flagging interest may have contributed to the haphazard look of the safety provision he depicted. But even if we take this into consideration there still remains the picture's content. The ladder, a symbol of precariousness, appears twice and the fire fighters depart while the ground is still smoldering.

We can approach Jerry's fascinating series from several viewpoints. Looking at the relationship of line and color, we see the interplay between graphic elements telling an intricate story and the expressive power of color which conveys the emotional significance of these events. The background colors seem to express general moods—aggressive affect building up in the first two paintings, depression accompanying the control of aggression in the third one, and a calmer (if somewhat precarious) mood in the last of the series.

Local color on the other hand accentuates the emotional connotation of various pictorial elements. Facts and feelings coincide when Jerry paints wildlife an earthy brown, while the alien fire fighters appear inhuman and eerie in their white asbestos suits and masks. (There may be racial overtones to Jerry's color choices.) Just like fire engines, fire-fighting helicopters are usually painted red and this color also appropriately expresses their aggressively controlling significance in Jerry's paintings.

We can also conceive of the series as a symbolic projection of psychic processes. We can see it as an image of the battle between impulse and control, or more specifically, as a symbol of the predicament of delinquency. We can focus on sexual symbolism and on the deadly love affair between Smokey and the fire fighters. Finally, we can speculate on Jerry's personality and his chances for rehabilitation. As with every good work of art the insights gained through these various approaches complement one another.

Jerry's relatively mature and complex personality is apparent in the intricate spatial arrangements he establishes and in the variety of figures he brings into action. The intertwining of two opposing dramatic events, the rescue of the forest and Smokey's downfall, also testifies to Jerry's highly differentiated inner life. Children have a way of imparting vitality to even the insipid creations of commercial art and adapting them to their needs. Jerry's Smokey has none of the poster's cuteness, but like his prototype he is humanoid.

This ambiguous state separates him from the wildlife that inhabits the forest. He stands alone, endangered by his intercourse with man, but through it he also becomes the instrument of salvation for the wilder species to whom he no longer quite belongs. Even though Jerry depicts the full-grown stag safe on his ledge and the infantile rabbit about to reach safety, neither of them could survive for long unless the forest is saved.

If Smokey is humanoid, the fire fighters appear mechanical and ghostly rather than human. Their behavior toward Smokey is contradictory. In the first picture one of them is floating directly toward his outstretched arms. In the second picture the same fire fighter is walking away from him, solely intent on salvaging the trees. In the third picture the fighter has turned again toward Smokey and is attempting a rescue, but the scene has an aggressively sexual tinge. The white figure is discharging white matter from a phallic instrument onto a passively supine figure whose belly is afire. The helicopter's huge phallic body hovering over the scene reiterates the theme of sexual menace. Inasmuch as Jerry's story externalizes his inner life, we have come upon an unconscious fantasy of deadly homosexual attack.

It is interesting that Jerry reaches far greater expressive depth in this picture than in the other three chapters of his story. The two figures around which the scene revolves are unremarkable, but the natural world that surrounds them eloquently expresses the many aspects of mourning. The background conveys the gray of undifferentiated depression. The trees seem lined up behind the two protagonists like mourners weeping bloody tears, their sorrow turned destructively against themselves. The black smoke spiraling upward, three times juxtaposed with the three sharply rising and falling mountain peaks, tells of the agitation that accompanies loss. The red and yellow smoldering ground embodies suppressed violence while the helicopter hangs in the sky like an enormous bloody cloud.

The painting dramatically depicts the high emotional cost of control achieved by violent measures, and the sadness of it. However, we cannot conceive of this picture as an expression of defeat. Since Jerry was pleased with his work we must conclude that the labor of mourning was at least in part successful and the final painting tells us how this was so.

At its very center we see the alien controlling forces departing. The overpowering phallic symbol has turned away and the white aggressors are carried along. The lookout they have left behind fits into the scene. It has Smokey's brown color and seems to stand for him. However fragile these controls represented by the lookout cabin may be, they have become assimilated. In preventing future conflagrations they may be more effective than Smokey had been.

Inasmuch as we can draw inferences about Jerry's personality from his paintings we perceive him as still being a delinquent who conceives of authority on infantile phallic terms. It is just as dangerous to submit to it as to give full reign to his impulses. His superego remains unreliable; his aggression is barely under control. However, Jerry is working at breaking the impasse. We can interpret the drama of Smokey's death as an act of exorcism. Jerry's infantile self is sacrificed and mourned so that he will have a chance to mature. Jerry's strong investment of the outside world seems a hopeful sign. Whatever tragedies may be enacted in the forest, the trees remain green and life in the woods is still desirable. It seems that Jerry wants to protect this world from harm rather than destroy it.

If we compare Jerry's last painting (Pl. XVI) with Carrol's house (Pl. XII) the difference between the borderline personality and the delinquent becomes apparent. Both boys must suppress destructive impulses that are smoldering below the surface. Neither of them has developed reliable defenses. But Carrol's internal struggles consume and isolate him and they distort his perception of the environment. There is no green grass left in his world. Jerry, on the contrary, is driven to escape into the world. Evading inner conflict, he may fail to mature. However, he is able to draw sustenance from the environment. Even though he cannot foresee the long-range consequences of his actions or plan for a distant future (his lookout appears to be a temporary structure) he is able to perceive the world around him realistically.

CERAMIC CLAY

The many examples of clay sculptures presented throughout this book testify to the great importance of ceramic clay for the practice of art therapy. To call attention to the material's specific qualities we need only to discuss further some of the sculptures already presented.

Clay and Regression

At first encounter, children often perceive clay as a toy. They are inclined playfully to enact their oral, anal, phallic, or genital fantasies with it.

Sara's Thanksgiving feast (Chapter III, pp. 45-46) is an example of this kind of play and we can think of innumerable birthday cakes, pizza pies, frankfurter rolls, and other edibles that children make for themselves and their friends. Such symbolic nourishment can be very comforting.

Clay can also stand for excrement. Young children whose control over their body functions is still shaky or older ones who have been brought up with excessive emphasis on cleanliness sometimes reject clay because it is too dirty. Such initial revulsions are soon forgotten except by children who have developed unusually rigid reaction formations against their anal impulses. More often we must lead children who have gleefully regressed into infantile anal behavior rather forcefully back to more age-appropriate, constructive work.

We have encountered the anal aspects of clay in Gregory's rudimentary creatures (Fig. 24, p. 118). Producing them was helpful for this child who was immobilized by his preoccupation with the process of elimination. He later became engrossed in constructing volcanoes and enacting eruptions with black and red paint. Children frequently use volcanoes as a symbol for anal explosiveness.

One must also be prepared for a certain amount of sexual play with clay. Penises are constructed by both boys and girls and masturbatory gestures are made with them. Intercourse is dramatized with the aid of clay sexual organs or crudely fashioned figures. We have encountered such behavior in its rawest form in blind Morris's productions (p. 000). More controlled and tender genital union was enacted by Samantha who created two bizarre sexual idols for this purpose (Figs. 21 and 22, p. 113).

The saga of Gertrude's, Joanna's, and Rachel's joint enterprise at making a family of horses in Chapter V (Figs. 43, 44, and 45) shows how clay can help children make the transition from sexual play to creative work.

Clay and Integration

The power of clay to stimulate integration is vastly more important for art therapy than is its propensity for inducing regression. Just as line lends itself well to depicting action and to flights of fancy, and as color has particular power to evoke emotion, the tangible earthiness of clay and its malleable, cohesive quality convey a sense of reality and substance.

Clay is therefore particularly helpful in art therapy with borderline children who are perpetually menaced by ego disintegration and must struggle to maintain a sense of stability in the face of the influx of primary-process thinking. However, children who are inclined to use art to establish severely distorted, systematized images of the world, comparable to adult paranoid schizophrenic productions, are apt to reject clay in favor of drawing material. The precision of the latter lends itself better to such purposes.

For fostering integration through sculptural work, the dignity of good-quality ceramic clay is essential. Plasticine, play dough, and other more easily managed materials can suffice for playful manipulation and may be used with individuals who cannot be expected to progress beyond this stage, although the earthiness of clay is highly desirable for them as well.

When the transition to formed expression can be even remotely expected, material should be offered that can be made to last and that will not through its shoddiness thwart the child's attempt to create esthetically valid forms. The use of ceramic clay requires access to a kiln, and routines of reclaiming unfired clay must be established. The expenditure of time and money is offset by the material's therapeutic effectiveness.

Wet clay coheres. Whatever comes apart can be joined again without trace of the preceding rift. When paper, pencil, and paint are used, mistakes and changes leave their mark. A child may have to begin anew many times before he reaches a satisfactory result. Clay, on the other hand, can be shaped and reshaped indefinitely. The ultimate outcome must be confronted, but failures and vain attempts along the road are not so painful.

The cohesive quality of clay makes it possible to shape separate elements and stick them together. This made it possible for blind Eduardo to assemble his mother's image from the individual parts he had made in the exact sequence in which he had imagined them (p. 65). Art therapists must be prepared to help children construct clay work solidly and to expend time and ingenuity in repairing sculptures.

The Theme of Birth

Forming shapes of living things out of clay carries overtones of exerting godlike powers even when the theme of birth is not directly touched upon. But the medium naturally lends itself to sculptured work that centers on the riddle of birth and procreation. We recall Eduardo's two images of his mother in her ordinary state and in the state of pregnancy (p. 66). We have seen Michael creating baby *Josephine* (Figs. 11 and 12). Daniela worked at understanding the physical process of pregnancy and childbirth by making a clay model of a womb with an embryo (p. 142).[13]

When children are dealing with the theme of human reproduction in their art, we must resist the inclination to rush in and enlighten them in any simplistic, didactic fashion. No child can fully integrate information about adult sexuality or pregnancy and birth although children can learn to repeat what we tell them.[14] Depending on imponderables such as their past life experience, their psychosexual development, and their present situation, they may be ready to deal with particular facets of these overwhelming facts. For instance, it would have been useless to try to instruct Gregory about the details of pregnancy and birth while his own body and his pathology told him convincingly that people are born through the intestines. It was sufficient victory to lure him out of the bathroom and make him want to produce his creatures with clay during art therapy sessions. Thoughtless didactic zeal might easily have nipped in the bud the complex psychic processes that were active when Sidney made his kangaroos. Our comments can be integrated best when we offer them in response to a child who spontaneously talks to us about his work. For example, several weeks before Michael made *Josephine* he modeled a clay penguin (Fig. 46), placed the figure on a slab of clay, and arranged a number of eggs around its feet. He explained that this was a father penguin who had just laid the eggs and was going to hatch them. I informed him gently that even among birds only mother birds can lay eggs. He was disappointed, but not angered to the point of destroying his penguin. Since Michael had initiated our conversation and we talked not

13. For an early description of sculpture used to elucidate concerns of sexual differences, impregnation, and birth, see Margaret Naumburg, *An Introduction to Art Therapy*, Case V.

14. For an excellent presentation of these pitfalls, see Selma Fraiberg, "Enlightenment and Confusion."

FIGURE 46. *Michael:* Penguin
and Eggs (approx. 6″ high)

about people but about the bird he had just made, he could take in what I was saying.

When he later made the eminently feminine baby *Josephine*, he was still working at coming to terms with the idea that women's procreative powers would be forever denied to him. By making the clay baby, he gratified his desires in a way that did not endanger his masculinity. At the same time he used the clay to envision clearly what girls are like and to establish that they are destined to become mothers.

Loss and Restitution

The substantial quality of clay also makes it a good medium for restoring what has been lost. When the sense of self is endangered, clay may help a child to restore his own image. We have seen an example of this in Dwayne's *Self-Portrait* in Chapter II (Figs. 5 and 6). Eduardo restored his mother's image when her protracted absence from home had made it hard for him to imagine her by purely mental efforts (p. 66).

Jasper: Ten-year-old Jasper used clay modeling in a similar way, but his task of restoring the absent was infinitely harder. When he was seven years old his mother had died of cancer after a long illness during which a leg had been amputated. His father was an ineffective man with a drinking problem. Once when he was drunk he overturned the mother's wheelchair. After her death, Jasper developed the idea that by causing his mother's fall his father had been responsible for her death. Jasper was hospitalized suffering from depression and from nightly hallucinations when he saw his mother's ghost flying across the bedroom and heard her voice calling to him.

Jasper liked art from the beginning. When his symptoms had abated after several months of treatment he entered the art room one day declaring that he had made up his mind to make a sculpture of his mother's head. He said he could not remember her face very well, but he did recall the shape of her hairdo and that her hair had been gray. While he prepared the material for constructing a large head he spoke of his mother's kindness to him. He stressed how she had refrained from meting out well-deserved punishment, saying that she had "spared him" many beatings. He spoke of no positive acts of giving or of care.

It was not easy to help Jasper produce a satisfactory image in the face of his inexperience as a sculptor, the vagueness of his memories, and his unconscious ambivalence toward his mother. A mother who had become progressively unable to fulfill her functions, had been horribly maimed, and had ultimately abandoned him through her death, could not fail to arouse intense aggression that conflicted with Jasper's equally powerful yearnings.

The conflict became apparent when Jasper, feeling quite helpless about recapturing his mother's features at all, declared he would change the head into a devil and impulsively placed two horns on it. At this point I intervened. Even though his mother's demonic qualities would have to be dealt with if Jasper was to be cured of his hallucinations and depression, it seemed important to help him first to restore her benign aspects if it was at all possible.

I removed the horns and told him that we should not give up so easily. I made him describe his mother's face to me as best he could and together we managed to construct an image that could conceivably stand for her. I then asked a volunteer helper[15] to carry on. Between them they completed the head to Jasper's satisfaction. After it had been fired Jasper spent much time painting it in lifelike colors, with particular emphasis on the gray hair. He also covered it with many layers of shiny shellac. The completed work (Fig. 47) bears evidence of Jasper's ambivalence. The blackened eyes and aggressively incised eyelashes in particular seem to tell of his mother's sinister, persecuting aspects. Her benign qualities nevertheless outweighed the malign ones. Jasper as well as the other children on the ward treated the head as an object that inspired respect mixed with tenderness, not fear. For a while Jasper was quite inseparable from the heavy head, carrying it around with him wherever he went. As a special favor he sometimes permitted his friends to hold it and they in turn were proud of the privilege. Jasper's mother's ghost had frightened the whole ward, so that the heavy, unghostlike head helped bind much communal fear. Eventually Jasper gave the head to his father to install in their apartment, and luckily his father was able to appreciate the reconciliatory gesture.

Did I do right when I prevented Jasper's aggression against his mother from gaining the upper hand while he made the head? His being able to complete it and his later treatment of it as a precious possession indicate that my intuition was sound. Had his aggression been too powerful the sculpture would either have turned into a devil in spite of my intercession or else would have come to a bad end in some other way.

Having been able to restore a positive image of his

15. Mrs. Phyllis Palombi, who has since become a registered art therapist.

FIGURE 47. *Jasper:* Mother's Head (approx. 8″ high)

mother, Jasper was in a better position for working on the fear and aggression her death had aroused without being overwhelmed by guilt. Much of this work was done in his psychotherapy. However, art therapy also played its part, and clay was again the preferred medium. He constructed a scene of his mother lying in state in an open coffin beneath a large golden cross. While he worked on it he spoke about the funeral and how frightening it had been when he was made to kiss her good-bye. He had feared that he might catch her disease when he touched her.

Children can only gradually assimilate a parent's death.[16] In his future life Jasper was undoubtedly destined to work at coming to terms with his mother's death in many ways. For the time being, having restored his mother's image and having laid her body to rest, Jasper was free to pursue more ordinary childlike interests in his art. His last sculpture before his discharge was a large horse, a subject that was at the time fashionable among the ward's children.

16. For a thorough psychoanalytic investigation of the effect of a parent's death on children's personality and development, see Erna Furman, *A Child's Parent Dies.*

Patrick: Our last example, twelve-year-old Patrick's[17] magnificent *Polar Bear* (Figs. 48 and 49), attains the quality of sculptural art in the full sense. Measuring approximately fourteen inches in length, it was made during ten sessions of intense struggle that extended over a period of five weeks. Patrick's chief problem was his impulsivity. At twelve years of age he terrified his mother by violent and erratic behavior. He was in many respects competent beyond his years, skillful with his hands, able to make household repairs, and helpful to women provided they treated him as a competent young man. He could not tolerate being in any way infantilized or treated disrespectfully.

He liked art and greatly admired the art therapist's skills. The working relationship established between them was in the main that of master and disciple, the implication being that disciples must submit to discipline and instruction but are destined ultimately to surpass their masters.

The way he tackled the making of his polar bear was indeed more like an adult artist's performance than that of a child. Having planned his subject matter beforehand, he looked for a suitable photograph to help him imagine a polar bear's shape. Subsequently he worked for many weeks exclusively on the body. He added the head only when the body had attained its final shape. At this point he did it easily. The well-defined features impart life and direction to the body while the head's smallness makes the body appear inordinately large by comparison.

When the sculpture had been fired, Patrick took great pains in mixing the right off-white color for the body and picked out the bear's features in black. The change from the brown of the clay to a light color counteracted the impression of excessive heaviness and helped accentuate the figure's movement.

17. For the case material of this passage I am indebted to Elizabeth Stone, A.T.R. It has been prepared with her cooperation and consent.

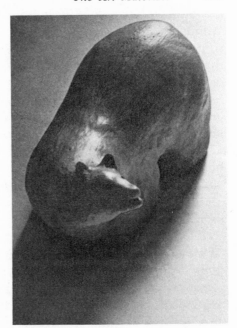

FIGURE 48. *Patrick:*
Polar Bear, front view
(approx. 14″ long)

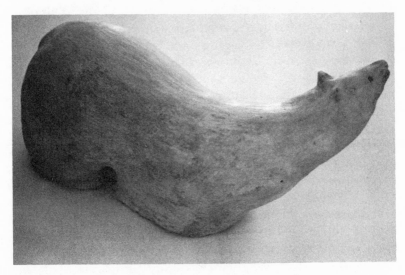

FIGURE 49. *Patrick:* Polar Bear, side view (approx. 14″ long)

Shortly before he finished it, Patrick had designated his animal as a she bear and he later produced a much smaller replica to stand for the mother bear's cub. Installed in Patrick's home, the group became one of the family's prized possessions.

It was no easy task for Patrick to wrestle the bear's voluminous shape from the heavy clay and to maintain it against the clay's tendency to collapse and lose shape. For many sessions the bear remained a formless hulk in spite of his efforts. However, Patrick's positive relationship with the art therapist as well as his obstinacy kept him at work. The battle to give form to the bear's voluminous body and to maintain the form against the pull of gravity seemed symbolic of Patrick's need to establish controls and to achieve a sense of identity through his own efforts rather than by relying on outside help.

In the course of time the clay's earthy beauty and its sculptural possibilities revealed themselves so that a sculpture of extraordinary quality came into being. We can confidently assume that processes of sublimation were active during the polar bear's creation. When art therapy was discontinued the completed work remained as a solid document of Patrick's emotional and artistic growth.

SCULPTURE WITH HARD MATERIALS

It is interesting that after he had completed the polar bear Patrick turned to even more exacting material by working in soapstone. Hard substances such as stone, wood, or blocks of plaster or other synthetic materials can be extremely useful for preadolescents and adolescents who need the challenge of working with matter that makes greater demands on physical strength, skill, and complex conceptual thinking than does clay. Unfortunately, space does not permit me to include any descriptions of such work in this volume.

CONCLUDING REMARKS

Having investigated art therapy and the art therapist's functions from many points of view, we must ask what qualities—other than those we expect from anyone who engages in some form of therapy—art therapists should develop to be well prepared for their work. I still believe, as I wrote in 1971,[18] that art therapists should be practicing artists or at least should have practiced art long and intensively and with joy, so that they have the technical ability, the empathy, and the commitment to art necessary to help others in their art. Equally important is the capacity of art therapists to enjoy the art of the children in their care—a capacity that is enhanced by their libidinal investment in their own art. This joy is a source of strength on which the children can draw, so that they in turn are better able to invest their own work highly and gain pleasure from it.

The mutual pleasure that grows up between adults who love their field and children who are inspired by and identify with their mentor's enthusiasm is so common that it may seem superfluous to make an issue of it. This shared pleasure is nevertheless only one of many different ways in which adults strive to mobilize children's energies for constructive work. We must distinguish it from simple praise and from material rewards. At best the latter confirm support that is also being conveyed in more subtle ways; at worst they are potentially harmful substitutes for the expression of genuine appreciation on the adult's part. Nothing good can come from an adult's dutiful effort to lavish extravagant praise on some childish undertaking in which he is unable to take any real pleasure or interest. As for material rewards, it is wise to resort to them mainly as an incentive for performing unpleasant duties or dull routine tasks, but to refrain from using them where it can be reasonably expected that the work itself will be gratifying.

18. Kramer, *Art as Therapy with Children.*

Rewards and punishments are invaluable for enforcing the rules and regulations needed in daily life but they have no power to inspire emotional investment. When children are conditioned entirely by systems of reward and punishment —however ingeniously devised—they are unlikely to experience inner commitment to any task or the resulting satisfaction in work well done.

The libidination of ego functions of which we are speaking begins long before praise or reproach can mean anything. It probably begins at the time of the symbiotic unity between infant and mother that reaches its peak at about four or five months of age.[19] At this time the infant responds with pleasure when its mother (or the mothering person) celebrates her joy in her baby's bodily existence and dawning mental faculties. The response is still part of the illusion of symbiotic oneness with the mother—there is as yet no awareness that this pleasure depends on another person's loving care. Later the mother's enjoyment of the infant's gradual emergence as a separate individual is celebrated in the ubiquitous mirroring games (such as pat-a-cake) that small children delight in, in the playful naming of body parts such as fingers and toes, and in innumerable kindred ways. Even though this early flow of pleasure has sensual qualities, it originates in the mother's ego and addresses itself to the infant's dawning ego and sense of self.

Mutual enjoyment of the child's accomplishments on the part of adult and child is evidently not the only motivating force of children's exertions. The desire for love and admiration generated in the Oedipal situation, identification with adults who are admired and envied, the manifold competitive strivings of childhood—all harness great quantities of aggressive and libidinal drive energy for constructive endeavors. However, it may well be that early experiences such as those we have described make possible

19. For a detailed description of this and subsequent phases, see Mahler, Pine, and Bergman, *The Psychological Birth of the Human Infant.*

the inner satisfaction in ego functions that sustains the individual even when external rewards are lacking. But if such satisfaction is to remain an actively sustaining force in an individual's life, the supportive experience must extend beyond early infancy. Adults must continue to greet their growing offsprings' efforts with benign interest throughout childhood and adolescence.

As art therapists we frequently work with children whose ego functions and sense of self have been insufficiently libidinized. Among them are children who have been grossly neglected, those for whom support was interrupted as soon as they ceased to be appealing babies and became troublesome toddlers, and others whose elders were too impulse-ridden to be able to support their children's growth consistently. Identification with dutiful but joyless parents can also deprive children of the inner contentment that should accompany the sustained effort of which they are capable.

Working with such children we cannot draw on a reservoir of experiences of mutual pleasure that can be perpetuated under the guidance of experts in a special field, a foundation educators rightly take for granted. We must try to lay this foundation by providing such experiences—sometimes for the first time—or by restoring pleasures these children have been deprived of too early.

Ordinary educative methods are usually ineffective with such children. Many of them have not learned to value any skills or talents they may possess and are therefore not prepared to identify with us on the basis of admiration for our skills or other enviable qualities. Even though many of them clamor vociferously for praise or material rewards for any token efforts they consent to make, rewards or praise fail to spur them on. Neither can we capitalize on the children's competitive spirit to engender enthusiasm. When self-esteem is abysmally low, competition does not act as a stimulus: it leads to despair. We must try to play down any competition for our attention and services as it arises. To stimulate productive work we must begin at the beginning, must celebrate any steps in ego functioning the child may make, much as a mother celebrates any signs of goal-directed behavior in her baby. Such an attitude may seem to infantilize the children, but actually we are addressing ourselves to the infantile level on which they are indeed functioning, cutting through the defiant or manipulative front such children often present to the world. But we must rejoice *only in real achievements*, however minute they may be—insincerity inevitably defeats our purpose.

In this spirit we will note any newly created color, any increase in the work's organization, any creative departure from empty stereotypes—in short, any real improvement. When we rejoice in improved behavior we will tie our comments to the child's main purpose. For example we might say "It's great that you didn't waste your art session fighting but used your time to paint a good picture," or "I'm glad that you managed to wait patiently and didn't tear up your good work until I had time to help you," and so on.

Naturally we will also show our pleasure in improvements in other aspects of life—in the children's mood, health, academic work, and so on. However, we will not jeopardize the dignity of the productive process by conveying the idea that we are using art as a means to an end and only want the children to produce because we hope that this will somehow improve their condition or their behavior. Lack of genuine respect for and disinterested pleasure in children's ego functions are a major cause of emotional illness and must not be perpetuated in the name of therapy. We are more likely to be rewarded by improvement in both art and life if we value children's art for its own sake.

Can we say anything about art therapists' relationships to their own art beyond the initial statement, that it is important to practice one's art? It seems to me desirable that mature art therapists should have transcended the search for identity and the quest for personal fulfillment that often mark the beginning of a lifelong involvement in art. They should have practiced art long enough and intensively enough so that it has become productive work, a gift to the world at large. (Only when it is the product of the artist's integrity does the artist's work enrich society's cultural life. Of course artists should never produce to please others in any opportunistic way.)

In saying that art therapists should have found themselves as artists, I do not mean to imply that their style should remain static; throughout their lives they must establish and reestablish their self-perception and their perception of the world in their art. However, even more than other artists, art therapists need to work through whatever personal concerns or conflicts may be the motivating power of their productive lives to the extent that their art is no longer purely subjective concern, but can stand on its own merit.

I feel that art therapists' engagement with art needs to be serious and honest, but it may be limited. There will always be those for whom the art of using art materials therapeutically eventually supersedes investment in their own work. While such an outcome can be very fruitful, I hope that many art therapists will be able to find equal satisfaction in the pursuit of their own art and in using their gifts in the service of others.

It would, of course, be unrealistic to expect that the many people who start their art therapy careers while still in their early twenties should have completed the initial search for identity through art which is part of the process of becoming an artist. For students still locked in their initial quest the adventure of art is barely begun. Nevertheless, their current experience of the healing quality of art and their recent discovery of the many ways in which self-expression in art can promote self-discovery[20] enable novices to empathize with disturbed people and greatly

20. See Mala Betensky's excellent formulation as set down in the title of her book, *Self-Discovery Through Self-Expression*.

help them to inspire confidence in the beneficial powers of art. However, as we have noted earlier (Chapter V) the similarity of their own search to the patient's predicament entails the danger of overidentification. Continued engagement in the arts and the pleasures and satisfactions it brings help art therapists maintain the distance necessary for empathic understanding that remains untainted by countertransference distortions. The most rewarding task of art therapists is to mobilize the power of art to lead the troubled children and adults in their care into a wider world beyond the narrow range of preoccupation with their own troubles. To be proper guides, art therapists must themselves have already made the same journey.

Bibliography

Ahrens, R. "Beitrag zur Entwicklung des Physiognomie- und Mimikerkennens." *Zeitschrift für Experimentelle und Angewandte Psychologie*, 2 (1953), 412–454, 599–633.

Alschuler, R. H., and Hattwick, L. W. *Painting and Personality: A Study of Young Children*. Chicago: University of Chicago Press, 1947 (rev. ed., 1969).

Arieti, Silvano. *Creativity, The Magic Synthesis*. New York: Basic Books, 1976.

Axline, Virginia. *Play Therapy*. Boston: Houghton Mifflin, 1969.

Bally, G. *Vom Ursprung und von den Grenzen der Freiheit*. Basel: Birkhauser, 1945.

Bender, Lauretta. *Child Psychiatric Techniques*. Springfield, Ill.: Charles C Thomas, 1952.

Bergman, Tesi, in collaboration with Anna Freud. *Children in the Hospital*. New York: International Universities Press, 1972.

Bernard, W. Viola; Ottenberg, Perry; and Redl, Fritz. "Dehumanization: A Composite Psychological Defense in Relation to Modern War." In Milton Schwebel, ed., *Behavioral Science and Human Survival*. Palo Alto, Calif.: Science and Behavior Books, 1965.

Bernfeld, Siegfried. *Antiautoritäre Erziehung und Psychoanalyse*. Frankfurt, Berlin, and Vienna: Verlag Ullstein, 1974.

———. "Bemerkungen über Sublimierung." *Imago*, 7 (1922), 333.

———. "Über Fascination." *Ibid.*, 14 (1928), 78–87.

———. "Zur Sublimierungstheorie." *Ibid.*, 17 (1931), 339.

Betensky, Mala. *Self-Discovery Through Self-Expression.* Springfield, Ill.: Charles C Thomas, 1972.

Bettelheim, Bruno. *The Empty Fortress.* New York: The Free Press, 1952.

———. *Love Is Not Enough.* New York: The Free Press, 1950.

———. *The Uses of Enchantment: The Meaning and Importance of Fairy Tales.* New York: Random House, Vintage, 1977.

Bloom, Leonard. "Aspects of the Use of Art in the Treatment of Maladjusted Children." *Bulletin of Art Therapy,* 4, No. 2 (1963).

Bornstein, Berta. "On Latency." In Ruth S. Eissler et al., eds., *The Psychoanalytic Study of the Child,* Vol. 6 (1951).

———. "Masturbation in the Latency Period." In *ibid.*, Vol. 8 (1953).

Brown, Claude. *Manchild in the Promised Land.* New York: Macmillan, 1965.

Burlingham, D. *Psychoanalytic Study of the Sighted and the Blind.* New York: International Universities Press, 1972.

Burns, Robert, and Kaufman, Howard. *Actions, Styles & Symbols in Kinetic Family Drawing.* New York: Brunner/Mazel, 1972.

Buytendjyk, F. J. J. *Das Spiel von Mensch und Tier.* Berlin: Der Neue Geist Verlag, 1933.

Cane, Florence. *The Artist in Each of Us.* New York: Pantheon, 1951.

Churchill, A. *Art for Preadolescents.* New York: McGraw-Hill, 1971.

Cole, Natalie R. *The Arts in the Classroom.* New York: John Day, 1940.

Conrad, Joseph. *The Secret Agent.* New York: Doubleday Anchor Books, 1953.

Crane, Rebecca. "An Experiment Dealing with Color and Emotion." *Bulletin of Art Therapy*, 1, No. 2 (1962).

Crawford, James. "Art for the Mentally Retarded: Directed or Creative." In Elinor Ulman and Penny Dachinger, eds., *Art Therapy in Theory and Practice*. New York: Schocken Books, 1975.

DiLeo, J. M. *Young Children & Their Drawings*. New York: Brunner/Mazel, 1970.

Eibl-Eibesfeldt, Irenäus. *Love and Hate*. New York: Schocken Books, 1974.

Eissler, Kurt R. "The Fall of Man." In Ruth S. Eissler et al., eds., *The Psychoanalytic Study of the Child*, Vol. 30 (1975).

――――. *Goethe: A Psychoanalytic Study*. Detroit: Wayne State University Press, 1963.

――――. *Leonardo da Vinci: Psychoanalytic Notes on the Enigma*. New York: International Universities Press, 1961.

――――, ed. *Searchlights on Delinquency*. New York: International Universities Press, 1949.

Eissler, Ruth S.; Freud, Anna; Hartmann, Heinz; Lustman, Seymour; and Kris, Marianne, eds. *The Psychoanalytic Study of the Child* (annual). 25 vols. New York: International Universities Press, 1945–70.

Eissler, Ruth S.; Freud, Anna; Kris, Marianne; and Solint, Albert J., eds. *The Psychoanalytic Study of the Child* (annual). New Haven: Yale University Press, 1971–.

Ekstein, Rudolf. *Children of Time and Space, of Action and Impulse*. New York: Appleton-Century-Croft, 1966.

――――. Wallerstein, Judith; and Mandelbaum, Arthur. "Counter-Transference in a Residential Treatment Home." In Ruth S. Eissler et al., eds, *The Psychoanalytic Study of the Child*, Vol. 14 (1959).

Erikson, Erik H. *Childhood and Society*. New York: W. W. Norton, 1963.

――――. *Youth in Crisis*. New York: W. W. Norton, 1968.

Erikson, Joan M. *Activity, Recovery, Growth*. New York: W. W. Norton, 1976.

Fraiberg, Selma. "Enlightenment and Confusion." In Ruth S. Eissler et al., eds., *The Psychoanalytic Study of the Child*, Vol. 6 (1951).

Freud, Anna. *The Ego and the Mechanisms of Defense*. New York: International Universities Press, 1946.

———. "Indications for Child Analysis." In Ruth S. Eissler et al., eds., *The Psychoanalytic Study of the Child*, Vol. 1 (1945).

———. *Normality and Pathology in Childhood*. New York: International Universities Press, 1965.

———. *The Psychoanalytic Treatment of Children*. New York: International Universities Press, 1946.

———. "The Role of Bodily Illness in the Mental Life of Children." In Ruth S. Eissler et al., eds., *The Psychoanalytic Study of the Child*, Vol. 7 (1957).

Freud, Sigmund. *The Complete Psychological Works*, standard ed., 24 vols., translated by Alix Strachey and Alan Tyson. London: Hogarth Press and Institute of Psychoanalysis, 1951.

Fukurai, Shiro. *How Can I Make What I Cannot See?* New York: Van Nostrand Reinhold, 1974.

Furman, Erna. *A Child's Parent Dies—Studies in Childhood Bereavement*. New Haven: Yale University Press, 1974.

Gantt, Linda, and Schmal, Marilyn Straus. *Art Therapy, A Bibliography*. Bethesda, Md.: National Institute of Mental Health, 1974.

Gaitskell, C. D., and Gaitskell, M. *Art Education for Slow Learners*. Peoria, Ill.: Charles A. Bennett, 1953.

Gitter, Leona L. "Art in a Class for Mentally Retarded Children." *Bulletin of Art Therapy*, 3, No. 3 (1964).

———. "Montessori and the Compulsive Cleanliness of Severely Retarded Children." In Elinor Ulman and Penny Dachinger, eds., *Art Therapy in Theory and Practice*. New York: Schocken Books, 1975.

————. "The Montessori View of Art Education." *Bulletin of Art Therapy*, 2, No. 1 (1962).

Goethe, Johann Wolfgang. *Warheit und Dichtung*. [The Autobiography of Goethe. Truth and Poetry: From My Own Life]. Translated by John Oxford. London: George Bell and Sons, 1891.

Gombrich, E. H. *Art and Illusion*. New York: Pantheon Books, 1960.

————. *Meditations on a Hobby Horse*. London: Phaidon Press, 1963.

Gonick-Barris, Susan E. "Art for Children with Minimal Brain Dysfunction." *American Journal of Art Therapy*, 15, No. 3 (1976), 67–73.

Gordon, E. I. *Art and Play Therapy*. New York: Doubleday, 1954.

Goodenough, F. L. *Children's Drawings. A Handbook of Child Psychology*. Worcester, Mass.: Clark University Press, 1931.

Greenacre, Phyllis. "The Childhood of the Artist: Libidinal Phase Development and Giftedness." In Ruth S. Eissler et al., eds., *The Psychoanalytic Study of the Child*, Vol. 12 (1957).

————. "Play in Relation to Creative Imagination." In *ibid*., Vol. 14 (1959).

————. "The Relation of the Impostor to the Artist." In *ibid*., Vol. 12 (1957).

Hammer, Emanuel F. *Clinical Application of Projective Drawings*. Springfield, Ill.: Charles C Thomas, 1958, 1967.

Harris, D. B. *Children's Drawings as a Measure of Intellectual Maturity*. New York: Harcourt, Brace & World, 1963.

Hartmann, Heinz. "Notes on the Reality Principle." In Ruth S. Eissler et al., eds., *The Psychoanalytic Study of the Child*, Vol. 11 (1956).

————. "Notes on the Superego." In *ibid*., Vol. 17 (1962).

————; Kris, Ernst; and Loewenstein, Rudolph. "Comments

on the Formulation of Psychic Structure." In *ibid.*, Vol. 2 (1946).

Hitzing, W. H., and Kiepenheuer, K. "The Child and Death." *Hexagon*, 4, No. 7, (1976).

Huizinga, Johan. *Homo Ludens*. Boston: Beacon Press, 1955.

Isaacs, Susan. *The Nursery Years*. New York: Schocken Books, 1972.

Jacobson, E. "The 'Exceptions': An Elaboration of Freud's Character Study." In Ruth S. Eissler et al., eds., *The Psychoanalytic Study of the Child*, Vol. 14 (1959).

———. "Observations on the Psychological Effect of Imprisonment on Female Political Prisoners." In Kurt R. Eissler, ed., *Searchlights on Delinquency*. New York: International Universities Press, 1949.

Jakab, Irene, ed. *Psychiatry and Art*. 4 vols. Basel: S. Karger, 1968–75.

Kellogg, Rhoda. *Analyzing Children's Art*. Palo Alto, Calif.: National Press Books, 1969.

Kläger, Max. *Jane C. Symbolisches Denken in Bildern und Sprache*. Basel and Munich: Ernst Reinhardt Verlag, 1978.

Klein, Melanie. "The Importance of Symbol Formation in the Development of the Ego." In *Contributions to Psychoanalysis*. London: Hogarth Press, 1948.

Koppitz, E. M. *Psychological Evaluations of Children's Human Figure Drawings*. New York: Grune & Stratton, 1968.

Kramer, Edith. "Art and Craft." *Bulletin of Art Therapy*, 5, No. 4 (1966).

———. "Art and Emptiness." *Ibid.*, 1, No. 1 (1961).

———. "Art Therapy and Childhood." *American Journal of Art Therapy*, 14, No. 2 (1975).

———. "Art Therapy and Play." *Ibid.*, 17, No. 1 (1977).

———. "Art Therapy and the Severely Disturbed Gifted Child." *Bulletin of Art Therapy*, 5, No. 1 (1965).

———. *Art Therapy in a Children's Community: A Study of the Function of Art Therapy in the Treatment Program*

of Wiltwyck School for Boys. Springfield, Ill.: Charles
C Thomas, 1958;   New York: Schocken Books, 1977.

————. "Autobiography of a Ten-Year-Old." *Bulletin of Art
Therapy,* 7, No. 3 (1968).

————. "Comment on *Unsolved Problems Concerning the
Relations of Art to Psychotherapy* by Lawrence Kubie."
American Journal of Art Therapy, 12, No. 4 (1973).

————. "A Critique of Kurt Eissler's *Leonardo da Vinci.*"
Bulletin of Art Therapy, 4, No. 1 (1964).

————. *Kunsttherapie mit Kindern: Handbuch der Kinder-
psychotherapie.* Munich: Gerd Biermann-Ernst Reinhardt Verlag, 1969.

————. "The Unity of Process and Product," in Symposium:
"Integration of Divergent Points of View in Art
Therapy." *American Journal of Art Therapy,* 14, No. 1
(1976).

————, and Ulman, Elinor. Editorial, "Art Therapy: Further Explorations and Definition." *American Journal of
Art Therapy,* 16, No. 1 (1976).

————, and Ulman, Elinor. "Postscript to Halsey's *Freud on
the Nature of Art.*" *Ibid.,* 17, No. 1 (1977).

Kreitler, Hans, and Kreitler, Shulamith. *Psychology of the
Arts.* Durham, N.C.: Duke University Press, 1972.

Kris, Ernst. "Neutralization and Sublimation." In Ruth S.
Eissler et al., eds., *The Psychoanalytic Study of the
Child,* Vol. 10 (1955).

————. "Psychoanalysis and the Study of Creative Imagination." *Bulletin of the New York Academy of Medicine,*
29, No. 4 (1953).

————. *Psychoanalytic Explorations in Art.* New York:
International Universities Press, 1952; New York:
Schocken Books, 1964.

Kubie, Lawrence. *Neurotic Distortion of the Creative
Process.* Lawrence: University of Kansas Press, 1959.

————. "Unsolved Problems Concerning the Relation of
Art to Psychotherapy. *American Journal of Art Therapy,* 12, No. 2 (1973).

————. Reply to Edith Kramer's Comment. *Ibid.*, 12, No. 4 (1973).

Kwiatkowska, Hanna Yaxa. *Family Therapy and Evaluation Through Art.* Springfield, Ill.: Charles C Thomas, 1978.

————. Symposium: "Integration of Divergent Points of View in Art Therapy. Technique Versus Techniques." *American Journal of Art Therapy,* 14, No. 1 (1976).

Lachman, Mildred. Symposium: "Integration of Divergent Points of View in Art Therapy. A Partnership with Other Expressive Arts; But Watch Out for Activity Groups." *American Journal of Art Therapy,* 14, No. 1 (1974).

Langer, Susanne. *Feeling and Form.* New York: Charles Scribner's Sons, 1953.

————. *Mind: An Essay on Human Feeling.* Baltimore: Johns Hopkins University Press, 1967.

————. *Philosophical Sketches.* Baltimore: Johns Hopkins University Press, 1962.

————. *Philosophy in a New Key.* New York: Mentor Books, 1948.

Lee, H. B. "The Values of Order and Vitality in Art." In G. Roheim, ed., *Psychoanalysis and the Social Sciences.* New York: International Universities Press, 1950.

Levick, Myra; Goldman, Morris; and Fink, Paul Jay. "Training for Art Therapists." *Bulletin of Art Therapy,* 6, No. 3 (1976).

Lewis, Nancy. *My Roots Be Coming Back.* New York: Touchstone Center for Children, 1973.

Lindsay, Zaidee. *Art and the Handicapped Child.* New York: Van Nostrand Reinhold, 1972.

Lindstrom, Miriam. *Children's Art: A Study of Normal Development in Children's Modes of Visualization.* Berkeley: University of California Press, 1957.

Lisenco, Yasha. *Art Not By Eye: The Previously Sighted Visually Impaired Adult in Fine Arts Programs.* New York: American Foundation for the Blind, 1972.

Lorenz, Konrad. *Behind the Mirror.* New York and London: Harcourt Brace Jovanovich, 1977.

———. *Evolution and Modification of Behavior.* Chicago: University of Chicago Press, 1965.

———. *On Aggression.* New York: Harcourt Brace Jovanovich, 1966.

———. *Studies in Animal and Human Behavior.* Cambridge, Mass.: Harvard University Press, 1971.

———, and Leyhausen, Paul. *Motivation of Human and Animal Behavior.* New York: Van Nostrand Reinhold, 1973.

Lowenfeld, H. "Psychic Trauma and Productive Experience in the Artist." *Psychoanalytic Review,* 1 (1941), 116.

Lowenfeld, Viktor. *Creative and Mental Growth,* 3rd ed. New York: Macmillan, 1957.

———. *The Nature of Creative Activity.* London: Routledge & Kegan Paul, 1952.

Machover, Karen. *Personality Projection in the Drawing of the Human Figure.* Springfield, Ill.: Charles C Thomas, 1952.

Mahler, Margaret. *On Human Symbiosis and the Vicissitudes of Individuation.* New York: International Universities Press, 1968.

———; Pine, Fred; and Bergman, Anni. *The Psychological Birth of the Human Infant.* New York: Basic Books, 1975.

Marshall, Sybil. *An Experiment in Education.* New York: Cambridge University Press, 1963.

Meares, Ainslie. *The Door of Serenity: A Study in the Therapeutic Use of Symbolic Painting.* Springfield, Ill.: Charles C Thomas, 1958.

———. *Shapes of Sanity.* Springfield, Ill.: Charles C Thomas, 1960.

Meyer-Holzapfel, M. "Das Spiel bei Säugetieren." *Handbuch der Zoologie,* 8, No. 10 (1956), 1–6.

276   BIBLIOGRAPHY

———. "Über die Bereitschaft zu Spiel- und Instinkthand-lungen." *Zeitschrift für Tierpsychologie,* 13 (1956), 442–64.

———. "Triebbedingte Ruhezustände als Ziel von Ap-petenzhandlungen." *Die Naturwissenschaften,* 28 (1940), 273–80.

Meyerhoff, Hilde. "Art as Therapy in a Group Setting: The Stories of Batja and Rina." *American Journal of Art Therapy,* 16, No. 4 (1977).

Midgley, Mary. *Beast and Man.* Ithaca, N.Y.: Cornell University Press, 1979.

Montessori, Maria. *Spontaneous Activity in Education.* New York: Schocken Books, 1965.

Münz, L., and Lowenfeld, V. *Plastische Arbeiten Blinder.* Brünn: Verlag Rudolf Rohrer, 1934.

Naumburg, Margaret. *Dynamically Oriented Art Therapy: Its Principles and Practice.* New York: Grune & Stratton, 1966.

———. *An Introduction to Art Therapy.* New York: Teacher's College Press, 1973.

———. *Schizophrenic Art: Its Meaning in Psychotherapy.* New York: Grune & Stratton, 1950.

———. *Studies of the Free Art Expression of Behavior: Problem Children and Adolescents.* New York: Grune & Stratton, 1947.

Olden, Christine. "Notes on the Development of Empathy." In Ruth S. Eissler et al., eds., *The Psychoanalytic Study of the Child,* Vol. 13 (1958).

———. "On Adult Empathy with Children." In *ibid.,* Vol. 8 (1953).

Orbis Statini Židovske Muzeum. *Children's Drawings and Poetry from Terezin.* Prague, 1962.

Paneth, Marie. *Branch Street.* London: George Allen & Unwin, 1947.

Peller, Lilli. *On Development and Education of Young Children.* New York: Philosophical Library, 1978.

Piaget, Jean. *The Origins of Intelligence in Children.* New York: International Universities Press, 1936.

———. *Play, Dreams, and Imitation in Childhood*. New York: W. W. Norton, 1951.

Piers, Maria W., ed. *Play and Development*. New York: W. W. Norton, 1972.

Pine, Fred. "The Concept of Borderline in Children." In Ruth S. Eissler et al., eds., *The Psychoanalytic Study of the Child*, Vol. 29 (1974).

———. "Libidinal Object Constancy: A Theoretical Note." *Psychoanalysis and Contemporary Science*, 3 (1974).

Pine, Sandra. "Fostering Growth Through Art Education, Art Therapy, and Art in Psychotherapy." In Elinor Ulman and Penny Dachinger, eds., *Art Therapy in Theory and Practice*. New York: Schocken Books, 1975.

Plank, Emma. "The Child Before the Operation." *Hexagon* (Roche), 4, No. 2 (1976).

———. "Leg Amputation in a Four-Year Old: Reactions of the Child, Her Family and the Staff." In Ruth S. Eissler et al., eds., *The Psychoanalytic Study of the Child*, Vol. 16 (1961).

———. *Working with Children in Hospitals: A Guide for the Professional Team*. Cleveland: Western Reserve University Press, 1962.

Prinzhorn, H. *Artistry of the Mentally Ill*. New York: Springer Verlag, 1972.

Redl, Fritz, and Wineman, David. *Children Who Hate: The Disorganization and Breakdown of Behavior Controls*. New York: The Free Press, 1951.

———, and Wineman, David. *Controls from Within*. New York: The Free Press, 1952.

Reich, Annie. *Psychoanalytic Contributions*. New York: International Universities Press, 1973.

Rhyne, Janie. *The Gestalt Art Experience*. Monterey, Calif.: Brooks-Cole, 1973.

———. Symposium: "Integration of Divergent Points of View in Art Therapy. Divergency and Growth in Art Therapy." *American Journal of Art Therapy*, 14, No. 1 (1977).

Robbins, A., and Sibley, L. B. *Creative Art Therapy*. New York: Brunner/Mazel, 1976.

Rorschach, Hermann. *Psychodiagnostics. A Diagnostic Test Based on Perception*. Berne: Hans Huber, 1942.

Rubin, Judith Aron. *Child Art Therapy*. New York: Van Nostrand Reinhold, 1978.

Sachs, Hanns. *The Creative Unconscious*. Cambridge, Mass.: Sic-Art Publishers, 1942.

Salant, Edna. "Preventive Art Therapy with a Pre-School Child." *American Journal of Art Therapy*, 14, No. 3 (1975).

Schachtel, Ernest G. *Metamorphosis*. New York: Basic Books, 1959.

———. "On Color and Affect." *Psychiatry*, No. 6 (1943).

———. "Projection and Its Relation to Character Attitudes and Creativity in the Kinesthetic Responses." *Psychiatry*, No. 13 (1950), 69–100.

Schaefer-Simmern, Henry. *The Unfolding of Artistic Activity*. Berkeley: University of California Press, 1948.

Schmidt-Waener, T. "Formal Criteria for the Analysis of Children's Drawings." *American Orthopsychiatric Journal*, 12 (1952), 95.

Sechehaye, M. *Autobiography of a Schizophrenic Girl*. New York: Signet Books, 1970.

———. *Symbolic Realization: A New Method of Psychotherapy Applied to a Case of Schizophrenia*. New York: International Universities Press, 1970.

Silver, Rawley. *Developing Cognitive and Creative Skills Through Art*. Baltimore: University Park Press, 1978.

Simon, Ellen. "Drawing Games in Art Therapy with Children." *American Journal of Art Therapy*, 17, No. 3 (1978).

Site, Myer. "Art and the Slow Learner." In Elinor Ulman and Penny Dachinger, eds., *Art Therapy in Theory and Practice*. New York: Schocken Books, 1975.

Spitz, R. A. "The Primal Cavity." In Ruth S. Eissler et al., eds., *The Psychoanalytic Study of the Child*, Vol. 10 (1955).

——, with the assistance of Wolff, K. M. "The Smiling Response." *General Psychology Monographs*, 24 (1946), 57–125.

Stember, Clara Jo. "Printmaking with Abused Children: The First Step in Art Therapy." *American Journal of Art Therapy*, 16, No. 3 (1977).

Storr, Anthony. *The Dynamics of Creation*. New York: Atheneum, 1972.

——. *Human Aggression*. New York: Atheneum, 1968.

Tanner, J. M., and Inhelder, B., eds. *Discussions on Child Development*. New York: International Universities Press, 1958.

Themal, Joachim H. "Children's Work as Art." *Bulletin of Art Therapy*, 2, No. 1 (1962).

Tinbergen, N. *The Study of Instinct*. London and New York: Oxford University Press, 1969.

Uhlin, Donald M. *Art for Exceptional Children*. Dubuque, Iowa: William C. Brown, 1972.

Ulman, Elinor. "Art Therapy: Problems of Definition." *Bulletin of Art Therapy*, 1, No. 2 (1961).

——. "A New Use of Art in Psychiatric Diagnosis." *Ibid.*, 4, No. 3 (1965).

——. "Psychotherapy and the Arts at Withymead Center." *Ibid.*, 2, No. 4 (1964).

——. Symposium: "Integration of Divergent Points of View in Art Therapy. Innovation and Aberration." *American Journal of Art Therapy*, 14, No. 1 (1974).

——. "Therapy Is Not Enough." *Bulletin of Art Therapy*, 6, No. 1 (1966).

——. "The War Between Therapese and English." *Ibid.*, 2, Nos. 2 and 4 (1964).

——, and Dachinger, Penny, eds. *Art Therapy in Theory and Practice*. New York: Schocken Books, 1975.

——, and Kramer, Edith. Editorial, "Art Therapy: Further Explorations and Definitions." *American Journal of Art Therapy*, 16, No. 1 (1976).

——, and Kramer, Edith. "Postscript to Halsey's *Freud and the Nature of Art*." *Ibid.*, 17, No. 1 (1978).

―――, and Levy, Bernard I. "An Experimental Approach to the Judgment of Psychopathology from Paintings." In Elinor Ulman and Penny Dachinger, eds., *Art Therapy in Theory and Practice*. New York: Schocken Books, 1975.

―――, Levy, Bernard I. "The Effect of Training on Judging Psychopathology from Paintings." *American Journal of Art Therapy*, 14, No. 1 (1974).

―――; Kramer, Edith; and Kwiatkowska, Hanna Yaxa. *Art Therapy in the United States*. Craftsbury Common, Vt.: Art Therapy Publications, 1978 (also in P. Valletutti, ed., *Interdisciplinary Approaches to Human Services*. Baltimore: University Park Press, 1977.

Vaessen, M. L. J. "Art or Expression: A Discussion of the Creative Activities of Mental Patients." *Bulletin of Art Therapy*, 2, No. 1 (1962).

Wadeson, Harriet. "The Fluid Family in Multi-Family Art Therapy." *American Journal of Art Therapy*, 15, No. 4 (1976).

Waelder, Robert. *Basic Theory of Psychoanalysis*. New York: Schocken Books, 1971.

―――. "The Psychoanalytic Theory of Play." *Psychoanalytic Quarterly*, 2 (1933).

Weissman, Stephen M. "Frederick Douglass, Portrait of a Black Militant: A Study in the Family Romance." In Ruth S. Eissler et al., eds., *The Psychoanalytic Study of the Child*, Vol. 30 (1975).

Williams, G. H., and Wood, M. *Developmental Art Therapy*. Baltimore: University Park Press, 1977.

Wilson, Laurie. "Theory and Practice of Art Therapy With the Mentally Retarded." *American Journal of Art Therapy*, 16, No. 3 (1977).

Winnicott, D. W. *The Maturational Processes and the Facilitating Environment*. New York: International Universities Press, 1965.

―――. *Therapeutic Consultation in Child Psychiatry*. New York: Basic Books, 1971.

———. *Through Paediatrics to Psycho-Analysis*. New York: Basic Books, 1975.

Wolf, Robert. "Art Therapy in a Public School." *American Journal of Art Therapy*, 12, No. 2 (1973).

Zierer, Edith; Sternberg, David; Fin, Regina; and Farmer, Mark. "Family Creative Analysis: Its Role in Treatment." *Bulletin of Art Therapy*, 5, Nos. 2 and 3 (1966).

Zierer, Ernest. *Kunst und Weltgezetz, Neue Wege ihrer Erforschung*. Stockholm: Nordiska Boktryckeriet, 1924.

———. *Neuaufbau der Kunstkritik: Einführung in die Absolute Tiefenanschauung*. Uberlingen: Verlag Seebote, 1932.

———, and Zierer, Edith. "The Integration Quotient in Creative Therapy." *Journal of the Hillside Hospital* (Glen Oaks, N.Y.), July 1960.

Index